MW01010436

JAMES
WHITE

JAMES WHITE

Innovator and Overcomer

GERALD WHEELER

REVIEW AND HERALD® PUBLISHING ASSOCIATION
HAGERSTOWN, MD 21740

The author assumes full responsibility for the accuracy of all facts and
quotations as cited in this book.

This book was
Edited by Clifford Goldstein
Copyedited by Jocelyn Fay
Designed by Trent Truman
Electronic makeup by Shirley M. Bolivar
Typeset: 11/14 Berkeley

PRINTED IN U.S.A.

07 06 05 04 03   5 4 3 2 1

R&H Cataloging Service
Wheeler, Gerald William, 1943-
    James White

    1. White, James Springer, 1821-1881. I. Title.

Abbreviations

EGW   Ellen G. White
JW   James White
WCW   William C. White

ISBN 0-8280-1719-0

DEDICATION

To

DON AND RON

because

WE ARE BROTHERS

CONTENTS

CONTENTS

PREFACE

THIS book does not duplicate Virgil Robinson's *James White,* which, even with its incident-by-incident approach to White's life (along with Arthur White's six-volume biography on Ellen White), nevertheless left out many aspects of the James White story. White was an incredibly complex and at times astoundingly contradictory man, and space does not allow me, as well, to explore every facet of his existence. A biographer could spend a lifetime studying him and not exhaust the depths of his personality, or his accomplishments, as he initiated almost everything that is the Seventh-day Adventist Church today. From church organization to publishing to education, health, and the church's worldwide mission, he was involved in the first stages of almost every major program, either as initiator or major participant.

Instead of trying to cover every event, I focus on certain patterns, seeking to show how they reveal him as a person and thus enable us to understand his relationship with, and impact on, the emerging Seventh-day Adventist Church. Though providing a historical framework of James White's life, I am more interested in how certain personality traits and events shaped him as a man and leader. In his later years in particular, he struggled with persistent problems best understood if examined in the context of their own history. Occasionally I will jump ahead of a strict chronology and follow a theme to its historical development, or even go back in time to trace a series of events that were just at that moment reaching their culmination.

Besides looking at his great accomplishments, we will also need to consider the reactions of some of those he had to deal with, his very human relationship with his wife, and his constant struggle with health and financial problems. Unless we first grasp the things that shaped these latter situations, we cannot fully appreciate how God worked through him.

This is the story of a man with great strengths and great faults. I have attempted to portray him in the spirit of how Ellen White said the Bible depicted its great men and women.

"Had our good Bible been written by uninspired persons, it would have presented quite a different appearance and would have been a discouraging study to erring mortals, who are contending with natural frailties and the temptations of a wily foe. But as it is, we have a correct record of the religious experience of marked characters in Bible history. Men whom God favored, and to whom He entrusted great responsibilities, were sometimes overcome by temptation and committed sins, even as we of the present day strive, waver, and frequently fall into error. But it is encouraging to desponding hearts to know that through God's grace they could gain fresh vigor to again rise above their evil natures; and, remembering this, we are ready to renew the conflict ourselves."*

I, of course, do not claim inspiration, but I hope to have shown the power of God in James White's life. I hope too that you will learn to respect him as much as I have and to acknowledge that whatever anyone accomplishes for God, it is only through our acceptance of His power.

I would like to thank those who helped in the research and preparation of this book. They include George Knight and Jerry Moon, of the Seventh-day Adventist Theological Seminary, Andrews University; Michael Campbell, doctoral student, Andrews University; Jim Nix and Tim Poirier, of the Ellen G. White Estate; Stanley Cottrell and Stan Hickerson, of the Adventist Heritage Ministry and its Historic Adventist Village at Battle Creek, Michigan; Jean Davis of Battle Creek, Michigan; and Robert H. Allen and Howard P. Krug of Rochester, New York. A special thanks to Jocelyn Fay for help in untangling often contradictory sources.

GERALD WHEELER

---

* Ellen G. White, *Conflict and Courage* (Washington, D.C.: Review and Herald Pub. Assn., 1970), p. 7.

FOREWORD

BEGINNING with Gerald Wheeler's *James White: Innovator and Overcomer*, the Review and Herald Publishing Association is inaugurating a much-needed series of biographies on the founders and shapers of the Seventh-day Adventist Church. This project is unprecedented in the denomination's history. Never has there been a concerted effort to systematically treat the lives and contributions of the men and women who have stood at the center of Adventism's development. The series will not only help us understand the individuals better, but will also shed additional light on the history of the Adventist movement.

The plan is to release one biography per year. Some of the individuals in the lineup for the next few years include Joseph Bates as Adventism's first theologian; Ellen White as a woman in a man's world and Adventism's prophetic voice; J. N. Andrews as Adventism's earliest scholar and missionary; W. C. White as his mother's assistant and a man at the center of action; and Ellet J. Waggoner as a leader in the revival of righteousness by faith. Each biography will focus on the individual's major contribution and will be written by a person well versed in his or her topic.

It is quite appropriate that the first volume is on James White, since he was the driving force behind the formation of Seventh-day Adventism as a denomination. As Wheeler's biography illustrates, James White founded the conference system, the publishing work, the health work, and the educational work of the church. Without White there would be no Seventh-day Adventism.

Wheeler's treatment not only features White's contributions in every area of denominational endeavor, but it also helps readers gain a better understanding of James White as a person. As Wheeler's fascinating picture of him indicates, White was not only a person of immense energy and multifaceted talents; he was also one with his share of human foibles. His contemporaries often witnessed him as opinionated and forceful. But then if he hadn't had such characteristics it is doubtful if he could have been instrumental in raising up a denomination virtually out of nothing.

As Wheeler's book makes clear, James was far from perfect. As are most leaders, he could be difficult to live and work with. Unfortunately, his problem became aggravated in the 1860s and 1870s as a result of several strokes. Yet White succeeded in spite of all his hardships.

James White: Innovator and Overcomer helps us see these points and many others. In providing us with a broader picture of White than we have had heretofore, Wheeler has utilized documents not fully mined in the past. This book takes its place beside Virgil Robinson's *James White* (1976) and White's autobiography, *Life Incidents* (1868)* as one of the few books to feature the man who did more than any other to shape Seventh-day Adventism. I highly recommend the reading of *James White: Innovator and Overcomer* to those who have an interest in Adventist history, biography, or nineteenth-century American Protestantism.

GEORGE R. KNIGHT
CONSULTING EDITOR
ANDREWS UNIVERSITY

---

* *Life Incidents* has been released by Andrews University Press to accompany Wheeler's biography.

James White at age 57

CHAPTER I

A MAN OF CONTRADICTIONS

TWENTY-FIVE hundred people crowded the Dime Tabernacle in Battle Creek, Michigan. Uriah Smith, editor of the *Review and Herald,* walked to the pulpit and began the funeral sermon. "No man is in this life immortal," he began in the hushed church, its silence broken only by his voice and the sound of people fanning themselves in the August heat. "Yet there are some men whose death is so far removed from all our calculations and expectations that we would fain persuade ourselves that we need make no provision in their cases for any such contingency, at least during the allotted period of three-score years and ten; that no such interruption is to occur in the charmed existence they seem to lead till in the natural course of years the period of their labor is over.

"Especially is this the case with those who have been engaged in lifelong public enterprises, and who have become largely identified with the movement to which they are devoting all their energies. We look at the work and inseparably connect it with the workmen; and so long as the former continues, we look for the latter also."[1]

James White, whom everyone had come to memorialize, was such a man. Who could imagine the Seventh-day Adventist Church without him? Having been its president and one of its three leading founders, White had not only established most of its organization and institutions but had guided them through financial and other crises. Whatever was Seventh-day Adventist he had either initiated or been responsible for its eventual acceptance. And now, suddenly, he was gone?

Uriah Smith began to summarize the tremendous contributions White had made to the young denomination. White had rallied the handful of former Millerites who had not given up their faith after the disappointment of October 22, 1844, and helped them accept the Sabbath and the sanctuary doctrines. He had founded Seventh-day Adventist publishing, including the *Review and Herald* and the church's first publishing house; he had spearheaded the church's organizational structure; he had been active in the development of its first medical institution and college; he had established a state conference and a second publishing house in California with its *Signs of the Times* church periodical; and he had raised large sums of money to evangelize Europe.

Smith then sketched White's character, describing him as always calm and cool during times of confusion and excitement, never given to fanaticism, skilled in judicious decision-making, never yielding to discouragement, and a careful planner. White, he said, was a man of strong friendships and generosity.[2]

But then Smith's memorial sermon took some strange twists: "Yet his position has been such as to make it almost inevitable that he should have enemies." It was not the kind of statement one would expect at a funeral. But even more startling, the *Review and Herald* editor added, "And some have thought that he was deficient in social qualities, and sometimes rigid, harsh, and unjust, even toward his best friends."[3]

What kind of man was James White that he could be eulogized, defended, and even criticized at his funeral? Uriah Smith was not alone in these convictions. Others would echo these thoughts in the following days. James White was, indeed, a man of startling contradictions.

His great strengths had helped found and build up the Seventh-day Adventist Church. Without him the denomination might not have come into existence, or at least achieved the shape and stability that it did. But his weaknesses, especially when aggravated by the illness that he struggled with during the later part of his life, had threatened to tear apart the fabric of his beloved Adventist Church. He was a man who could elicit great love and admiration, or leave people frustrated and puzzled. At times not even his own wife could understand him. But few would deny that he had accomplished far more than most men and women ever could, even despite his personality problems.

As we shall see, his life shows what the power of God can accomplish through the clay vessels that are finite human beings—even when the vicissitudes of life shatter that fragile vessel. Frail vessels are, after all, what God has to work with. He has no plaster saints. The Lord took this tall, lanky, would-be teacher from Maine and turned him into a mighty preacher and apostle.

---

[1] *In Memoriam: A Sketch of the Last Sickness and Death of Elder James White, Who Died at Battle Creek, Michigan, August 6, 1881, Together With the Discourse Preached at His Funeral* (Battle Creek, Mich.: Review and Herald Press, 1881), p. 22.

[2] *Ibid.*, pp. 25-33.

[3] *Ibid.*, p. 34.

ChApTeR II

MADE IN MAINE

MAINE is a land of forest and river, mingling with the ocean along a rugged coastline. Countless bays indent the coast. Rivers probe everywhere inland. Endless forests stretch north to Canada, and even today much of the state is sparsely populated by small towns and villages. The region is a world of fleeting springs, delightful summers of sharp blue skies, glorious autumns of brilliant color, and long dark winters.

It was into this world of rugged beauty that James Springer[1] White was born August 4, 1821, in the township of Palmyra, Somerset County, Maine—the year after Maine entered the union as the twenty-third state. In his book *Life Incidents*[2] he claimed that he was descended from Pilgrims aboard the *Mayflower,* but recent research questions the idea. Genealogical records published in 1900 traced his lineage back to John White of Salem, reported to be in New England by 1638. James's mother was a granddaughter of Samuel Shepard, a noted Baptist minister. The boy was the middle child of nine born to John and Betsey White.[3]

His ancestors had left Massachusetts and immigrated to Maine, then still part of Massachusetts. The culture and environment of both Massachusetts and Maine would shape his outlook on life, and that perspective would influence the denomination he cofounded.

PURITAN CULTURE

Massachusetts became the center of what's called "the Puritan culture," a worldview that distinguished itself by distinctive attitudes and practices involving wealth, education, dress, food, building styles, social relationships, and, of course, religion.[4] Particular characteristics of Puritan culture that would mold James White and the emerging Seventh-day Adventist Church to various degrees included a congregation-oriented church structure, an emphasis on education, a strong work ethic, egalitarianism and low class consciousness, and a tendency to live in small rural communities.[5] The people of New England worshiped in what David Hackett Fischer calls "the meeting and lecture" style,[6] as opposed to the liturgical style of Anglican Virginia, the communal religious life of Baptists, or the spontaneous spirituality of the Quakers in the Delaware Valley of the Middle Atlantic states. Puritan preaching began with a text and analyzed it in great detail. Such an approach emphasized the intellect more than the devotional life, though it could elicit quite an emotional response when dealing with what the believer must do to be saved. Such careful study of the biblical text provided an intellectual seedbed for both the Millerite movement and the Seventh-day Adventist Church. The pattern of meeting and the sermon as lecture on the biblical text linger among the Anglo Seventh-day Adventist churches of North America and dominate traditional evangelistic presentations throughout much of Adventism.

THE DISTRICT OF MAINE

Though carrying a strong community sense, Puritan culture particularly focused on personal religion, responsibility, and self-improvement. Those New England settlers who pushed north into the part of Massachusetts that would become Maine modified Puritan culture in new ways. Although the state of New Hampshire divided them, Massachusetts governed the territory of Maine. The District of Maine, as it was called, felt that it was treated as a colony, and a militant separatism arose. This would create a strong sense of independence. War and other disasters had made the settlement of Maine difficult, forcing the people to learn endurance and persistence. James White's life would mirror that of his rugged birthplace.

The people of Maine soon became known as social reformers. Unlike that of its parent, Massachusetts, the first constitution of Maine rejected the idea of an official church or religious requirements for elected officials. The territory of Maine abolished slavery in 1788—long before some of the other Northeastern states—and many of its citizens became ardent abolitionists during the 1830s. The Baptists and Congregationalists especially opposed slavery. The first total abstinence society in the United States was founded in Portland, Maine, in 1815, and the state had some of the first United States prohibition laws. In 1846 they sought to stop the sale of alcohol except for medical and industrial purposes. Then in 1851 Maine outlawed the manufacture and sale of alcoholic drinks.

The people of Maine gained the reputation of being the Yankees of the Yankees as they stressed their traditional traits of honesty, thrift, frankness, self-reliance, thoroughness, and ruggedness. Maine's long cold winters and the rugged geography of forest, river, and coastline profoundly shaped its settlers. Outsiders came to regard "Mainers" as low-keyed personalities with the ability to spend long hours by themselves and who could make do with whatever was at hand, characteristics that were manifest in James White's life (though no one would ever accuse him of being "low-key"). Sometimes these traits would serve him well, other times not. Occasionally he would transcend them. But he would always remain a son of Maine, reflecting, for example, the warmth and loyalty of its people once they overcame their reserve and established close friendships.

If he had been born elsewhere, he would have been a different person. And if the Seventh-day Adventist Church had formed, for example, among the Cavalier culture of the southern United States or the Quaker culture of the Middle Atlantic states, it would probably have been a quite different denomination. It is significant that of the three founders of Seventh-day Adventism—James and Ellen White and Joseph Bates—two were born in Maine, the third in Massachusetts.

DEACON WHITE

James White's father, John White, a proper son of New England, had tilled the thin rocky soil of his gently rolling farmland for 15 years by the time of James's birth. John had purchased the farm shortly after moving to the township of Palmyra at the age of 21 and remained there 51 years. Only 20 acres of the heavily forested property had been cleared when he arrived. Through the years he lumbered off more of the dense forest and collected the countless rocks into fence walls in order to keep the stones from breaking his plow.

He also taught voice. His students included his own children. One time he and James and two daughters traveled to a religious meeting. During the trip they stopped at a hotel for the night. That evening the four of them sang hymns to the guests. The next morning when John started to pay his bill, the innkeeper told him that the singing had more than paid for their lodging. In fact, if they wanted to sing for his guests in the future, the White family could stay for free. John's interest in music was transferred to James, who would publish the first Seventh-day Adventist hymnals.

A devout Christian, in June 1828 John established what was probably the first Sunday school in the state of Maine.[7] Fifty years later James White would remember how it shaped his life. The father also conducted daily morning and evening family worships. Three sons would become ministers (one a Baptist, another in the Methodist Episcopal Church, and James White first a Christian Connexion, then a Seventh-day Adventist, preacher).

The elder White seems to have been a religious seeker, a trait he would pass on to James. First a Congregationalist, he joined a group of Calvinistic Baptists after a Baptist minister came to the area and convinced him that immersion was the right form of baptism. He was a deacon in his Baptist congregation for 10 years. Then he became interested in the teachings of the Christian Connexion, an influential denomination in nineteenth-century New England. His Baptist congregation called a special meeting to exclude him from their fellowship because of his association with the more liberal denomination. White left them and soon joined the Christian Connexion.[8] He served the latter as a deacon for nearly 40 years and attended every monthly conference meeting of his church, missing only one during all that time.[9]

CHILDHOOD PROBLEMS

James White was a sickly child. At the age of 2 or 3 he came down with what was diagnosed as worm fever. The condition produced severe fits or seizures, and he was sick for weeks. Although he recovered, he suffered from crossed eyes. "I am reported to have been . . . a feeble, nervous, partially blind boy," he wrote later.[10] At the age of 7 he accompanied his brothers to the primitive local school. "How different now the opportunities for an education to those we found in the old Palmyra schoolhouse a half century ago," John White, James's oldest brother, observed late in life. "Every winter we would get over in old Webster as far as [the word] booby—then go home and work it all out of body and brain. And next winter, repeat the farce."[11]

Whether because of vision problems, dyslexia, or some other difficulty, James White seemed unable to learn to read. He said the letters of words all ran together. Concluding that he would remain illiterate, he dropped out of school to help on the farm. At 15 he was baptized into the Christian Connexion. And by the time he was 18 he was six feet tall and quite physically strong.

THIRST FOR EDUCATION

But as he developed physically, his eyesight began to improve, and he could now make out individual letters. Although 19 years old, he enrolled as a beginning student at the local academy in St. Albans, Maine. During his brief schooling he would study up to 18 hours a day. He exemplified the Puritan New England drive to get an education. Although many of his friends advised him to stick to farming, he immersed himself in his schoolwork, an example of how he would drive himself the rest of his life. His father gave him a suit of clothing, the $3 for the tuition, and a weekly supply of bread. Each Monday James walked the five miles to the academy. Saturday evening he would return and pick up the bread from home. The school term lasted only 12 weeks. Eventually the schoolmaster, C. F. Allen, handed him a certificate that allowed him to teach elementary grade subjects.

Deciding that he wanted to pay for his own education, James searched for work as soon as school ended. When he heard of an opening at a sawmill on the Penobscot River, he walked the 40 miles to take the job. Lumbering and wood products were one of the most important parts of the Maine economy, and remain so even today. The Penobscot River was constantly clogged with floating logs. The mills loaded ships—almost to the sinking point—with cut boards. The many sawmills produced so much sawdust that it raised the river bottom. To allow vessels to continue to travel it, the channel had to be dredged several times through the years.

Unfortunately, shortly after he started work, White severely cut his ankle and had to drop out for several weeks. The injury left him with a limp for a number of years, and he was not able to put much weight on his left heel for the rest of his life. But by the end of the summer he had managed to save $30, and after collecting his clothes and books back at home in Palmyra, he enrolled for a three-month term at the Methodist Episcopal school at Reedfield, Maine, about 50 some miles southwest of Palmyra.

Because of poverty, James had to survive on cornmeal pudding (which he prepared himself) and raw apples. But he studied so hard that when the session ended the headmaster assured him that after another semester White could enter college. That winter he taught at a large school and saved his money, planning to continue his education. His life would take a sudden turn, however, and his total length of formal education would consist only of the 12 weeks of elementary school and 29 weeks beyond that. But he had already set the pattern: he had overcome both physical and educational problems. James White was an overcomer, and throughout the rest of his life he would triumph over challenges that would have defeated many others.

JAMES WHITE MEETS THE MILLERITES

John White began to read William Miller's lectures on the Second Coming, but James regarded the Baptist lay preacher's ideas as fanatical. A lecture by a James Hall at the church in Palmyra confirmed his opinion. But when James White's mother supported Millerism, her son had to take it seriously. She calmly answered his objections. Soon he began to come under a growing conviction that Miller might be right.

After being encouraged to attend religious meetings held by a "Brother Oakes, of Boston," he accepted the Millerite teachings and decided that Christ would indeed return soon. In addition, White became impressed that he should present the Second Coming concept to his former students. But, wanting to continue his education, he enrolled in Newport Academy instead. A local minister named Bridges rode along with him the few miles to the school and spent the journey talking about preaching, a subject James would rather have not heard discussed. Once at school he became convinced that he should tell his former grade school students. Thoughts of Christ's return made it impossible for him to concentrate on his studies. Even physical labor and prayer would not get the idea out of his mind. Finally in desperation he set out for his former school in Troy, Maine, where he had been teaching. As he did, peace replaced his inner turmoil.

Impressed to stop at one house, he encountered a man who had earlier that day buried his son and was not sure that he could cope with his grief. James told him that Christ could help him through the experience. The next morning White asked for a drink of water at a log cabin two miles away. There he ran into a young woman who had attended James's school the previous winter. She recognized him and invited him in. James asked for permission to pray with her and her family. The woman not only agreed but insisted that she invite neighbors. Within a short time 25 people gathered in the house. After asking how many were Christians, he discovered that none were. He then encouraged them to accept Christ. Despite the common misconceptions of today, a large number of early Americans had little or no contact with Christianity. They were just as unchurched as modern Americans. Many little communities had no churches or ministers.

After praying with the children and neighbors, James searched for more of his students. He even prayed in the home of the nonreligious man who had hired him to teach the previous school year. Within a few days he had found the rest of the students. Between teaching and preaching, he made an impression on at least one of them—a 7-year-old girl that he had carried on his back through snowdrifts to school when he was the teacher. Thirty years later she and her mother came to hear him at a Seventh-day Adventist camp meeting at Wanseca, Minnesota. They attended, though they were not Sabbath observers.[12]

Assuming that he had performed his duty, White returned to Newport Academy. But he could not shed the impression that he must continue to preach. White had a good friend named Elbridge Smith, who had been his school roommate at St. Albans and Reedfield. They often discussed their dreams and hopes. One day James told Smith about his belief that the Lord would return about 1843 and that he felt that he should preach it. Smith, although not a Christian (and recognizing that he might not be the best person to give advice on what James should do) told White that he should follow the convictions of his heart.[13]

YOUNG PREACHER

Struggling with the idea, James realized that to accept it would end any further education. But did he really have the ability to preach? He decided to test his talent by announcing a religious meeting in the Troy townhouse. People crowded in to hear him. But after attempting to speak for a time, he gave up in embarrassment. Afterward a woman came up to him, called him "Elder White," and asked him to dinner at her house. Her use of the title "Elder" greatly disturbed him.

A little later people urged him to speak in the presence of two other young preachers, but after 20 minutes he abruptly sat down in confusion. Going off by himself in the woods, he tried to analyze his failure. Finally he concluded that even though he was trying to work for God, what he really wanted was success in the secular world. But after more struggle he decided to spread the Millerite teachings. Thus, he resigned from his teaching post.

During September 1842 he heard William Miller, Joshua V. Himes, and other Adventist speakers at Castine, Maine. William Miller's intelligence, kindness, and humility especially impressed him. The next month James attended an Adventist meeting in the large tent that they had erected in Exeter, Maine. Convinced of the Second Coming, he gave in to the compulsion to preach it.

One of the visual aids the Millerite movement developed was a prophetic chart printed on cloth. White used his meager savings to obtain one, along with some Millerite books. His father offered him one of the family horses, and an Elder Moses Polley supplied James with a patched-up saddle and part of a bridle that James managed to repair. Then he set out as an itinerant evangelist. He began by holding meetings in Palmyra, though their results were, he felt, sparse. Then a schoolteacher friend in Burnham, who had just lost an eye, asked White to substitute for him for a week. James agreed, deciding to hold religious meetings during the evenings at the schoolhouse. People crowded it to hear him speak on the Second Coming. At his final meetings he invited them to accept salvation. Sixty responded, coming to the front of the room, where White prayed with them. But a sense of inadequacy made him write to his brother Samuel for help. His older brother had already been a minister for five years. Samuel spent six weeks with the people, baptized them, and organized a church.

Someone suggested that James preach in the communities along the Kennebec River as far as Brunswick, Maine. No Adventist preacher had yet penetrated that area. Even though his light clothing offered little protection from the frigid climate, one January morning in 1843 White set out on a preaching tour. Near Augusta, Maine, the present state capital, someone offered him a place to stay. Soon he received a request to speak at a school not far from the Kennebec River. People packed it, even filling the windows and door. Although the Millerite movement attracted great interest, it was a controversial topic and generated equally intense opposition, as White soon discovered. The next night some troublemakers attempted to drive him out of town. One of them threw a spike, hitting James in the head. The spike bounced off and fell onto his Bible. Picking up the spike, White stuck it into his pocket.

A local individual had invited a noted Universalist editor to the meeting to rebut James's sermon. Universalism, which taught that God would eventually save everyone, saw little need for the Second Coming. When the man asked James to urge the people to remain for his presentation, White replied that the audience could do as they wished, that he could not make any claim on them. Only about 25 remained.

The next night the people again crowded the schoolhouse. But a mob of several hundred, who either opposed the idea that Christ would return or just wanted to stir up some trouble, decided to stop the meeting. Just before James White started to speak, several individuals warned him that because of his lack of cooperation with the Universalist editor the previous night, the mob would close down the meeting. James replied that if it was God's will, so be it. Then he began to pray. But realizing the hostility of the mob, he stood by the pulpit and prayed with his eyes open. When he started his lecture, snowballs hurled through the open windows began to splatter on the ceiling and walls above and behind him. The mob's screaming drowned out his words. The melting snowballs dripped from the ceiling and soon soaked his Bible and clothing.

Finally, closing his Bible and speaking as loudly as he could, James began to describe the day of judgment. "Repent and be converted," he declared, "that your sins may be blotted out. . . . Turn to Christ and get ready for his coming, or in a little time from this, on rocks and mountains you will call in vain. You scoff now, but you will pray then."

When the shouting became more subdued, James pulled from his pocket the nail that someone had thrown at him the night before. Using it as an object lesson, he said, "Some poor sinner cast this spike at me last evening. God pity him. The worst wish I have for him is that he was this moment as happy as I am. Why should I resent his insult when my Master had them driven through his hands?"

"The hands of Jesus were nailed to a cruel cross," he proclaimed. "Why should His followers expect better treatment?" Then to dramatize his point, James stretched his hands against the wall behind him as if he too had been crucified. The gesture caught his audience's attention. Taking advantage of the shift in mood, he spoke of Christ's love and urged his audience to accept the divine offer of salvation and then prepare for Jesus' soon return. Nearly 100 rose to their feet when White asked the crowd who would be willing to follow Christ.

After closing the meeting with a prayer, James took his books and prophetic chart and left the school building. As he approached them, the members of the mob outside opened a path for him. One individual took James's arm and guided him through the crowd.[14]

After several more meetings in the same schoolhouse, White moved on to other schoolhouses along the Kennebec River, generally spending only a couple nights at each spot. At a place called Litchfield Plains, he began the meeting with what would become a common practice with him. An estimated 1,000 people had packed the building, filling even the aisles and the speaking platform. A drone of voices filled the room as he pushed his way through the crowd. To quiet them and get their attention, he began to sing a contemporary Advent hymn.

"You will see your Lord a-coming,
 You will see your Lord a-coming,
 You will see your Lord a-coming,
 In a few more days,
 While a band of music,
 While a band of music,
 While a band of music,
 Shall be chanting through the air."[15]

James White spent four months on his first speaking itinerary. Finally on April 2 he started for home. The snow was still deep, and he did not reach Palmyra until April 5. Reports indicate that during the winter months of 1842-1843 more than 1,000 people responded to his preaching. A few days after he returned to Palmyra the Christian Connexion ordained him to the ministry.

¹ James White does not seem to have used Springer. In fact, there exists no known legal record that it was even part of his name.

² James White, *Life Incidents, in Connection With the Great Advent Movement, as Illustrated by the Three Angels of Revelation XIV* (Battle Creek, Mich.: Steam Press of the Seventh-day Adventist Pub. Assn., 1868), p. 9.

³ References for incidents recorded in Virgil Robinson's *James White* (Washington, D.C.: Review and Herald Pub. Assn., 1976) have been occasionally omitted to save space. Consult Robinson for sources.

⁴ See David Hackett Fischer, *Albion's Seed: Four British Folkways in America* (New York: Oxford University Press, 1989), pp. 13-74. Fischer offers the challenging thesis that English settlers replicated in the New World four regional cultures from the British Isles (Puritan, Cavalier, Quaker, and that of the English/Scottish border counties) and that these cultures continue to affect American life today. New England reflects Puritan culture, the Middle Atlantic states Quaker culture, Virginia and the rest of the coastal South the Cavalier culture, and Appalachia the English/Scottish borderlands' culture. Other regional cultures have developed as an intermingling of these four cultures, the Jewish and Central European influences in New York City, and Hispanic influences in the American Southwest and West Coast.

⁵ For a concise list of regional characteristics of Colonial times, including that of Puritanism, see Fischer, pp. 813-815.

⁶ *Ibid.*, p. 117; see his fascinating description of Puritan churches and religious services, pp. 117-125. It might make an interesting study to compare Puritan worship with that of early Seventh-day Adventists.

⁷ James White, "Sabbath-Schools," *Review and Herald*, Aug. 22, 1878.

⁸ The new denomination liked to spell "Connection" as "Connexion."

⁹ James White, *Life Incidents*, pp. 10, 11.

¹⁰ *Ibid.*, p. 12.

¹¹ John White letter, June 26, 1878.

¹² JW to WCW, July 1, 1875.

¹³ James White, *Life Incidents*, pp. 23, 24.

¹⁴ *Ibid.*, p. 78; see also Robinson, p. 24.

¹⁵ James White, *Life Incidents*, p. 94.

Chapter III

THE CHRISTIAN CONNEXION

THE Christian Connexion (or Christian Church) that ordained James White was the first indigenous American religious movement, an example of the Restorationist tradition that sought to return Christianity to what it thought was the New Testament pattern of belief and organization. Developing simultaneously in at least three major regions of the United States, Restorationism represented a reaction to the religion of the time. One strand—especially in Calvinist-oriented New England—rejected the passiveness of much American Protestantism. In an attempt to make individual religious life more personal, active, and practical, the Christian Connexion movement preached "gospel liberty," which meant that all believers must base their faith on what they themselves discovered to be the teachings of the Bible, and that their understanding would keep growing.

The Christian Connexion movement formed when a number of New England congregations left the Methodist, Baptist, and Presbyterian communities of faith and united, about 1810, under the leadership of Alexander Stone.[1] In the twentieth century the Connexionists considered joining the Freewill Baptists, then in 1931 merged with the Congregationalists to form the Congregational Christian Church.

THE BIBLE—THE ONLY RULE OF FAITH

"In the rise of the Christian Church," one nineteenth-century writer observed, "we have seen that one of the great fundamental principles for which they all strongly contended, was, the right and duty of *private judgment,* and taking the Bible, and that alone, as the *only* rule of *faith* and *practice.* They also contended that *Christian character* should be the only test of *Christian fellowship,* and that it would be just as consistent to blame God for not giving all faces alike, as to blame Him for not giving all the same mind, in order that they might believe alike."[2]

One prominent Christian Connexion minister saw his denomination emerge "not so much to establish any peculiar and distinctive doctrines, as to assert, for individuals and churches, more liberty and independence in relation to matters of faith and practice, to shake off the authority of human creeds and the shackles of prescribed modes and forms, to make the Bible their only guide, claiming for every man the right to be his own expositor of it, to judge, for himself, what are its doctrines and requirements, and in practice, to follow more strictly the simplicity of the apostles and primitive Christians."[3] His denomination fought any "infringement of Christian liberty."[4]

Elias Smith, a former Freewill Baptist who became a prominent Christian Connexion leader, "argued that every last Christian had the 'unalienable right' to follow 'the scripture wherever it leads him, even an equal right with the Bishops and Pastors of the churches . . . even though his principles may, in many things, be contrary to what the Reverend D.D.'s call Orthodoxy.'"[5] The Christian Connexion took Scripture seriously and felt that it must be continuously explored. If they should interpret some biblical teaching incorrectly, further study would surely correct it. Truth was progressive, an insight that especially shaped Sabbatarian Adventists and the eventual Seventh-day Adventist Church. The idea is enshrined in the preamble to the denomination's Statement of Fundamental Beliefs.

Elsewhere in the United States, the Disciples and Christian Churches also emphasized Restorationism. They had evolved out of the Campbellites and Stonites in the Ohio River valley region. Christianity, the Restorationist leaders taught, had become encrusted with many unbiblical traditions and doctrines. Believers must study the Bible and recover the primitive Christianity of the New Testament. They must restore the teaching and practice of the pure church that Jesus had founded. So strongly did they believe that nonscriptural elements had crept into Christianity that whatever contemporary religious bodies taught or did, they seemed to automatically reject.

THE CHRISTIAN CONNEXION
AND SEVENTH-DAY ADVENTISM

James White was not the only member of the Christian Connexion who would pioneer the Seventh-day Adventist Church. Joseph Bates, active in Christian Connexion circles, accepted Millerism and eventually convinced the congregation of the Washington, New Hampshire, church to accept the Advent doctrine. The Washington church was a former Christian Connexion church built in the early 1840s. The Christian Connexion's openness toward the scriptural teachings of others continued among the congregation's members, and Rachel Oaks Preston, a neighboring Seventh Day Baptist, convinced its Methodist minister, Frederick Wheeler, and others in it to accept the seventh-day Sabbath doctrine. It became the first Sabbatarian Adventist congregation. A number of members would become prominent in the Seventh-day Adventist denomination, including Daniel, William, and Cyrus Farnsworth; Newell Mead; and Worcester (known as Wooster) Ball. Uriah Smith also had contact with the congregation and was converted there.

Christian Connexion churches had been particularly receptive to Millerite teachings, and many Christian Connexion ministers and members had become Millerites.[6] In fact, Joshua Himes, who more than anyone else enabled William Miller to become nationally known, was a Christian Connexion minister. He wrote that every member had the right to be his or her own expositor of Scripture and that "diversity of sentiment is not a bar to church fellowship."[7]

After 1844, when most other denominations refused to let Sabbatarian Adventists use their facilities, Christian Connexion congregations still allowed them to meet in their buildings. During the 1850s conferences of Sabbatarian Adventists met regularly in Christian Connexion churches. Such gatherings attracted Christian Connexion members who then converted to Sabbatarian Adventism.[8] Not only did many future Seventh-day Adventist leaders and thinkers come from Christian Connexion backgrounds, but other believers read Christian Connexion writings. We see their theological arguments in Seventh-day Adventist articles for several decades.[9] James White often quoted Christian theologian William Kinkade in his *Review* articles.[10]

SHAPING SEVENTH-DAY ADVENTISM

General Conference archivist and church historian Bert Haloviak, who has studied the Christian Connexion extensively, has shown how this strong contact with the Christian Connexion movement would shape the future Seventh-day Adventist Church. He sees "a direct linkage" in three fundamental areas, as well as in many details.

Organizational Structure: The Christian Connexion influence reveals itself in the early Sabbatarian Adventist suspicion and even hostility toward any ecclesiastical structure beyond the local congregation. One Christian Connexion historian depicted his people in the following manner: "When asked 'of what sect they were?' the reply was, 'None.' 'What denomination will you join?' 'None.' 'We will continue as we have begun—we will be Christians. Christ is our leader, the Bible is our only creed, and we will serve God free from the trammels of sectarianism.'"[11] Early Sabbatarian Adventists would have described themselves similarly.

Because Christ alone was head of the church, the Christian Connexion local conferences as well as the General Conference were more advisory organizations than controlling bodies. Sharing the Christian Connexion emphasis on the Bible as the basis for everything they did, early Seventh-day Adventists opposed not only creeds but even titles that they felt were nonscriptural.

Social Attitudes: The pioneer Adventists shared the Christian Connexion approval of temperance and health reform, manual labor, religious freedom, and a prominent role for women within the church. Both groups opposed slavery. These social concerns would manifest themselves in many Seventh-day Adventist Church programs, as well as in James White's personal life. He felt a strong concern for the welfare of others throughout his life. For example, shortly before his death he and his wife, Ellen, went out riding through Battle Creek, Michigan. As they passed an African-American woman who supported her five children by taking in washing, James commented, "Wife, we must look after this poor woman. Let us not, amid our busy cares, forget the poor souls who have so hard a struggle to live. It is well always to pay them more than they ask; and you may have clothing and provisions that you can spare them. It will be a small matter to us, but may be a great help to them. . . . Living where these poor people do, surrounded by the miasm of the millpond, they must have constantly to battle with disease and death. If I had means at my command, I would build suitable houses on high land to rent to these poor people. We will see what can be done to make their hard lot more comfortable."[12]

Theology: Early Seventh-day Adventists joined the Christian Connexion in rejecting the doctrine of the Trinity, holding an Arian view of Christ, and relegating the Holy Spirit to nothing more than a manifestation of God's power. At first the Christian Connexion denomination had included both Trinitarians and non-Trinitarians. While Alexander Stone was apparently a non-Trinitarian, he did not make it an issue for membership. But when fellow Restorationist Alexander Campbell, founder of the Disciples of Christ, attracted many from the Christian Connexion to his Trinitarian movement, those who stayed with the Connexionists were overwhelmingly non-Trinitarian. They shared Joshua Himes's belief "that there is one living and true God, the Father almighty, . . . That Christ is the Son of God . . . [and] the Holy Spirit is the power and energy of God, that holy influence of God by whose agency . . . the wicked are regenerated, converted and recovered to a virtuous and holy life."[13] Also Sabbatarian Adventists and Connexionists stressed obedience to God's law and sanctification; both denied the imputationist and substitutionary views of the atonement.[14]

Thus, although James White had absorbed much good from the Christian Connexion, he had also accepted some of its errors. Like the Christian Connexion, he concluded that the Trinity was unbiblical. In a series of articles entitled "The Faith of Jesus," he would deal with the argument raised by those who rejected the continuing obligation of obeying God's commandments, especially the Sabbath one. Such critics claimed that the commandments of God mentioned in the New Testament were not the Ten Commandments but the requirements of the gospel. He dismissed them by declaring, "To assert that the sayings of the Son and his apostles are the commandments of the Father is as wide from the truth as the old Trinitarian absurdity that Jesus Christ is the very and eternal God."[15]

But reflecting the Christian Connexion emphasis on a growing understanding of truth, James White would lead the emerging Seventh-day Adventist Church to reject two major Christian Connexion positions. The first, as we shall see in chapter 10, was that of organization. He would spur Sabbatarian Adventists into developing an organizational structure.

The other issue was theological. One's understanding of the doctrine of the Godhead shapes how a person views the doctrine of salvation, or soteriology. Arian groups who regard Christ as a created being tend to emphasize human obedience as the major factor in human salvation. Christian Connexion theologian William Kinkade, for example, wrote, "When God changes a sinner, and writes his law on his heart, and makes him love God with all his heart, and his neighbor as himself, every attribute of the divine Being harmonizes in his pardon and salvation. Justice is satisfied, because the man is made just, and renders to God and man the service that justice requires of him."[16] As for the idea of a substitutionary atonement, Kinkade dismissed it, saying, "God blesses his people because they are obedient and holy, and not because some other person is obedient and holy instead of them."[17]

Christian Connexion historian J. R. Freese stated that members of his movement "generally, reject the popular theology that teaches that 'Christ died to reconcile his Father to us.' . . . The true doctrine, as conceived by the Christian is, that Christ's death 'placed the world in *salvable* ground, while it releases us from no obligation of obedience, and annuls no threatening of damnation denounced against the obdurate.' This view of the subject leaves justice with God, free moral agency with man, and faith and good works, with the grace of God, as the only means, whereby to secure eternal life."[18]

For many decades some Seventh-day Adventists agreed with such viewpoints. Joseph Bates stressed that keeping the commandments was the only "entrance to 'life,'" and "to break them was sure 'death' (eternal)."[19] Pioneer scholar and theologian John Nevins Andrews wrote, "By faith in the atonement of the Savior our hearts are cleansed from sin, and we receive the 'renewing of the Holy Ghost.' Then with that perfect love to God restored to us, which Adam lost at his fall, we are prepared to render acceptable obedience to God, and thus to fulfill 'the righteousness of the law' (Rom. 8:3, 4, 7)."[20]

James White, however, had a stronger grasp on the biblical reality that salvation was solely through Christ. Speaking of the Millerite message in 1850, he declared that it "weaned us from this world, and led us to the feet of Jesus, to seek forgiveness of all our sins, and a free and full salvation through the blood of Christ."[21] While he urged his fellow believers to "humble ourselves before the mighty God, and obey and honor him by keeping his commandments," he immediately added, "We must seek a full and free pardon of all our transgressions and errors, through the atonement of Jesus Christ, now while he pleads his blood before the Father."[22] In his last days, White would make Christ's role in salvation a major emphasis in his preaching and writing. He would powerfully stress our dependence upon the holiness of Another. Unfortunately, his death would prevent him from accomplishing all that he desired. His wife, and others, would have to finish his dream.

---

[1] Jerry Moon, "Trinity and Anti-Trinitarianism in Early America," in Woodrow Whidden, Jerry Moon, and John H. Reeve, *The Trinity* (Hagerstown, Md.: Review and Herald Pub. Assn., 2002), p. 186.

[2] J. R. Freese, *A History and Advocacy of the Christian Church* (1852), p. 40.

[3] Joshua V. Himes, in J. N. Brown, *Encyclopedia of Religious Knowledge* (Battleboro, Vt.: Fessenden and Co., 1836), p. 362.

[4] *Ibid.*

[5] Nathan Hatch, *The Democratization of American Christianity* (1989), p. 76.

[6] Bert Haloviak, "A Heritage of Freedom: The Christian Connection Roots to Seventh-day Adventism (Some Pertinent Documents)" (General Conference Archives, November 1995), pp. 8, 9.

[7] Himes, p. 362.

[8] Haloviak, p. 3.

[9] John Loughborough, for example, based part of his response to a question on the Trinity (*Review and Herald,* Nov. 5, 1861) on a discussion of the subject by a Christian Connexion minister named Nicholas Summerbell. See Haloviak, "Some Great Connexions: Our Seventh-day Adventist Heritage From the Christian Church," (General Conference Archives, May 1994), pp. 13, 14.

[10] *Ibid.*

[11] N. Summerbell, *History of the Christian Church* (1873 ed.), p. 519.

[12] *In Memoriam,* p. 55.

[13] Himes, p. 363.

[14] Bert Haloviak, "A Heritage of Freedom"; Haloviak, "Some Great Connexions." (General Conference Archives, May 1994).

[15] *Review and Herald,* Aug. 5, 1852.

[16] William Kinkade, *The Bible Doctrine of God, Jesus Christ, the Holy Spirit: Atonement, Faith and Election.* 4th ed. (1908), pp. 246, 247.

[17] *Ibid.,* p. 218.

[18] Freese, pp. 68, 69.

[19] JW to Leonard and Elvira Hastings, Apr. 27, 1848.

[20] John Nevins Andrews, *Thoughts on the Sabbath and the Perpetuity of the Law of God* (1851), p. 9. Tradition says that Adventist pioneers did not preach righteousness by faith before 1888, but historical evidence suggests that this is not completely correct. As for

Andrews himself, he preached the efficacy of Christ's shed blood and death during the 1860s and 1870s. He wrote in his last-known letter: "My feet are on the Rock of Ages and . . . the Lord holds me by my right hand" (quoted in Joseph G. Smoot, "John N. Andrews: Faithful to His Service," *Adventist Heritage* [Spring 1984], p. 5).

[21] James White, "The Third Angel's Message," *The Present Truth,* April 1850, p. 66.

[22] *Ibid.,* p. 69.

CHAPTER IV

ACCEPTING "A WILE OF THE DEVIL"

DURING the summer of 1843 James visited Portland, Maine, and worked with an Elder John Pearson, Jr. Pearson coedited an Advent paper called *Hope of Israel* and would later publish—in a pamphlet titled *The Christian Experience of William E. Foy Together With the Two Visions He Received in the Months of January and February 1842*[1]—the first two visions of William Foy. An African-American Freewill Baptist preacher, Foy was the first of several who would receive visions and a prophetic call during the Advent movement.[2] James did not know it then, but he would soon encounter still another individual whom God would call. He later recorded that it was at this time that he first noticed Ellen Harmon and began to admire her personality. "She was then a Christian of the most devoted type," he wrote. "And although but 16, she was a laborer in the cause of Christ in public and from house to house."[3]

When Joshua Himes visited Portland shortly after October 22, 1844, and told its discouraged Adventists that they should prepare for another cold Maine winter, White reported that his feelings were almost uncontrollable. He wept like a child.[4] Numbly James helped his father and brothers harvest whatever crops there were as they prepared for winter.

After the emotional high of the months before October 22 and then the trauma of when Christ did not come, the Millerites responded in a number of ways. Most abandoned any thought of Christ's immediate return. They either crept back to their previous churches or lost all interest in religion. Some, such as White, clung to their belief in the Adventist doctrine and tried to figure out why Christ had failed to appear.[5] Perhaps He would still return before too long? A few of them—again including James—began to set new dates. He looked for the Second Coming to happen during 1845[6] by interpreting the "fourth watch" of Matthew 14:25 to imply that Christ would delay His return for a year. "Do we *know* what watch the Lord is coming?" he asked an Adventist believer named Jacobs. "Certainly. Three [watches] have passed, and there is but four. All who see this light will receive a certainty that before the 10th day of the 7th month, 1845, our King will come, and we will watch, and like Noah, know the day. . . . Awake! Awake! Awake! Ye heralds of the Jubilee, and tell the scattered flock, The morning cometh."[7] And others slipped into all kinds of religious aberrations and fanaticism.

Sometime during the winter of 1844-1845, White heard that Ellen Harmon had had a vision relating to the Millerite movement, one given to her as she prayed with four other women in an attempt to find meaning in their spiritual disappointment. For people to have visions was not an unknown phenomenon in New England, especially in the Wesleyan/ Methodist tradition of the time. Ellen Harmon's vision depicted Christ guiding God's people out of a world of darkness while at the same time warning them not to give up their spiritual journey. For them to now turn back would imperil their eternal existence. The vision also taught that the disappointed Millerites must not doubt their experience. Because it endorsed what the Millerites had gone through, the vision would have caught White's attention even if he had not already become aware of Ellen as a person.

James White heard, in her account, assurance of God's leading. The Lord, having been with them in the past, would continue to remain with them in the future. They were right to cling to their hope of the Second Coming. Christ would return. White would use the vision to rally those receptive to Ellen Harmon's spiritual gifts, and in the process he would form a new Adventist community.

One William Jordan and his sister, Sarah, decided to travel by sleigh to Orrington, Maine, a town on the Penobscot River and about 100 miles away. Earlier he had borrowed a horse from James White. Now he decided to return the animal and suggested that Ellen Harmon accompany them. It would give her a chance to relate her visions to a larger group. When Jordan stopped to leave the horse, he introduced her to James.

During much of 1845 James and Ellen focused their attention on relating her visions, dealing with fanaticism, and waiting for Christ to return. Many shared James White's conviction that Christ would appear on the tenth day of the seventh month, 1845. But Ellen Harmon saw in vision that they would be disappointed again.[8]

Also many Adventists concluded that if the Second Coming was indeed near, then it would not be right to marry. James shared this attitude. In October 1845 he called marriage "a wile of the devil."[9] He even declared, after an Adventist couple had announced their marriage, that they had "denied their faith"[10] in the Lord's immediate return. But he was simply reflecting the viewpoint of many Adventists, who felt that "such a step seemed to contemplate years of life in this world."[11]

In time, however, James White and Ellen Harmon realized that this present life might go on longer than they had assumed, and that Ellen had a divinely ordained role in this present life. She was God's contemporary messenger, and she needed to travel widely to present that message. Because travel was dangerous and physically demanding on the stagecoach lines, canal boats, and early railroads, she needed help and protection. In frail health and weighing only 80 pounds, she would often faint, remaining breathless for several minutes. In addition, contemporary culture disapproved of a woman journeying alone. Thus she could hardly go by herself, nor did any male relative have the time to accompany her. "It was necessary that she should have one or more attendants," James concluded. "Either her sister Sarah or Sister Foss traveled with her. And as neither her aged father nor feeble brother were suitable persons to travel with one so feeble, and introduce her and her mission to the people, [I], fully believing that her wonderful experience and work was of God, became satisfied that it was [my] duty to accompany them."[12]

For a time James White escorted her and another woman companion, but that raised questions of propriety. Criticism could destroy her prophetic influence. Already Ellen's mother had written to her, "Come home, Ellen, my daughter. False reports are being circulated about you. You should not be traveling all over the countryside like that. It is not fitting and proper for one of your age to do this."[13] When Ellen decided it would be best to return home, James rowed her and the Jordans 20 miles down the Penobscot River to Belfast, Maine, where they boarded a coastal steamer for Portland. Returning upriver, James and two friends were attacked by a mob. One of the ruffians horsewhipped James, then the men dragged them to jail for the night. The next morning the three went on their way with wounds and bruises.[14]

THOUGHTS OF MARRIAGE

Finally White decided that Ellen needed "a legal protector, and that we should unite our labors."[15] His admiration for her mission and Christian character had deepened into something else. Ellen said that he concluded that he "should [either] have to go away and leave me to go with whomsoever I would, or we must be married."[16] James felt that "God had a work for both of us to do, and he saw that we could greatly assist each other in that work. As she should come before the public, she needed a lawful protector; and God having chosen her as a channel of light and truth to the people in a special sense, she could be of great help to me."[17]

But the decision did not come hastily. White said "it was not until the matter of marriage was taken to the Lord by both, and we obtained an experience that placed the matter beyond the reach of doubt, that we took this important step."[18] They would marry even though most of their fellow Adventists regarded marriage as a denial of faith in an imminent return of Christ.[19]

James soon began to write others about the marriage plans. "Sister Ellen says that the way is made plain," he told a believer named Collins. "We are published [the approaching marriage had been publicly announced, a tradition of the time called "publishing the banns"; it gave people opportunity to bring up any reason why the marriage should not take place]; we shall be married perhaps Monday."[20] Though startled at first, people began to accept the idea. James and Ellen, meanwhile, discussed the possibility of moving farther west, maybe to Dartmouth.

By now James was 25, Ellen 18. On Sunday, August 30, 1846, a Portland, Maine, justice of the peace married them in (ironically enough) a civil ceremony. As the couple recited their vows, she barely reached his shoulder. James was more than six feet, Ellen five feet two inches. Their marriage certificate consisted of a small printed form stating: "This certifies, that Mr. James S. White and Miss Ellen Harmon of Portland were this day joined in marriage according to the laws of this State, by me, Charles Harding, Justice of the Peace." There would be no honeymoon. It was not yet a widespread custom (besides, they had no money anyway). As James observed many years later, they entered married life "penniless, with few friends, and broken in health. Mrs. White has suffered ill health from a child, . . . and although I had inherited a powerful constitution, impru-dence in study at school, and in lecturing . . . had made me a dyspeptic [someone with digestive problems]."[21]

Ellen fainted many times a week during the first year of marriage,[22] and they had few possessions. He wrote to his friends the Hastings that "all that we have including clothes, bedding, and household furniture we have with us in a three-foot trunk, and that is but half full. We have noth-ing else to do but to serve God and go where God opens the way for us."[23]

A LOVING BUT HUMAN FAMILY

Though some might have dismissed their union as a marriage of con-venience, love did exist between them, and it would grow, despite (and maybe even because of) many trials. James and Ellen White were two hu-mans who struggled in a harsh, difficult world.

We can witness their relationship developing through the years in the letters between them. The natural reserve of two New Englanders did not often encourage them to express their emotions, but it did show. For ex-ample, in early October 1860, about three weeks after the birth of their fourth child, John Herbert, she told James, who was traveling: "You may be assured I miss your little visits in my room, but the thought you are doing the will of God helps me to bear the loss of your company."[24] A short time later, after commenting about Herbert's development, she ex-pressed her loneliness that James's "place at the dining room table is va-cant."[25] The next month she happily wrote him that "one more week brings you home. We shall all be rejoiced to see you home again."[26]

Those sentiments continued through the years. In 1874 she assured him that "I have the highest estimate of your ability."[27] As James traveled to camp meetings and other appointments, Ellen wrote to him that "I have no special news to write to you, except I greatly desire to see your face and look forward to the time with great pleasure."[28] A week later she added: "All will be rejoiced to see you here and none more so than your Ellen."[29] The next year she observed that "my husband is very attentive to me, seeking in every way to make my journeyings and labor pleasant and re-lieve it of weariness."[30] Before James's death she described him as "my crown of rejoicing."[31] And a quarter century after his death she referred to him as "the best man that ever trod shoe leather."[32]

James White also expressed similar feelings. "Marriage marks an important era in the lives of men," he wrote. "'Whoso findeth a wife findeth a good thing, and obtaineth favour of the Lord,' is the language of wisdom. Proverbs 18:22. . . . We were married August 30, 1846, and from that hour unto the present she has been my crown of rejoicing."[33]

He would especially seek her companionship during periods of sickness or depression. Late in October of 1877 Ellen wrote to her son and daughter-in-law about how James was "so lonesome I have to ride out with him and devote considerable time to keep him company. Father is quite cheerful but talks but little."[34] About a year later she confided to her daughter-in-law, "I am his constant companion in riding and by the fireside. Should I go, shut myself up in a room, and leave him sitting alone, he would become nervous and restless. . . . He depends on me and I shall not leave him in his feebleness."[35]

FAMILY SUPPORT AND OPPOSITION

The couple spent their first year of married life at her parents', first briefly in Portland, then Gorham, Maine, where her father, Robert Harmon, Sr., bought a farm.

Until recently it has been difficult in most cultures for a couple to make a living by themselves. To survive, people had to live together in extended families. Neighbors and even whole villages worked together to raise enough food and manufacture other necessities. The Bible repeatedly urges people to aid each other. As early Christians were expelled by their natural families, the church became their new extended family, providing material, emotional, and spiritual support. James White experienced the pain of being rejected by part of his family. His brother John, writing to their sister, Anna, attacked James's involvement in the Millerite movement. "I deeply regret that Brother James has fallen into the snare of the devil and Mr. Miller," he declared, relegating the 2300-day teaching to the work of a sick imagination.[36] John's wife rejected the Adventist shut-door teaching:[37]

> "O! What a cruel work has Satan wrought
> Upon the brain of our dear brother James.
> The door of mercy shut to sinful man?
> Not yet! Thank God; for Christ is pleading still

Before His Father's throne; with wounded hands
And feet and side, and temples pierced there
With sword and thorns; saying 'Father, spare them.
I have bled, and groaned. And sweat, and died.'
Not yet! Oh, no! My soul prays God not yet
Has pity ceased to flow for fallen man.
But from the rocky heights of Calvary
I see its crimson tide of mercy flow
To wash away the guilty stain of sin."[38]

Modern industrialized society now enables couples and even single persons to earn a living on their own. More and more modern Westerners live by themselves. But the time of James and Ellen White's early marriage was closer to the ancient preindustrial world, when people could survive only within extended families. Reflecting this pattern, the couple received help from those relatives sympathetic to their beliefs. But such family resources were extremely limited. James White was modern in the sense that he found it difficult to share the home of Ellen's parents.

For James to preach the Advent message, and Ellen her visions, without the aid of independent wealth, their fellow believers also had to become a vital part of their extended family and financially support them. Many did. Sometimes, though, it would lead to resentment and tension.

[1] Portland, Maine: The Pearson Brothers, 1845.

[2] For additional information on Foy, see Delbert W. Baker, *The Unknown Prophet* (Washington, D.C.: Review and Herald Pub. Assn., 1987).

[3] *Life Sketches: Ancestry, Early Life, Christian Experience, and Extensive Labors, of Elder James White, and His Wife, Mrs. Ellen G. White* (Battle Creek, Mich.: Steam Press of the SDA Pub. Assn., 1880), p. 126.

[4] James White, *Life Incidents*, p. 182.

[5] Apparently White did struggle with some kind of doubt. See JW to Gilbert Collins, Aug. 26, 1846.

[6] James White, *A Word to the "Little Flock"* (Brunswick, Maine: 1847), p. 22.

[7] JW to Enoch Jacobs, Sept. 20, 1845.

[8] James White, *A Word to the "Little Flock,"* p. 22.

[9] *Day Star,* Oct. 11, 1845.

[10] *Ibid.*

[11] *Life Sketches* (1888), p. 126.

[12] *Ibid.,* p. 238.

[13] Quoted in Margaret Rossiter Thiele, *By Saddle and Sleigh* (Washington, D.C.: Review and Herald Pub. Assn., 1965), p. 106. Mrs. Harmon's concern may have been motivated by reports of Israel Dammon (or Demmen) trial. A Portland, Maine, newspaper named Ellen in its account. Dammon was arrested and brought to trial because of his fanatical behavior. See Frederick Hoyt, ed., "Trial of Elder I. Dammon Reported for the *Pscataquis Farmer,*" *Spectrum,* August 1987, pp. 29-36. For a discussion of this controversial incident, see Rennie Schoepflin, "Scandal or Rite of Passage? Historians on the Dammon Trial," *Spectrum,* August 1987, pp. 37-50.

[14] *Ellen G. White: Her Friends and Fellow Workers,* p. 13; "Interview" with James White; cf JW to Enoch Jacobs, Sept. 6, 1845.

[15] *Life Sketches* (1888), p. 238.

[16] EGW manuscript 131, 1906.

[17] *Life Sketches* (1888), p. 126.

[18] *Ibid.* (1880), p. 126.

[19] *Ibid.*

[20] JW to Gilbert Collins, Aug. 26, 1846.

[21] *Life Sketches* (1880), p. 127.

[22] JW to Elvira Hastings, Aug. 22, 1847.

[23] JW to Leonard and Elvira Hastings, Apr. 27, 1848.

[24] EGW to JW (letter 10, 1860), Oct. 12, 1860.

[25] EGW to JW (letter 12a, 1860) October 1860.

[26] EGW to JW (letter 14, 1860), Nov. 19, 1860.

[27] EGW to JW (letter 41, 1874), July 11, 1874.

[28] EGW to JW (letter 44, 1874), July 17, 1874.

[29] EGW to JW (letter 47, 1874), July 23, 1874.

[30] Ellen G. White, *Daughters of God: Messages Especially for Women* (Hagerstown, Md.: Review and Herald Pub. Assn., 1998), p. 261.

[31] *Life Sketches* (1888), p. 125.

[32] Ellen G. White manuscript 131, 1906.

[33] *Life Sketches* (1888), p. 125.

[34] EGW to Children (letter 25, 1877), Oct. 16, 1877.

[35] EGW to WCW and Mary White (letter 4d, 1878), Jan. 22, 1878.

[36] John White to Anna White, June 1846, quoted in Robinson, pp. 40, 41.

[37] We can get a sense of the role the various concepts of the shut door concept played in early Adventism through a number of statements in James White's early letters.

"When I think of my strange course for nearly two years, sometimes the thought rushes over me that it is all wrong: I mean my course. I have no doubt as to the Advent history, shut door and all, not one. But I have sought with intense interest for heavenly wisdom and I will believe that God has led me. Amen" (JW to Gilbert Collins, Aug. 26, 1846).

"Do not think Brother James is getting formal [as in the "organized" churches] or is going to try to convert people to the Advent faith. No, its [sic.] too late. But its [sic.] our duty on some occasions to give a reason for our hope I think, even to *swine*.

"I have no doubt as to the Advent history, shut door and all, not one" (*ibid.*).

"The brethren are strong on the Sabbath and Shut Door." "So the Shut door and Sabbath is [sic.] the present truth. These truths will form and keep up the same mark of distinction between us and unbelievers as God made in 1844" (JW to Leonard and Elvira Hastings, Aug. 26, 1848).

Writing about a general meeting at the house of Stockbridge Howland in Topsham, Maine, he stated that "the principal points on which we dwell as present truth are the 7th day Sabbath and Shut Door" (JW to Leonard and Elvira Hastings, Oct. 2, 1848).

In an addition to one of James White's letters, Ellen White saw in vision that Brother Stowell of Paris, Maine, was wavering on the shut door and Sabbath. She felt that she had to visit him, had visions there, and strengthened his faith (EGW to Leonard and Elvira Hastings [letter 5, 1849], Apr. 21, 1849).

James believed that Miller, Brown, Fassett, Shipman, Porter, Hale, Cook, and others taught the shut door (JW to Leonard Hastings, July 21, 1850).

For a discussion of the various usages and understandings of the term *shut door*, see George R. Knight, *Millennial Fever and the End of the World: A Study of Millerite Adventism* (Boise, Idaho: Pacific Press Pub. Assn., 1993).

[38] John White to Anna White, June 1846, quoted in Robinson, p. 41.

CHAPTER V

THE FOUNDATION OF A
NEW MOVEMENT

THE Whites worked together as a team. "Our meetings were usually conducted in such a manner that both of us took part," he later wrote. "I would give a doctrinal discourse, then Mrs. W. would give an exhortation of considerable length, melting her way into the tenderest feelings of the congregation. . . . While I presented the evidences, and sowed the seed, she was to water it. And God did give the increase."[1] They went from place to place, planting the seeds of a new church. Few people during their lifetimes would travel as much as they did.

THE HAZARDS OF NINETEENTH-CENTURY TRAVEL

During a time of primitive or nonexistent roads, a journey could be easier in the winter, because people could resort to sleighs, which could cut across any snow-covered landscape. When the Whites did not use sleighs, carriages, or farm wagons, they employed the horse-drawn stages, canal boats, and primitive railroad trains of the 1840s and 1850s. The couple often wrote about their traveling trials.[2] The rough-riding stage coaches had to negotiate the crude roads hacked through the forests and mountains of the northeastern United States. Such roads could be dusty in dry weather or bottomless mud during rain or the spring thaw. Because of the mud, road builders in many areas made so-called corduroy roads by paving them with logs. Naturally the bumpy logs would shake any vehicle to pieces as well as make for an extremely uncomfortable ride. The lack of heavy road construction equipment meant that road builders did not remove rocks and other obstruction but just ran roads over or around them.[3] Bridges were few, and travelers either forded the streams and rivers or crossed on primitive ferries. Wagon-makers would determine the size of wheels they used by the depth of river crossings on the route a wagon would travel on.

Mule- or horse-drawn canal boats were perhaps the most comfortable early form of transportation. The explosion of canal building across such states as New York, Ohio, and Indiana during the 1820s opened up travel to many areas. Canal boats came in three types: those that transported only freight, those that carried both freight and a limited number of passengers, and those devoted exclusively to passengers. Once, when the Whites were traveling with Joseph Bates, the couple transferred from a mixed freight-passenger craft to a passenger liner. Unfortunately, Bates still had the money for their fare. When he tried to leap from one vessel to the other, he fell into the canal.

For much of the nineteenth century passenger-carrying ships regularly traveled along the New England coast. They were especially popular because of the lack of good roads. In 1847 the Whites boarded a vessel in Portland, Maine, bound for Boston. A strong storm blew up and nearly sank the ship.

Early trains were especially dangerous. Many pioneer railroads first used wooden rails topped with a layer of iron. Sometimes the iron strap would break free from the wooden rail, curl upward, and then rip open the bottom of the wooden coaches as they passed over. Soon the wooden rails were replaced with all-iron ones. But the early iron rails were brittle and could break easily, derailing the primitive passenger coaches. Also, any object that got on the rough tracks could cause a wreck. Primitive braking systems and overheated friction bearings constantly contributed to accidents. The crude suspension systems meant the cars jolted and bounced on the rough track. Trains were slow. Even during the 1870s when the Whites frequently traveled to the West Coast, trains averaged only 20 miles per hour. And they were drafty.

The all-wood construction of the railroad cars meant they would splinter in a wreck. During cold weather the wood- or coal-burning stoves in each passenger coach could tumble over and set the car ablaze. Those who visit the Railroad Hall of the Museum of American History at the Smithsonian Institution in Washington, D.C., will get an idea of the dangers that early railroad passengers faced. The small wooden Camden and Amboy passenger coach shows the fragility of the passenger cars the Whites rode as they traveled to present the Sabbatarian Adventist teachings. The steam locomotives could not only explode in a wreck, scalding the crew to death, but would hurl fragments of metal into the rest of the train. Train wrecks were constant until the end of the nineteenth century, and the statistics of deaths and injuries for the nineteenth century are appalling.[4] If any form of transportation had comparable statistics today, the government would immediately shut it down.

One time, in Michigan, the Whites boarded a train at Jackson. For some reason James, who had traveled constantly for years, felt uncomfortable about the trip. Several times he mentioned his unease but insisted that they had to go. The Whites and those who had accompanied them to the station that evening prayed for protection. James and Ellen then boarded one of the coaches. Ellen told her husband that they must move to another car. Even there she felt uncomfortable.

Just three miles west of the station the locomotive struck an ox lying on the track. Locomotives did not yet have cowcatchers to push animals and other objects out of the way. The collision derailed the engine, killing the engineer, a fireman, and several passengers. The Whites' coach violently jerked back and forth, then jolted to a stop. When Ellen opened a window, she saw that the engine and cars ahead of them had run off the track, but theirs had stopped about 100 feet behind the rest. Somehow its crude link and pin coupler had come unfastened, allowing their coach to roll to a stop behind the rest of the train. Its chain and bolt had not broken but lay on the end platform. One end of the car they had first boarded now rested on top of the cars that had been ahead of it. The baggage car containing their trunk of books was still intact. (Because Sabbatarian Adventists did not yet have any system of distributing Adventist books, the Whites would carry a supply along with them to sell at each place they visited. The sale of such books also paid their traveling expenses.)

After they hastily exited the car, James carried his wife across a swampy area. They walked a half mile to the nearest dwelling. Ellen remained there while he rode with another man back to Jackson in order to find doctors for the injured.

Another time, even though their train derailed after traveling only nine miles, they had to wait five hours for rescue. The passengers went hungry until James remembered that he had brought three pounds of crackers with him, which he shared with them.

Besides the constant danger from wrecks, the trains were uncomfortable; either too cold or too hot during the winter, and stifling during the summer. Tobacco smoke made even stations unbearable, and the Whites would have to pace the platform outside to find fresh air. Trains often ran late, and because the Whites would constantly miss connections, they would have to spend hours waiting for the next train. Many times they would reach their destination long after dark. Trains did not yet have dining cars, and the Whites would have to live on the cold food they had brought in a basket or reheat it on the dangerous stoves in each coach. Because safe and comfortable hotels were few and far between, and because the Whites' funds were at first almost nonexistent, they had to depend upon the hospitality of local believers. Constantly being in other peoples' homes gave them little privacy, and was both physically and emotionally exhausting.

ISOLATED BELIEVERS

But despite the inconveniences, the Whites journeyed from one individual or group of believers to another. They felt divinely compelled to do so. Such travel was especially vital during the early days of the Sabbatarian Adventist movement. Believers might live 30 miles or more from the nearest fellow Adventist, and with little or no transportation, their sense of isolation was intense. Readers of early Sabbatarian Adventist publications often wrote about how months or even more than a year might go by before they heard a sermon or attended an Adventist meeting. The Whites understood that feeling. They had experienced it themselves. James White wrote to his friend Stockbridge Howland that "here is not one soul that we can meet with or unite in serving the Lord." The sense of isolation could also make him irritable, as when he continued, "Oh, I am sick of our ungodly, hypocritical, dishonest, cheating neighbors."[5] The loneliness often led White to refer to himself and other Adventist believers as "outcasts."[6] His powerful spiritual witness and leadership during such travels was a vital factor in the survival of the Sabbatarian Adventist movement.

James captured the confidence of the isolated believers and encouraged their faith. His personality and the strong friendships he formed with those early believers were just as important as Adventist doctrine itself in establishing the core of the early Sabbatarian Adventist movement. And social relationships held it together just as much as a common body of belief. Many of those White became friends with would be the first leaders of the Seventh-day Adventist Church. Strong loyalties developed between him and them.

In addition, the Whites brought the Sabbath teaching to new areas. Joseph Bates had introduced them to the concept of the seventh-day Sabbath early in 1846. At first they questioned the idea of its observance, thinking he was wrong to stress one commandment more than the others. But a 48-page tract that Bates published in August 1846 encouraged the couple to accept it shortly after they married. At first the White's Sabbathkeeping created some tension with Ellen's parents. But the Harmons also studied Bates's tract and were observing the Sabbath by August 1848. And some point during this period Ellen asked her husband to rebaptize her, perhaps in recognition of her acceptance of the Sabbath doctrine.[7]

To spread Ellen's visions, James printed a broadside (a single-page publication) in 1846, then a 24-page pamphlet entitled *A Word to the "Little Flock"* came off the press in Brunswick, Maine, during May 1857. In it he wrote that "Dreams and Visions are among the signs that precede the great and notable days of the Lord. And as the signs of that day have been, and still are fulfilling, it must be clear to every unprejudiced mind, that the time has fully come, when the children of God may expect dreams and visions from the Lord. . . .

"The Bible is a perfect, and complete revelation. It is our only rule of faith and practice. But this is no reason, why God may not show the past, present, and future fulfilment of His word, in these *last days,* by dreams and visions; according to Peter's testimony. True visions are given to lead us to God, and His written word; but those that are given for a new rule of faith and practice, separate from the Bible, cannot be from God, and should be rejected."[8]

In 1862 White supplied a balanced and carefully reasoned introduction on prophecy and other spiritual gifts to M. E. Cornell's book entitled *Miraculous Powers.* Cornell's book sought to show that spiritual gifts still continued in various denominations. James later issued the introduction as a separate 23-page tract entitled "Perpetuity of Spiritual Gifts."[9]

EARLY ADVENTIST WORSHIP

In contrast to the lecture and meeting approach of so much New England religion, Ellen Harmon White's visions exemplified a more charismatic style of worship that help distinguish early Adventism. Such experiences balanced the intellectual emphasis of prophetic charts and biblical discourses by introducing a more personal and emotive element in spirituality and worship. Adventist religion was not just reason and theory—it was also emotion and individual spirituality. God spoke not just through the study of Scripture but also through a sense of the personal presence of the Holy Spirit and His working in individual lives. True religion was an encounter with God, a Spirit-induced feeling as well as the clear testimony of the printed word. It must let Him lead through His Spirit (in some ways echoing the Quaker spirituality that had shaped the Middle Atlantic states). God worked through more spiritual gifts than the inspired Word alone.[10] We see this in action, for example, in an account of some incidents that James White recorded in the *Review and Herald.*

"We went to the house feeling that we had nothing for the people. We told brethren on the way that we could not decide on any subject, and wished them to select. We sung a hymn, and had great freedom in prayer; sung again, but felt perplexed as to duty. In this state of mind, knowing not what to do, we gave liberty to others to use the time, when Mrs. W arose and spoke with much freedom. The place was filled with the Spirit of the Lord. Some rejoiced, others wept. All felt that the Lord was drawing very near. How sacred the place. Those present will never forget that meeting. When seated, Mrs. W began to praise the Lord, and continued rising higher and higher in perfect triumph in the Lord, till her voice changed, and the deep, clear shouts of Glory! Hallelujah! thrilled every heart. She was in vision.

"Unknown to us there was a poor, discouraged brother present, who had thrown his armor down, in consequence, in part, at least, of neglect by his wealthy brethren, and was returning to strong habits which threatened the happiness of himself and family. A most touching and encouraging message was given for him. By the grace of God he raised his head that very evening, and he and his good wife are again happy in hope. Monterey church will never forget that evening. At least they never should. . . .

"In the afternoon the Lord's Supper was partaken by the believing assembly. But while in prayer at the commencement of the meeting, awful solemnity rested down upon the place. Most all wept, several aloud. The scenes of Calvary came vividly up, and we all felt that it was good to weep before the Lord. . . .

"Sabbath, the 17th, we spent with the church at Battle Creek, and enjoyed freedom and a blessed season in speaking upon the unity of the church of Christ and perpetuity of the Gifts. We gave it as our opinion that instead of undervaluing what Gifts are manifested among us, it would be better to thank God for what we have, and pray for more."[11]

Adventist religion was not just what one believed but also what the Holy Spirit could do in each life. Believers sought not only propositional truth but transformed lives. Such encounters with God and the changes they produced could be striking, even charismatic. An Adventist named G. W. Holt declared of one Adventist gathering that "the power of God was manifest in our first meeting. The preaching of Bro. Cornell was not with enticing words of man's wisdom, but in demonstration of the Spirit and of power. The spirit of confession was cherished in our meetings. And as heart-felt and deep confessions were made, the cry for mercy from a broken heart, was breathed forth with earnestness and fervency that we scarce ever witnessed before. The Lord heard, and souls were set at liberty. Shouts of 'glory' from full hearts might have been heard afar off. Parents confessed to children, and children to parents. Some have been converted, and are going to Mount Zion with their parents. . . . The conversation we hear now, is about 'gold, white raiment and eye-salve, and less about farms, houses, horses and other things of this world.'"[12]

To James White, one of the most important of these spiritual gifts which could change lives was the gift of prophecy—and it was manifested through Ellen White. He would defend the integrity of her gift, and of her role, through their years together. White would especially stress that, because of her limited education and other limitations, she accomplished all that she did only through a true prophetic gift.[13]

Unfortunately, sometimes it was easier to accept her prophetic gift when it was directed to others than to himself. But when she had a message for him—as we shall see later, that could be another matter.[14]

ELLEN WHITE'S FIRST LITERARY ASSISTANT

James especially helped her with her writing, particularly the grammatical part. She was insecure about her writing ability. In 1873, frustrated by her literary limitations, she wrote in her diary that she was not a "scholar," a term used at the time for simply being a student, and that she was "not a grammarian."[15] But James had been a teacher. She wrote that "while my husband lived, he acted as a helper and counselor in the sending out of the messages that were given to me. We traveled extensively. Sometimes light would be given to me in the night season, sometimes in the daytime before large congregations. The instruction I received in vision was faithfully written out by me, as I had time and strength for the work. Afterward we examined the matter together, my husband correcting grammatical errors and eliminating needless repetition. Then it was carefully copied for the persons addressed, or for the printer."[16]

James would continue to help her editorially for the rest of his life, though sometimes it frustrated him because of time limitations.[17] "I have so much writing," he once lamented, "that to have her book added would kill me."[18] And when he suffered from depression brought on by the strokes he faced later in life, he could write, "I have felt an interest in [her] writings that no language can express, and at the same time have felt terribly grieved at some things."[19] (He did not elaborate on what he had in mind.) Then, at those times, he no longer wanted to counsel his wife; instead, he wanted to control her.[20]

A GROWING FAMILY

James's first son, Henry Nichols, was born August 26, 1847. The name honored the son of Otis Nichols, the Whites' good friends at Dorchester, Massachusetts. Both James and Ellen had to be frequently away from the child because of travel. The boy would stay with friends. White would often write, inquiring about the child. "How is my dear little Henry?" he asked the Howlands. After requesting a letter about the boy, the father told them, "Kiss Henry for me." Then echoing the parenting style of the time, James added, "Whip him if he is not a good boy. That agrees with the good Book."[21] A few months later he proudly declared to friends, "Henry is well and has grown wonderfully. He is a real good boy."[22] White would send his love to his sons.[23] In addition, he often included notes to the children of those he wrote to.[24]

In October 1847 the couple accepted an invitation from the Howland family of Topsham, Maine, to share the second floor of their home. Located at the corner of Main and Elm streets, it was a large house for the time, 30' x 40', with two full stories and a partial one under the roof. The Whites borrowed furniture to set up housekeeping. James cut firewood and worked on railroad construction to support himself. He crushed and hauled stone at a railroad cut on what is now the Guilford/Springfield Terminal Railway a few miles north of Freeport, Maine. His foreman had been a rough, swearing man named George Cobb, who later became a Seventh-day Adventist.[25]

The Whites received a request to attend a Bible conference at Rocky Hill, Connecticut, in April 1848. It would be the first general gathering of Sabbath-observing Adventists.

During the summer of 1848 James White and some others mowed hay in the fields near the Albert Belden home at 87 and a half cents an acre in order to earn money so that they could travel to conferences around New York State. The horse-drawn mowing machine did not yet exist, so he had to do it all by hand-held scythe. His labor earned him $40, and from then on he would devote himself full-time to ministry.

JAMES WHITE, PUBLISHER

At the Dorchester, Massachusetts, conference during November 1848 Ellen received a vision that James must start a periodical to disseminate the doctrinal understandings developing among the little group of Sabbath-observing Adventists. James intended to use the new journal to spread knowledge of the Sabbath among Adventists. "Unless they keep the commandments of God," he believed, "they will be lost. I do not expect that many of them will receive the truth, yet we have a duty to do to them."[26] In contrast to his letter to Collins of August 26, 1846 (see pp. 44, 45), his understanding of the purpose of the Sabbatarian Adventist movement was expanding.

Because of financial and other problems, however, he could not publish anything immediately. Then, with the aid of a 75-cent Bible and a concordance with both covers missing, he began during the summer of 1849 to prepare articles for an eight-page publication he named *Present*

Truth. White was able to get 1,000 copies printed, on credit, at a Middletown, Connecticut, printer. He then borrowed a horse and buggy belonging to Albert Belden to transport them Rocky Hill, Connecticut. There a small group of believers folded, wrapped, and addressed the magazines. After they prayed for God's blessing on the new periodical, James White put them in a carpetbag and walked the eight miles back down the gently rolling Connecticut River Valley to the Middletown post office to mail them. He issued the first four issues from Middletown during July through September of that year. Consisting largely of articles he had written himself, they helped create a sense of community for the scattered Sabbath-observing Adventists. Later issues would originate in Oswego, New York, and Paris, Maine.

At first the meager results of his publishing efforts and the lack of funds left him discouraged. People did not seem interested in the periodicals. "As for the poor little paper, it has so little sympathy, and (I fear) so few prayers that I think it will die."[27] His fellow pioneer, Joseph Bates, didn't see much need for Sabbatarian Adventist periodicals.[28] Bates thought tracts and pamphlets were all that the movement required.

In his January 10, 1850, letter White includes an account of a vision Ellen had on the need to publish more. "I saw," she wrote, "that paper [James's new periodical], and that it was needed. That souls were hungry for the truth that must be written in the paper. I saw that if the paper stopped for want of means, and those hungry sheep died for want of the paper, it would not be James's fault, but it would be the fault of those to whom God lent His money to be faithful stewards over, and they let it lie idle; and the blood of souls would be upon their garments. I saw that the paper should go; and if they let it die they would weep in anguish soon. I saw that God did not want James to stop yet; but he must *write, write, write, write,* and speed the message and let it go. I saw that it would go where God's servants cannot go!"[29]

By 1850 he had published the first of several songbooks and hymnals that he would produce through the years. Entitled *Hymns for God's Peculiar People That Keep the Commandments of God and the Faith of Jesus,* it was a 48-page pamphlet containing 53 hymns. The songs consisted only of words without music. He produced seven other hymnals and supplements between 1852 and 1861. White obtained many of the selections by encouraging Sabbatarian Adventists to send in their favorites, and he tried to include as wide a variety as possible.

While working on the 1861 edition, for example, he announced in the *Review,* "Not a type is set on the new Hymn Book yet. Please send in good Hymns and Tunes, and point out defects in those in the old Book. We want the best Hymn Book in the world. We [I] dare not take the whole responsibility of selecting. Neither have we the least idea of leaving this important work to any one or two men. Let us all take hold and have an admirable Book that will suit all so far as possible." [30]

White also requested church members to compose hymns about the Sabbath and other topics of interest to Sabbatarian Adventists. The 1855 volume was the first to include some music, and the 1861 volume had 529 songs. He was proud of his skill and success at music publishing. "All I have ever done in that line was well done. Our last Hymn Book was a miserable failure simply because others controlled." [31]

The sale of such hymnbooks provided a way to finance other projects as well as give James funds to help others. A son (Edson White) worked with him on songbooks for many years, and later Ellen White's nephew (Frank E. Belden) also entered the music publishing business.

Friends and relatives continued to help the Whites. In the spring of 1849 Albert Belden, of Rocky Hill, Connecticut, sent them some money and an invitation to live in the area. That June they moved to the Middletown/Rocky Hill region. Clarissa Bonfoey, who had taken care of Henry White while his parents traveled in New York, inherited some household furnishings from her mother. She suggested that she join the Whites, share with them her household goods, and work for them while James and Ellen wrote and traveled in ministry. They accepted her offer, and together with Miss Bonfoey moved into an unfinished part of Albert Belden's house on his farm two miles from Rocky Hill.

FANATICISM AND FRACTURE

As we have already seen, when Christ did not come on October 22 the Millerites had coped with their disappointment in a variety of ways. The various forms of fanaticism espoused by those who did not immediately abandon their belief in the Second Advent would linger and trouble the evolving Sabbatarian Adventist movement. One major theme among such fanatics was that Christ had indeed come on October 22, but in a spiritual way. He now lived in the perfect person of His people. Those who advocated the concept also believed that God's people were now in the seventh millennium since sin had entered the world. An eternal Sabbath had begun.[32] Because by definition a Sabbath is a time to abstain from work, those who taught the concept concluded that they should no longer hold jobs or do any other labor. Because they considered themselves spiritually in heaven, they attempted to demonstrate that fact by taking literally Christ's injunction to humble themselves and become as little children (Matt. 18:3, 4). They crawled around on their hands and knees like infants and refused to use chairs and tables. Ellen Harmon had had to oppose both the no-work and the false-humility doctrines. In addition, the fanatics claimed that since they were already in heaven, they should be like the angels who do not marry. But they could have spiritual wives—usually someone other than their legal spouses—in a nonsexual relationship. The fanatics practiced foot washing between the sexes and other customs guaranteed to shock their conservative New England neighbors.

Such fanaticism had so fractured the Adventist community in Paris, Maine, that they did not meet together for a number of years. Like so many other New England towns, Paris was part of a cluster of settlements, each usually bearing a geographical designation (West Paris, South Paris, etc.). For a time the village prospered, until the railroad passed it by and the county seat moved from Paris to South Paris. Paris contained many large homes, including that of Hannibal Hamlin, Abraham Lincoln's first vice president. The village itself perched on a long ridge.

In some ways one could say that the ridge symbolized the barriers that had thrust themselves up between the various members of the little group of believers. As you look west from the little community, especially in the evening, you will notice several ranges of low hills, one rising behind the other and culminating in the White Mountains of New Hampshire. The view itself portrayed the impact of what happened at Paris would have on the rest of James White's life. The reaction to this and succeeding events there would keep rising to create bitterness, distrust, and tragedy between the Whites and two local families, the Andrewses and the Smiths. As we shall see, those feelings would spill over into the Sabbatarian Adventist movement at large and linger for decades.

Sometime after October 22, 1844, the Edward Andrews family had invited the Stowell family to live with them in their large but simple house. The Stowells' 15-year-old daughter, Marion, read the tract on the Sabbath by Thomas M. Preble, who had labored with William Miller and Joshua V. Himes. Convinced by its arguments, the girl shared it with her older brother, Oswald. The two of them decided to observe the seventh-day Sabbath. Then she gave it to Edward's son, John Nevins Andrews, also 15 years old. Soon he, his parents, and seven other families in Paris accepted the Sabbath. But the new belief could not overcome the spirit of fanaticism that continued to plague the group. Almira Stevens, wife of Cyprian Stevens and the mother of John Andrews' future wife, Angeline, portrayed the period after October 22 as "sad and painful." The experience had created "divisions and subdivisions" and shattered the relationships between the little group until "each heart stood aloof."[33] Her own husband had been one of those whose fanatical behavior Ellen White before her marriage had to confront.[34] Another involved in the "no work" aberration had been Edward Andrews, John's father.

During March of 1846 John's aunt, Persis Sibley Andrews, reported in her diary that "we called upon brother Edward—who—poor deluded man—with his family still believe in the speedy coming of Christ—that the day of grace has been past this year. They have done no labor for more than two years and have lived in constant expectation that every day the world wo'd be consumed by fire. They have nearly expended all the property of their little community of 'Saints' & nearly exhausted the charity & patience of their friends so that 'if time continues' as Edward s'd he expected they wo'd be obliged to go to work. Some very likely families well situated with $3000 to $4000 of property have spent their all & and what is worse have kept their children from school & from industry & educated them only in cant & delusion."[35]

The "seventh millennium" theory that Edward Andrews followed would remain a problem in the church. Edward's son, John Nevins Andrews, would later publish his own version of it, and variations of the concept have plagued Seventh-day Adventism until the present day. Finally, in 1849, Ellen White had a vision that informed her that she and James should go to Paris and confront the fanaticism. Accompanied by Stockbridge Howland, they journeyed from Topsham to Paris for a meeting on September 14. There a man named F. T. Howland (no kin to Stockbridge) disrupted the meeting that the Whites had with the local Adventists. Stockbridge Howland prayed, then rose from his knees, pointed at the fanatic, and said, "You have torn the hearts of God's children and made them bleed. Leave this house, or God will smite you." The man fled. With his departure the attitude of the others began to change. As they acknowledged their faults to each other, the hostility and barriers broke down, and the fanaticism began to recede. "I would exchange a thousand errors for one truth," 20-year-old John Nevins Andrews proclaimed. He would always consider that meeting the moment of his conversion. The Paris Adventists once more started to worship together regularly.

From the Cyprian Stevens family would come not only the wife of John Nevins Andrews but also that of Uriah Smith. The two pioneer leaders would have a close relationship because of their wives. But it would be a relationship that would occasionally cause the Whites much grief. The character traits that had led Edward Andrews into fanaticism would eventually trigger new problems that would spread through the web of family ties and repeatedly threaten the Seventh-day Adventist Church itself. And Cyprian Stevens may still have rankled from the time Ellen had reproved him for his earlier fanaticism. The early Sabbatarian Adventists had the same feelings and emotions as any other human beings, and unfortunately hurts—real or imagined—could last a long time.

Although James traveled constantly to develop the fledgling movement, whenever possible he would publish an issue of a periodical. During the months of August, September, and November 1850, he printed five issues of the *Advent Review,* four in Auburn, New York, and the fifth in Paris, Maine. The publication had as its goal reaffirming certain positions advocated by the Millerite movement. The opening sentence of the first issue declared: "Our design in this review is to cheer and refresh the true believer, by showing the fulfilment of Prophecy in the past wonderful work of God, in calling out, and separating from the world and nominal church, a people who are looking for the second advent of the dear Saviour."[36] Although the periodical contained material by William Miller, Joshua V. Himes, Sylvester Bliss, and other longtime Adventists, it presented nothing that was particularly Sabbatarian Adventist. White would start a third publication for that purpose.

After an exhausting trip the Whites had made to Sutton, Vermont, the local believers raised $175 to buy them a horse and carriage, the first of a number of such gifts through the years. Ellen chose as her horse a slightly swaybacked dapple chestnut named Charlie. The animal liked to pluck apples as they passed an orchard and chew on them as he traveled along.

THE REVIEW AND HERALD

In 1850 the Whites moved in with the Edward Andrews family. James wrote that he had chosen the rural area to save expenses.[37] Edward had offered them free room and board. The Andrews home was two blocks from a local printer, G. L. Mellen and Company, that also housed the post office. Mellon would print the final issues of the *Present Truth* and the *Advent Review*. A meeting of Sabbatarian Adventist leaders at Paris authorized the new publication directed at fellow believers. Calling it the *Second Advent Review and Sabbath Herald*, White, as editor, stated that the periodical intended "to be strictly confined to those important truths that belong to the present time. We hope to be able to send you this enlarged size of the paper quite often, containing a simple and clear exposition of those great and sanctifying truths embraced in the message of the third angel."[38] The journal listed no subscription price, but suggested that those who could should send in donations while the poor would receive it free. Each issue listed the names of donors and the amounts they gave.

Unfortunately, White could not immediately keep his promise of frequent issues because of finances and other difficulties. But although at first it came off the press spasmodically, the publication replaced both the *Present Truth* and the *Advent Review*, and by 1853 it became a weekly publication that continues today (the *Adventist Review*). The first issue listed a "Publishing Committee" that included James White. In August 1851 the masthead identified him as editor. For the rest of his life he would serve either as its main editor, corresponding editor, or one of a group of editors.

Beverly Beem and Ginger Hanks Harwood have explored the role that the *Review and Herald* played in the formation of the early Seventh-day Adventist Church. They found that its letters to the editor described the *Review* "as 'teacher,' 'a welcome visitor,' and 'meat in due season.' One writer says, 'The *Review* has not been an idle servant here. It has traversed this region round about, and has been like the leaven of the scriptures.'

To its readers, it brings comfort and encouragement: 'I feel I should almost faint by the way, were it not for the *Review and Herald* which comes weekly bringing the blessed tidings of the kingdom and the prosperity of the cause.' It is loved 'for the precious truth you send forth to the scattered flock.' Another says concerning the *Review,* 'I thank my heavenly Father that there are servants giving meat to those who are hungry and thirsty, and to those who have fed on husks long enough.'"[39]

Beem and Harwood observe that "for many Sabbatarian Adventists it was only through the *Review* that they participated in the ordinary functions of a religious community. The connection with a larger band of believers the *Review* provided was critical for individuals living out their spiritual journey without the comfort and accountability afforded by a local congregation. The theme of loneliness and isolation appears repeatedly through these letters. It reflects the spiritual challenge of these early Adventist believers to maintain their stance. 'I am situated alone, as regards any of our faith and practice. The paper being all the teacher I have, is a welcome visitor,' says one writer. Another writes, 'Being so situated that I seldom have the privilege of meeting with any one of like precious faith, I truly hail the *Review* as a welcome messenger.' And another writer says, 'I feel lonesome here, having no one to speak to on the Sabbath, but I have your papers which cheer my heart.' And another voice says, 'There are no Sabbath keepers here by myself and companion. We feel very lonely, and I know not what we should do without the *Review.*'"[40]

The periodical's part in shaping and teaching doctrine is immediately obvious. But equally vital, as Beem and Harwood demonstrate, was its role in forming Sabbatarian Adventist spirituality and community. This involved not only articles but letters. They contained the personal testimony of Adventists as they sought and worked through their own religious experience. Believers then shared it through the pages of the *Review,* and that spirituality spread to other Adventists.

The fact that James White printed such material reminds us that Adventist life was a spiritual relationship as much as a body of teaching. Adventism was a personal, spiritual experience as well as a set of beliefs. James encouraged this role of the *Review* when he announced in its pages: "Wanted—On our table a large pile of spirited and interesting articles and communications, from, not only the Corresponding Editors, but also every

interested believer of present truth in the land. Where are the pens conse-
crated to the cause of truth? Where are those all over the land who we are
constrained to believe might, and therefore ought, to have a few thoughts
to utter in behalf of the message, or a few familiar words of exhortation or
experience, for the encouragement of their brethren and sisters?"[41]

In the words of Beem and Harwood, "producing the Review allowed
James White (and the group most closely associated with him) to create
and sustain a dialog that reflected . . . God's redemptive activity [among
Sabbatarian Adventists] and utilize it to reinforce faith in Christ's soon appearing. The pages of the Review allowed the group to promote their understanding of the Spirit-led religious life. The subjects selected,
arguments utilized, statements printed and items attended established a
field of discourse and set the standard for normative belief and spiritual
experience. The paper legitimated forms of spiritual practices and expectations discounted or discouraged in other religious circles and utilized
them as a demonstration of the reality of spiritual gifts as remarkable as
those given at Pentecost."[42]

James White's sensitivity to spirituality and the believer's relationship
to God would also emerge during later years in his growing awareness of
the need to emphasize it more among Seventh-day Adventist believers.

In addition to doctrinal and spiritual issues, the Review became the
community arena in which believers debated and worked through such
fundamental problems as church structure and organization. Without this
vital publication the Seventh-day Adventist Church would never have
come into existence or would have been long delayed.

POISONED RELATIONSHIPS

After the Whites had been with the Andrews family for a short time,
Edward and James came to a verbal agreement that the Whites would pay
$20 rent a year and $1 a week for food. As he began thinking about it,
though, James decided that it was not really a good arrangement.
Eventually he discovered that the local newspaper editor paid only $1.50
for board at a local tavern-hotel, a deal that James considered "worth more
than twice what we two dyspeptics got selecting the plainest [fare] from a
farmer's table."[43] Local tradition claimed that it was easier to till land on the
tops and sides of the hills, so pioneer hilltop farms such as Andrews' were

quite small and barely fed the family, let alone earned money to buy food from elsewhere.[44] Digestive problems prevented James from eating meat, butter, or any greasy food—the most common items a subsistence farming family such as the Andrewses could offer. White grumbled that the Andrewses usually served only corn bread and potatoes seasoned with a little salt and a few spoonfuls of milk. Because he and Ellen often stayed up to midnight or even 2:00 or 3:00 in the morning reading proofs for the new publication and constantly drove themselves, they needed more nourishing food. Between the poor diet and all that he was trying to accomplish, he was destroying his health. Soon he could barely walk the two blocks to the printshop. Also tension existed between the Whites and some of the local believers, making the situation at the Andrews home even more uncomfortable. James apparently reproved the shortcomings of some in either the Andrews or the Stevens families. And he did it so forcefully and with typical Maine bluntness that the people in Paris never forgot it. But considering the personalities of some of those involved, whoever might have dealt with them would have probably encountered a similar reaction.

Realizing that he had to do something to avoid "utter starvation," James found another place for him and Ellen to stay. Unfortunately, his decision upset Edward Andrews. Spurred on by the Cyprian Stevens family, Edward began to claim—according to White—that James had cheated him out of $8. What exactly happened is difficult to reconstruct, but we do know that for many years Edward Andrews expressed skepticism of both James White's leadership and of Ellen White's visions. He explained his lack of confidence in them by repeatedly bringing up the charge that James had defrauded him of the $8.[45] Could you trust a man, he argued, who would do that or believe in a prophet who would permit it? His attitude would poison not only fellow family members but many others in the emerging denomination. Both James and Ellen would frequently have to deal with the issue.

THE CASE OF N.A.H.

In 1850 James encountered another type of problem that would haunt him the rest of his life. That year he met a man we now know only by the initials N.A.H. The man was poor and extremely discouraged. People often donated money to White for various needs, and now he decided to use some of it. He gave N.A.H. $20, an amount then equivalent to several weeks' pay. James also offered him his own coat. Clothing was not yet mass-produced in the quantities that it is today, and since it was still largely handmade, proportionally expensive. Few people could afford more than a few items of clothing, unlike today, when we worry about how to clean out our closets and dispose of out-of-style garments. To give clothing away then was equivalent to donating furniture, major appliances, or even used automobiles today. In addition to the coat and money, James talked fellow believers into buying N.A.H. a horse and carriage.

Both James and Ellen would donate clothing to others the rest of their lives. J. O. Corliss, who had been one of a number of young ministers that the Whites had live with them while they learned ministerial skills through apprenticeship, reported that he had seen James give away as many as three overcoats to poor preachers during a single winter.[46] He provided a coat to L. R. Conradi for the young man to wear at his graduation.[47]

Near the end of 1850 the Whites received an invitation to attend a general meeting of Sabbatarian Adventists in Waterbury, Vermont, on January 18 and 19, 1851. Because James had already lent his own horse and carriage to John N. Andrews in order that John and Samuel Rhodes could visit believers in Vermont and what was then known as Canada East, he and Ellen would have to go to the expense of taking public transportation. First they traveled by train to Boston and northwest to New Ipswich, New Hampshire, to stop at the Leonard Hastings family. Leonard's wife, Elvira, had died February 28, and the Whites must have wanted to see how he and the children were doing.[48] A friend then drove them to Washington, New Hampshire. A 15-mile ride next brought them to the home of a Stephen Smith. Smith had been struggling with spiritualism. Perhaps, James thought, attending the Waterbury meeting would help the man get his religious bearings. White handed him $5—the money they had planned to use to pay their fare—to buy a horse. They would all ride in an open sleigh. Along the way they contacted a believer named Joseph Baker. But Baker, because of poor health and general discouragement, had decided to remain home. Again dipping into his funds, James offered him $5 so the man could travel in comfort by train.

As for the Whites, they rode in the open sleigh for three days to reach Waterbury. They did not even have a heavy robe to stay warm. Ellen later wrote that it would take years for James to recover from the exposure to cold that he endured on the trip.[49] When the Whites arrived at Waterbury, they discovered that many of those in attendance had been circulating rumors that James and Ellen had a better horse than they really needed—and far worse, were using the funds people had donated for the new *Review* for their own living expenses. Even Joseph Bates was involved in the whispering campaign. One of those most active in bringing the charges against James was N.A.H., the man White had befriended some months earlier. At the end of the meeting the participants collected an offering to help defray the expenses of those who had come long distances. But they did not offer the Whites any financial assistance even though the couple may have traveled farther than anyone else.

The allegations about the Whites' personal finances continued. A Sabbatarian Adventist in Massachusetts wrote James a long letter chastising him for what the person believed to be White's extravagant lifestyle. If his requests for financial aid for the *Review* produced such a backlash, perhaps James should stop its publication. At last reaching a decision, he composed a note for the next issue stating that it would cease. Then he explained to his wife that the burden of trying to get the publication established now threatened to kill him and that it was best to give up. The announcement caused her to faint.

The next morning, while praying at family worship, Ellen had a vision that informed her that James must continue the *Review*. If he did, God would make it possible. Though never again did White consider the idea of not publishing, he would repeatedly have to meet attacks on his financial and business practices, attacks and charges so extensive and divisive that, at times, his fellow church leaders would have to convene committees to investigate and respond to them.

During his seven-month stay in Paris, Maine, James managed to publish only 13 issues of the *Review and Herald*. Frequent invitations to meetings and conferences kept him away, and when he was gone, he had no one to substitute as editor, for other members of the little publishing committee were also too busy to take care of the *Review*.

WESTWARD TO NEW YORK

From June 25 through July 1, 1851, James convened a general meeting of Sabbatarian Adventists near Ballston Spa in eastern New York. It took place in the barn of Jesse Thompson, a fairly well-to-do lawyer, farmer, and frequent financial contributor. Having no large churches or other buildings of their own, early Adventists often met in barns. The session dealt with a number of topics. We do not know if it discussed the future of the *Review* and where it should be published, but soon afterward White decided to move to Saratoga Springs, a few miles away, where they would also print the periodical. Moving from Paris, Maine, he and Ellen spent several weeks in Jesse Thompson's 21-room home. They then borrowed furniture from fellow believers and rented a house in Saratoga Springs.[50] The house was large enough for them to have at least some of their children with them. They contacted Clarissa Bonfoey in Rocky Hill, Connecticut, to bring their second son, Edson (named after another good friend, Hiram Edson), with her.[51] Henry, however, would continue to stay at the Howland family home in Topsham, Maine, and would not rejoin the family until the fall of 1853. On August 5, 1851, the same day that James White sent out the first numbers of volume II of the *Review,* Ellen's sister, Sarah Harmon, married Stephen Belden. The couple would be the parents of the prominent Seventh-day Adventist hymn writer, Franklin E. Belden.

One of the things James did during their nine-month stay in Saratoga Springs was to help his wife compile her written accounts of the visions she had had since her first one in Portland seven years previously. He published them as *A Sketch of the Christian Experience and Views of Ellen G. White.* Most of the chapters consisted of reprints of earlier broadsides or articles. Because they had already set much of the material for a *Review Extra,* it cost White $100 ($5 per 100 for a total of 2,000 copies) to have the 64-page pamphlet printed. It would be republished in 1882 as the first section of *Early Writings.*

James not only edited and wrote much of each issue of the *Review* during those periods when he was home from his constant travel, he did the mailing. "We are unusually well, all but myself," he wrote to Stockbridge Howland. "I cannot long endure the labors of traveling and the care of publishing. Wednesday night we worked until two o'clock in the morning, folding and wrapping Number 12 of the *Review and Herald,* then I retired and coughed till daylight. Pray for me. The cause is prospering gloriously. Perhaps the Lord will not have need of me longer, and will let me rest in the grave. I hope to be free from the paper. I have stood by it in extreme adversity; and now when its friends are many, I feel free to leave it, if someone can be found who will take it."[52] He did not know that he would have to lead the publication through much more turmoil and difficulty.

Concerned about how to increase circulation of the publishing house's products, Samuel W. Rhodes suggested that each Sabbatarian congregation or group select a member to handle church publications. The individual would make sure that subscribers received their periodicals, correct addresses, and collect funds.[53] James immediately put the plan into operation.

While at Saratoga Springs he concluded that to do his own printing, he needed a pressman. He met Lumen V. Masten at the printing company where he had his work done. Although Lumen's widowed mother was a devout Methodist, and he himself was interested in religion, he did not belong to a denomination. James talked him into joining the little Sabbatarian Adventist group as foreman of this embryonic publishing entity. Masten would train some of the Sabbatarian Adventists in the printing arts.

James called another meeting in March 1852 at Thompson's home. It began March 12 in Thompson's large parlor. Besides the Whites and Thompson, there were Joseph Bates, Hiram Edson, Frederick Wheeler, John Nevins Andrews, Samuel W. Rhodes, Washington Morse, and Joseph Baker. They decided to move the publishing program to Rochester, New York, and to purchase their own printing press. The participants voted a three-person committee that included Hiram Edson to collect funds for the equipment and to conduct the *Review's* financial operation. The next issue of the *Review* carried both an appeal for funds to pay for the printing equipment, and a notice that the periodical would suspend publication until things were ready in Rochester. White had to borrow money to ship their paper stock, printed pamphlets, and meager personal belongings.

---

[1] *Life Sketches* (1888), p. 127.

[2] See, for example, JW to Leonard Hastings, Mar. 22, 1849; EGW to Leonard and Elvira Hastings, Mar. 23, 1849.

[3] For an example of a road just running over ledges of rock, see the photo in Mark Ford, *The Church of Washington, New Hampshire* (Hagerstown, Md.: Review and Herald Pub. Assn., 2002), p. 51.

[4] Although describing the latter part of the nineteenth century, Randall R. Butler II,

"Overland by Rail, 1869-1890," in Gary Land, ed., *The World of Ellen G. White* (Washington, D.C.: Review and Herald Pub. Assn., 1987), pp. 63-76, and Otto L. Bettmann, *The Good Old Days—They Were Terrible!* (New York: Random House, 1974), pp. 171-181, show the continuing problems of both rail and water travel. A good summary of the dangers of train travel appears in Oliver Jensen, *The American Heritage History of Railroads in America* (New York: American Heritage Wings Books, 1975), pp. 178-189.

[5] JW to Leonard and Elvira Hastings, Oct. 2, 1848.

[6] For example, see JW to Gilbert and Deborah Collins, Sept. 8, 1849.

[7] James White, *Life Incidents*, p. 273.

[8] James White, *A Word to the "Little Flock,"* p. 13, May 30, 1847.

[9] Issued as part of the Seventh-day Adventist Library series, set 3, vol. 8, no. 9.

[10] Interestingly, White records an incident of glossolalia that at least some Sabbatarian Adventists considered as support for beginning the Sabbath at 6:00 p.m. When a believer named Chamberlain spoke in an unknown tongue, someone interpreted it as "Give me the chalk; give me the chalk." Another person found a piece of chalk, and Chamberlain drew a diagram that he used as an argument for the 6:00 p.m. time (see JW to "My Dear Brother," July 2, 1848). And as late as 1860 James records that after a session of intense prayer, "We all lay on the floor under the power of God" (JW to EGW, Nov. 6, 1860). Even to the end of his life he could conduct quite emotional worship and revival services (see, for example. JW to EGW, Apr. 11. 1880).

[11] James White, "Report of Meetings!" *Review and Herald,* Oct. 22, 1857.

[12] G. W. Holt, *Review and Herald,* Feb. 5, 1857.

[13] See, for example, JW to EGW, Mar. 20, 1880; JW to WCW, May 4, 1880.

[14] See also, for example, JW to WCW, Apr. 10, 1879.

[15] Ellen G. White, *Selected Messages* (Washington, D.C.: Review and Herald Pub. Assn., 1980), book 3, p. 90.

[16] *Ibid.,* p. 89. James could be a heavy editor on her writings. One time he told Willie White, "Carefully revise Vol. 1 [of *Spiritual Gifts*], throwing out every sentence and word unnecessary, and much of long quotations of scripture" (JW to WCW, Jan. 4, 1879). When they reprinted bound copies of the *Testimonies* he wanted to leave out material that he feared critics of the Adventist Church would seize on (JW to EGW, Mar. 4, 1880).

[17] JW to WCW, May 7, 1876.

[18] JW to WCW, Dec. 19, 1878.

[19] JW to WCW, May 7, 1876.

[20] On January 1, 1873, James summarized his attitude toward his wife's vision in a 16-page document entitled "A Solemn Appeal to the Ministry and the People." Arthur L. White quotes from the pamphlet, then discusses some of the tensions between James and Ellen over the relationship of her gift to his life. See Arthur L. White, *Ellen G. White: The Progressive Years* (Washington, D.C.: Review and Herald Pub. Assn., 1986), pp. 425-445. We will also look at this tension later in this book.

[21] JW to Brother and Sister Howland, Nov. 19, 1848.

[22] JW to Brother and Sister [Hastings?], Mar. 22, 1849.

[23] See, for example, JW to "Dear Brother," Oct. 11, 1860.

[24] For example, see JW to Gilbert and Deborah Collins, Feb. 10, 1850.

[25] *In the Footsteps of the Pioneers* (Silver Spring, Md.: Ellen G. White Estate, 1990), p. 17.

[26] JW to J. C. Bowles, Oct. 17, 1849.

[27] JW to Leonard and Elvira Hastings, Jan. 3, 1850.

[28] JW to Leonard Hastings, Jan. 10, 1850.

[29] *Ibid.*

[30] James White, in *Review and Herald,* Feb. 5, 1861.

[31] JW to J. Edson White, Aug. 5, 1872.

[32] Variations of this Sabbath millennium idea have troubled the Seventh-day Adventist Church to the present day.

[33] *Present Truth,* December 1850, p. 16, in Ron Graybill, "The Family Man," *J. N. Andrews: The Man and the Mission,* ed. Harry Leonard (Berrien Springs, Mich.: Andrews University Press, 1985), p. 15.

[34] Arthur L. White, *Ellen G. White: The Early Years* (Washington, D.C.: Review and Herald Pub. Assn., 1985), pp. 95, 96.

[35] Persis Sibley Andrews Black diary, Mar. 11, 1846, in Leonard, p. 17.

[36] *Advent Review,* May 1850.

[37] James White, *Life Incidents,* pp. 292, 293.

[38] *Second Advent Review and Sabbath Herald,* November 1850.

[39] Beverly Beem and Ginger Hanks Harwood, "'My Soul Is on the Wing for Glory': The Roots of Adventist Spirituality, 1850-1863" (paper presented at the Adventist Society of Religious Studies Annual Meeting, Denver, Colo., Nov. 16, 2001), p. 9.

[40] *Ibid.*

[41] James White, in *Review and Herald,* Nov. 24, 1859.

[42] Beem and Harwood, p. 5. In their paper they cite a number of examples of the manifestation of such gifts.

[43] JW to E. P. Butler, Dec. 12, 1861.

[44] Diane and Jack Barnes, comp., *The Oxford Hills: Greenwood, Norway, Oxford, Paris, West Paris and Woodstock* (Dover, N.H.: Arcadia Publishing, 1995), p. 7.

[45] JW to E. P. Butler, Dec. 12, 1861, in Graybill, pp. 18, 19.

[46] J. O. Corliss, "James White, A Leader of Men," *Review and Herald,* Aug. 23, 1923.

[47] L. R. Conradi to EGW, Aug. 16, 1891.

[48] A letter of condolence and encouragement that James White had written to Leonard on March 18, 1850, still survives.

[49] *Life Sketches* (1888), p. 282.

[50] *Ibid.*

[51] Ellen G. White, *Life Sketches* (Mountain View, Calif.: Pacific Press Pub. Assn., 1915), p. 141.

[52] *Ibid.*

[53] *Review and Herald,* Aug. 19, 1851.

Chapter VI

THE REVIEW IN ROCHESTER

ORIGINALLY incorporated in 1817 as Rochesterville (shortened to Rochester in 1822) and named after Colonel Nathaniel Rochester, the city grew rapidly after the opening of the Rochester-Lockport section of the Erie Canal. The four waterfalls and swift-flowing current of the Genesee River fostered the development of grist (flour) mills. Barges on the Erie Canal carried the flour they produced to distant customers. The canal and other developing forms of transportation in the area, as well as its proximity to what was then known as the "West," may have helped attract the Whites there. They would find travel fairly easy in the surrounding area.

Like the state of Maine, Rochester was active in many social movements. It was the center of the Anti-Masonic Party, it was a station on the Underground Railroad, and it was the publishing center for several abolitionist periodicals, including one by Frederick Douglass. The home of Susan B. Anthony, the city was the focus of the women's suffrage and women's rights movements. Also it was (at Hydesville) the birthplace of the modern spiritualism movement through the activities of Margaret and Katherine Fox. Not far away is Hiram Edson's farm (Port Gibson) where Edson came to an understanding of October 22, 1844, and of Christ's high-priestly ministry in the heavenly sanctuary. It was also near Hill Cumorah, where Joseph Smith claimed to have found an ancient book inscribed on golden tablets that he then translated as the *Book of Mormon*. In a single afternoon one can drive to sites important to the Seventh-day Adventist Church, spiritualism, and the Church of Jesus Christ of Latter-day Saints.

Because it was the home of the Sabbatarian Adventist publishing house, Rochester was for a number of years also the headquarters of the Sabbatarian Adventist movement. In addition, it would be the home of many prominent church members.[1] The Whites would often visit there even after they had moved away. Mount Hope Cemetery contains the graves of many early Sabbatarian Adventists, including James White's brother and sister, and John Nevins Andrews' wife and daughter.

In April 1852 the Whites rented a large house on 124 Mount Hope Avenue for $175 a year. The property was at the time on the edge of the city limits. (The street has been renumbered twice, and the present site of 124 Mount Hope Avenue is not the original location of the house the Whites lived in.) Besides using it as living quarters, they planned to install the printing press there, in the hope of saving $50 a year on office space. After the Whites furnished the house with two bedsteads costing 25 cents each and six nonmatching chairs for $1, they found four more chairs lacking seats for 62 cents. A board perched across two empty flour barrels served as a table. Their meals were equally frugal, as they substituted sauce for butter and turnips for potatoes. Beans became their staple item of diet. They would supplement their food supply from a nearby garden.

When spring came James hired someone to plow the garden, and as the man did so he found many small potatoes left from the previous summer. A drought had discouraged the previous tenants from expecting a crop worth anything, and they had left the potato patch untouched. The mild winter had kept them from freezing. When with typical Maine frugality Ellen White began to collect them in a metal pail, James's foreman announced that he was quitting. Masten refused to work for anyone whose wife was reduced to scavenging the previous year's potato crop. Fortunately he accepted her explanation that she felt it her duty not to let anything go to waste.

THE FIRST PRINTING PRESS

When the new printing press did not arrive by the announced startup of the beginning of May, James had the May 6, 1852, *Review and Herald* printed by a commercial press in Rochester. Its masthead listed a publishing committee of Joseph Bates, John Nevins Andrews, and a Joseph Baker. The periodical announced itself as free but urged readers to support it financially "as the Lord has prospered them." The Review staff who would live in the house straggled in, one or two at a time. As more and more crowded in, the Mount Hope Avenue residence ran out of room. By

October of 1852 the Whites moved the little publishing organization to a rented third-floor office at Stone's Block, No. 21, on South St. Paul Street in downtown Rochester. (At the time of this writing [summer 2002] a Kinko's quick-print franchise occupied the approximate location of the Review office.) Money loaned by Hiram Edson (who had sold one of his farms)[2] and funds raised through donations had enabled White to buy the small press and a font of type for $652.93. Because the donations eventually totaled $655.84, they had $2.91 left over.

The press would be the first piece of communal property ever owned by Sabbath-observing Adventists. No longer would they be dependent on commercial companies who might print the Review on Sabbath. But the printing press itself would cause another problem. It had to have an official owner, and James was it by default. Before long people would become suspicious of where money, raised for Sabbatarian publishing, was really going. But for the moment that was still in the future. The first issue of the Review printed in Rochester carried the date May 6, 1852. The last issue would be the one on October 30, 1855.

In August 1852, to provide material for children and youth, James began the Youth's Instructor. Its Sabbath school lessons would be one of the first means of unifying the scattered Sabbatarian Adventist believers. Although preparing the early lessons himself, he soon turned the responsibility for the periodical to others. The publication lasted until 1970, when the church replaced it with Insight.

Until 1853 the publishing house used donations to underwrite the printing of the tracts, which it then gave away. That year it put prices on the publications and sold them. The Review had no external support. To keep it from total collapse, as well as support himself and the rest of his staff, James sold Bibles, concordances, Bible dictionaries, atlases, medical books, charts, and stationery. Later, when he saw ministers and other church employees involved in some side business, he began to regret the example he had set during those difficult times in Rochester. In 1867 he observed that "I should have been supported in my calling, and had nothing to do with selling [non-Adventist] books."[3] Such experiences would eventually motivate him to develop a system to pay church employees enough in order that they could devote their efforts full time to the church.

The Whites and a staff of a dozen printers, preachers, and writers lived as an extended family. The publishing house employees themselves received little more than room and board. Often they would work 10, 12, even 18 hours a day, walking home from the downtown office as late as 2:00 or 3:00 in the morning.

The residents of the boarding house were, by today's standards, young. In 1853 they included—besides James (age 32), Ellen White (age 26), and their sons Henry (age 6) and Edson (age 4)—a printing crew consisting of foreman Lumen Masten (age 24); Warren Bacheller (age 14), an apprentice or printer's devil; Fletcher Byington (age 20), another apprentice; George Amadon (age 21), printer; and Oswald Stowell (age 25), printer.

Annie Smith (age 25) helped James White with the editing and production when he was on one of his many extended preaching tours, and her brother, Uriah (age 21), wrote and did anything else necessary, such as trimming the edges of the signatures with a penknife. While the printing was done on South St. Paul, the stitching, trimming, and addressing took place at the Mount Hope Road dwelling.

Clarissa Bonfoey (age 32) took care of Edson during his parents' extended absences. James White's brother Nathaniel (age 22), and his sister Anna (age 25) joined the group, as did two of Ellen White's relatives, her sister Sarah Belden (about age 30) and brother-in-law Stephen Belden (age 24). Stephen took care of business details, and Sarah acted as a housekeeper. John N. Loughborough (age 21) and his wife lived elsewhere in Rochester. He would assist in the pressroom or punch holes in the signatures so they could be sewed together. John Nevins Andrews, by now 24, would stop by between preaching trips. Young as they may seem today, in a century when life expectancy was only in the 40s, half or more of their lives were already over.

Indeed, four of them would soon be dead.

Despite James White's difficulties with John Andrews' father, he and the son usually got along well. John would sometimes address his letters to him and Ellen "Very dear Brother and Sister White" and sign them with "much love." The Whites and Andrews expressed a great deal of affection for each other. As happened so frequently among the early Sabbatarian Adventists, John's health gave way. During the young man's sickness James provided the best room in the boarding house, fed him for free, and supplied wood to heat his room. Appealing to the New York believers to raise money to buy

John some decent clothes, White himself headed the list of contributors with a pledge of $100. But as close as Andrews and the Whites would become through the years,[4] at times their relationship could be rocky, accentuated by silence and misunderstanding alternated with confession and forgiveness.[5] But despite it all, he would be one of the greatest supporters of both James and Ellen. Even though James White occasionally questioned Andrews' support, John's consistent defense of him helped preserve James's leadership and influence in the developing church.[6]

ANNIE SMITH

Annie Smith had given up her dreams of a career in literature and art to join the Whites. Her mother had told Joseph Bates her concerns about her daughter's religious apathy. He suggested that she write to Annie, asking her to attend a series of meetings he would hold in the home of an Elizabeth Temple in Boston. The night before the first meeting Bates had an unusual dream. In it he saw every chair in the room filled except the one near the door. Just as he opened his Bible to begin his sermon, a young woman took the last seat.

That same night Annie had an almost identical dream. When Bates saw Annie enter—she had gotten lost and arrived late—he immediately switched from his planned topic to the one he remembered presenting in his dream, the Adventist view of the Old Testament tabernacle service. Afterward he approached Annie. "I believe this is Sister Smith's daughter, of West Wilton," he said. "I never saw you before, but your countenance looks familiar. I dreamed of seeing you last night." Impressed by how the incident had duplicated her own dream, Annie accepted the Sabbatarian message.[7]

A month later the 23-year-old woman sent the *Review* a poem, "Fear Not, Little Flock." In an accompanying letter she said, "It is with much reluctance that I send you these verses, on a subject which a few weeks since was so foreign to my thoughts. Being as it were a child in this glorious cause, I feel unworthy and unable to appreciate a subject of such *moment,* but as I've written for the world, and wish to make a full sacrifice, I am induced to send."[8]

Impressed, White not only printed the poem and her letter, but after talking to Joseph Bates about her he also urged Annie to come to Saratoga Springs, New York, where he was then living, to help him as a copy editor. Probably he had already learned from her mother something of her talents and education. Both Mrs. Smith and her daughter had belonged to the Millerite movement, but after October 22 the girl had drifted away. She had studied at the Charlestown Female Seminary in Charlestown, Massachusetts, near Boston. In addition, she had taught in area grammar schools and had contributed to a literary magazine named *The Ladies' Wreath* and had been published in New York.

Besides literature, she was also interested in art. Annie had strained her eyes while sketching a scene of Boston from Prospect Hill in Somerville. For eight months she could hardly use them. Now she told White that she could not accept the offer because of her eye trouble. He told her to come anyway, and after she arrived he held a prayer and anointing service. Her vision quickly healed. A few months later she accompanied the Whites to Rochester.

James White could be hard to work with. He drove others as hard as he did himself. Annie Smith wrote a poem that may suggest James's desire for editorial perfection:

"What news is this falls on my ear?
What next will to my sight appear?
My brain doth whirl, my heart doth quake—
Oh, that egregious mistake!
'Too bad! Too bad!!' I hear them cry,
'You might have seen with half an eye!
Strange! Passing strange!! How could you make
So plain, so blunderous a mistake!'

~ ~ ~

Guilty, condemned, I trembling stand,
With pressing cares on every hand,
Without one single plea to make,
For leaving such a *bad mistake*."[9]

Despite White's sometimes difficult personality, Annie became quite close to him and Ellen. Her mother wrote that she loved the Whites. Besides copyediting, James sometimes handed her total editorial responsibility for the *Review* while he and Ellen went on preaching tours. She also wrote at least 45 poems and hymns for the *Review* and *Youth's Instructor*. Apparently she fell in love with John Nevins Andrews. Some evidence suggests that she may have believed that he would marry her. But John's interest in her was not romantic.

The years in Rochester were a period marked by poverty, illness, and sometimes great discouragement. The publishing house could have easily collapsed and the Sabbatarian Adventist movement with it. After all, the *Review* was the main channel of communication for the widely scattered believers. The *Review* announced meetings and provided news of the slowly emerging church, and the pamphlets and books presented Sabbatarian Adventism's beliefs to nonmembers. The Seventh-day Adventist Church could have been stillborn without it.

THE CONSTANT THREAT OF ILLNESS

The American population as whole struggled with constant illness and high mortality. The group on Mount Hope Avenue were not immune from the problem either. When John Loughborough first met the Whites, James took him to a prayer session for Oswald Stowell. The printer had come down with severe attacks of pleurisy. The local physicians with their limited skills and medical knowledge had given his case up as hopeless. James anointed Stowell, then prayed. As White rose from prayer, Stowell announced that he was fully healed and would be able to work the next day.

A cholera epidemic raged through the area. At night the publishing house family would hear the rumbling of carriages transporting the dead to nearby Mount Hope Cemetery (a magnificent Victorian cemetery established in 1838 as America's first municipal cemetery and full of sculptured art), and during the day they would see wagons go by loaded with plain pine coffins. White feared that such epidemics might force him to suspend operations for several weeks at a time.[10]

When James Edson contracted the disease, his parents prayed for the boy's healing. Ellen took her 3-year-old son in her arms and rebuked the disease in Jesus' name. To James and Ellen's relief the child immediately felt somewhat better. "They need not pray any more," Edson told his mother, "for the Lord has healed me."[11] But his full recovery was slow. For three days he did not eat anything.

His parents had been planning a two-month series of speaking appointments that extended east to Bangor, Maine. They hesitated to leave with the child so sick, but then decided to go unless Edson's condition worsened. To make their first appointment, they had to depart in two days. James and Ellen prayed that if their son began to eat, they would take it as a sign that God approved of their journey. The second day the child asked for broth.

While they were gone on the extended speaking tour, their foreman, Lumen Masten, contracted cholera. Although he worked with the Whites and the other Sabbatarian Adventists, he had not accepted Christ. The woman who ran the boarding house where he stayed—as well as her daughter—died from the disease. Now Masten had no one to take care of him because of the widespread fear of his disease. Finally staff members of the Review and Herald stayed with him until his condition seemed to improve, then took him to the Mount Hope Avenue house. There Masten had a relapse. His physician tried everything he knew to save him, eventually concluding that his case was hopeless. He told Masten that he would not survive the night.

The Review workers could not bear to see him die without any religious hope and began to pray around his bed. Masten also prayed that God would forgive his sins. All night the Review people pled that God might spare him in order that he could repent and obey God's commandments. Finally, after he committed himself to God and said he would observe the Sabbath, he began to feel better.

When the doctor arrived the next morning, he mentioned that about 1:00 that morning he had commented to his wife that Masten had probably died. When someone told him that the foreman was still alive, he hurried up the stairs to Masten's room. Feeling the man's pulse, he declared that the young man was better and the crisis had passed. It was not his medical skill that had saved him, he said, "but a higher power." Soon Masten returned to work, now a fellow believer. It was the type of incident that the people at the publishing house needed to sustain their faith. Not every experience, however, would turn out so well.

The threat of tuberculosis was constant. Close confinement in unsanitary conditions and bodies weakened from poor diet make people especially vulnerable to this disease, known then as consumption. Every year tuberculosis would kill many, including some in James's own family.

When his brother and sister, Nathaniel and Anna White, arrived, both were probably already infected. Nathaniel had until then been somewhat apathetic to religion. But the Review family worships made an impression on him, and he accepted Christ and the seventh-day Sabbath, which his brother and his friends had advocated.

He died May 6, 1853, age 22, and the Whites buried him in the city's Mount Hope Cemetery. The death left James and the others despondent since Nathaniel was the first member of the Rochester group not to be healed in answer to prayer. For a while depression and a high fever confined James to bed. Nevertheless he embarked on his first trip to Michigan.

Anna White also accepted Sabbatarian Adventism. James made her editor of the *Youth's Instructor*. She shared her brother's interest in music publishing and compiled (in 1854) the first Adventist children's hymnal. But tuberculosis took her next, and she died November 30, 1854. She was 26.

The tuberculosis spread to others of the Review family. Luman Masten, the foreman, died in 1854. By November Annie Smith exhibited the first stages of the disease. A month later she began coughing blood. Having returned home, she sought hydrotherapy treatments, but they did not help. Annie knew she would soon die. James White, who received a salary of only $4 a week when he was paid at all, sent her a gift of $75. The young woman determined to complete one last project—a long poem titled "Home Here and Home in Heaven," and include it in a little book of poetry. She lived less than 10 days after its publication, dying at age 27 on July 26, 1855. A poem she had written in honor of Anna White after her death was now sung as a hymn at Annie Smith's funeral.

> "She hath passed Death's chilling billow,
>   And gone to rest:
> Jesus smoothed her dying pillow—
>   Her slumbers blest."[12]

DISAPPOINTED ROMANCE

A month after Annie Smith's death Ellen White wrote to John Andrews, who was courting Angeline Stevens, daughter of Cyprian Stevens, of Paris, Maine. Ellen urged him to marry the girl and "that after you had gone thus far it would be wronging Angeline to have it stop here. The best course you can take is to move on, get married, and do what you can in the cause of God. Annie's disappointment cost her her life."[13] Mrs. White intimated that Annie Smith's disappointment that John did not marry her led to the depression that reduced her resistance to the tuberculosis. The painful question was Why had John shown enough of an interest in her that she jumped to the conclusion that he was considering marriage?

"I saw that you [John] were injudicious in her case," Mrs. White continued, "and it all grew out of a mistaken view you had of James. You thought he was harsh and impatient toward Paris friends, and you stepped right in between Annie and us; sympathized with her in everything. The interest manifested for her was undue and uncalled for, and showed that you had a great lack of confidence in us."[14]

One Adventist historian has suggested that Mrs. White was telling Andrews that, believing James had been too harsh and critical in the past toward some of the believers in Paris, John had sided with Annie against James. Annie jumped to the conclusion that his sympathy was motivated by love for her "when, in fact, it grew out of opposition to James White. When Annie discovered the truth, she was devastated."[15]

James continued to publish when he and Ellen were not traveling. By now they had a back list of about 30 publications. Most early books and pamphlets were reprints of articles from the *Review,* a number of which White had written himself. Through the years he would author several books. He considered preparing books one of his most important tasks[16] and kept his hand in it even when he relinquished control of other aspects of Adventist publishing. His own titles included:

The Second Coming . . . ; A Brief Exposition of Matthew Twenty-four (after several editions rewritten as *His Glorious Appearing*).

Bible Adventism; or, Sermons on the Coming and Kingdom of Our Lord Jesus Christ (several editions).

Life Incidents in Connection With the Great Advent Movement (1868).

Sketches of the Christian Life and Public Labors of William Miller (1875).

The Early Life and Later Experience and Labors of Elder Joseph Bates (1878).

Life Sketches . . . of Elder James White, and His Wife, Mrs. Ellen G. White (1880).

At the time of his death he was planning a major book exalting the role of Christ in the plan of salvation.

White's literary style emphasized careful reasoning and balance. While he seemed to enjoy polemical parry and thrust, it was not the major element of his approach. He would examine what the biblical text taught on a topic, then deal with objections that others might raise against the Adventist conclusions. Although he had no formal theological training, he would quote from contemporary commentaries and religious writers. At times he would even cite elements of Greek that he had picked up to bolster his argument. White's articles, tracts, and books have stood the test of time better than many other early Seventh-day Adventist writers. His writings have an authority and sensibility that convinces even the twenty-first-century reader.[17]

The task of evangelism, as well as that of nurturing isolated groups of Sabbatarian Adventists, kept the Whites constantly on the road. For example, shortly after cholera struck Edson and he was still not fully recovered, the couple spent two months traveling as far east as Bangor, Maine. As they rode along Ellen would tie the child to her waist in order to not drop him if she fell asleep. At each appointment James would do most of the preaching, he would sell books, and he would promote Adventist periodicals. Immediately leaving one conference for the next, they would stop at noon along the road to feed the horse and eat a quick lunch. Then James would use their food box or his top hat to write on as he would start articles for the *Review* and the *Instructor*.

While they were in Rochester, James established the first known Adventist Sabbath school. Once again he founded another core institution of the Seventh-day Adventist Church.

Believers had occasionally muttered fears that donations to the *Review* were winding up in James White's pocket (everything *was*, technically, in his name). When someone in 1854 made a definite accusation, the *Review*'s publishing committee, consisting of J. N. Andrews, R. F. Cottrell, and Uriah Smith, repudiated the charges.[18] But James would have to meet similar charges again. Also, the publishing committee continued to ignore his request that they take charge of the business aspects of the publishing entity.

In the spring of 1854 the Whites moved to 109 Monroe Street. During their stay there Ellen went into vision. At James White's urging a Dr. Fleming and another physician examined her while she experienced it.

The two medical doctors were impressed by the fact that she did not seem to breathe.[19]

During 1853, 1854, and early 1855 James visited Michigan. Because of swamps and other difficult terrain, its settlement had lagged behind other states carved out of the Northwest Territory. But development finally took off after it became a state in 1837 as new roads and water transportation brought great numbers of settlers to its southern part. In many ways it was culturally an extension of New England and would be more receptive to Sabbatarian Adventism than New England itself had been.

By now White was once again running out of strength. He still worked 14-18 hours a day editing and publishing the *Review, Youth's Instructor,* and various books and tracts while at the same time finding money to keep the publishing house from financial collapse. In addition, he had responsibility for all those living in the house on Mount Hope Avenue. Then his brother, sister, and two others of his publishing house staff died. The stress of dealing with it all had, he felt, brought him close to the grave. James wrote in the *Review* that only a complete change in circumstances would restore his health. Finally he determined to do something even if it meant leaving the publishing house.[20] He wrote a document that he titled "Private," in which he acknowledged that he had broken his own health through overwork. In this personal covenant he listed seven points that he vowed to do, including that he and Ellen would spend more time teaching their children.[21]

WHERE SHALL THE PUBLISHING HOUSE GO?

Just about this time White began to get invitations to move the publishing company elsewhere. In March 1855 members in Vermont sent a check for $492 with the suggestion that the publishing house relocate there. Not to be outdone, the Michigan believers made a counter proposal. The Michigan request seemed to especially intrigue White. "The brethren in Battle Creek and vicinity are generally awake to the wants of the cause," he commented, "and are anxious to establish the Review office in that place. They are able and willing to do so, and manifest much anxiety to relieve us of those cares and responsibilities which we have too long borne. The climate, water, prices of rent, fuel, provisions, etc., seem favorable to the location."[22]

To be sure, he decided to visit Vermont and let the Sabbatarian Adventists there present their case. His summer 1855 tour of the eastern churches included Vermont. Either James could not make up his mind or he was hoping to receive better offers. "'Providence' does not open the way for the press in Michigan," he reported. "The way is abundantly opened in Vermont. Follow the opening providence of God."[23] Three weeks later he commented in the *Review* that "unless the friends of the cause in some more central position shall take their responsibility, it will be proper that the friends and supports of the cause in Vermont should take it."[24] He also reiterated his previous resolution to escape the impossible load, which was destroying his health. Besides, he further emphasized, the publishing program was not his responsibility alone, but that of all Sabbatarian Adventists. "We shall no longer bear the burdens we have borne in Rochester; neither shall we move the Office, East or West. The Office is the property of the church. The church must wake up to this matter, and free us from the responsibilities that have been forced upon us, and which we have reluctantly taken. We must have freedom and repose, or go into the grave."[25] Unfortunately, when things later improved, he would find it difficult actually to accept such "freedom and repose."

On August 24 he questioned whether Vermont was the right place. "My mind is west, say Wis. Ill. Or Iowa or Minnesota. But I mean to stand by the press till it is well established."[26]

Finally he wrote to a Battle Creek friend, Abram Dodge, that he had picked Michigan, because of the efforts of Henry Lyon, Dan Palmer, Cyrenius Smith, and J. P. Kellogg. They had collected $1,200 to purchase a lot and construct a small building. After directing them to put up a 32' x 25' structure of two story and a half on three-fourths, James suggested a number of points on how he would like to see the relocation handled.

1. The publishing house should be the property of the Sabbatarian Adventist believers as a whole.
2. Or as an alternative, at least three or more persons would own it.
3. Uriah Smith would serve as resident editor. James White, Roswell F. Cottrell, John Nevins Andrews, and J. H. Waggoner would be corresponding editors. They would supply reports of their travels among the churches, and would give articles to Smith. All five would have equal authority.

4. A finance committee of Cyrenius Smith, Henry Lyon, and one other individual would receive all funds for the *Review and Herald,* pay all bills, and set periodical/book prices.

5. James White would retain the current inventory of books and use the income from their sales to pay off debts incurred while operating the publishing house.[27]

James did not expect that it would be possible to move the publishing house before the next spring. But the Michigan believers immediately went to work. After all, they had already become strong financial supporters of his work.[28]

---

[1] For background information and a tour guide of Adventist historical sites, see Robert H. Allen and Howard P. Krug, *Rochester's Adventist Heritage: Tour Guide and Biographical Overview* (Rochester, N.Y.: Adventist History Project, 2002).

[2] Edson seemed to have a farm to sell whenever the believers needed money.

[3] *Review and Herald,* Mar. 26, 1867.

[4] James White allowed Andrews to bury family members in the White family burial plot in Mount Hope Cemetery, but John Nevins would not allow James to deed over the property until after Andrews' wife died. White gave Andrews the burial plots for a nominal sum. Source: Robert H. Allen, of Rochester, New York.

[5] J. G. Smoot, "John N. Andrews," p. 6. See also Joseph G. Smoot, "The Churchman: Andrews' Relationship With Church Leaders," in Harry Leonard, ed., *J. N. Andrews,* pp. 42-74.

[6] *Ibid.*

[7] Ron Graybill, "The Life and Loves of Annie Smith," *Adventist Heritage,* Summer 1975, pp. 15, 16.

[8] *Ibid.,* pp. 16, 17.

[9] *Ibid.,* p. 17.

[10] JW to Uriah and Harriet Smith, Aug. 29, 1854.

[11] Ellen G. White, *Life Sketches,* p. 144.

[12] Graybill, "The Life and Loves of Annie Smith," p. 20.

[13] EGW to J. N. Andrews (letter 1, 1855), Aug. 16, 1855.

[14] *Ibid.*

[15] Graybill, "The Family Man," p. 20.

[16] JW to J. Edson White and WCW, Dec. 30, 1872.

[17] For an example of his literary and theological style, see his tract "Perpetuity of Spiritual Gifts."

[18] *Review and Herald,* Nov. 7, 1854.

[19] Arthur L. White, *Ellen G. White: The Early Years,* pp. 302, 303.

[20] James White, "The Office," *Review and Herald,* Feb. 20, 1855.
[21] James White, "Private," 1855.
[22] James White, in *Review and Herald,* May 15, 1855.
[23] JW to "Brother," Aug. 3, 1855.
[24] James White, in *Review and Herald,* Aug. 7, 1855.
[25] *Ibid.*
[26] JW letter, Aug. 24, 1855.
[27] JW to Abram Dodge, Aug. 20, 1855.
[28] JW to Brethren in Jackson, Michigan, Dec. 5, 1852.

CHAPTER VII

A HOME FOR THE WHITES

BATTLE CREEK was nestled at the juncture of the Kalamazoo River and a stream named after an 1824 Indian skirmish with a party of surveyors. Together the two sources supplied ample water for both a growing population and industry. The large areas of open prairielike countryside made raising grain and farm animals easy. Flour and feed industries sprang up along the creek and river. Founded in 1831 as Milton, and then renamed after the creek, the settlement was in 1850 incorporated as a village, becoming officially a city in 1859.

Besides connecting the town with Detroit and Chicago, the Michigan Central Railroad transported the products of the four flour mills, two woolen factories, and a couple iron foundries (one specializing in steam engines) to distant markets.[1] Later the Peninsular Railway (eventually renamed the Grand Trunk Western) would build through the city, and it and the Michigan Central would give Seventh-day Adventists links to much of the United States. The nation's railroads not only gave mobility to people; they enabled ideas to spread faster than ever.

The shrill of train whistles, the chugging of locomotives, and the rumble of train wheels drifting up from the tracks only a short distance away was a constant background to life in the Battle Creek Adventist community. Railroad schedules frequently appeared in the *Review and Herald* and other Seventh-day Adventist publications, and James White referred to the Michigan Central as "one of the very best [rail]roads in the Union."[2]

When the Whites and the rest of the party of 14 that had been in Rochester arrived in Battle Creek in early November 1855, the village had already grown to 3,000. That year alone new settlers had added 100 private homes to the bustling community. As with the rest of Michigan, many townspeople had come from New England, and the style of the buildings they constructed echoed their origins. That and the rolling hills north and south of the town must have seemed pleasantly familiar.

Besides a four-story brick building with an Ionic facade, Battle Creek contained a good selection of grocery, drug, book, and dry goods stores. Livery stables, blacksmith shops, saddle and harness shops, and feed mills catered to the needs of the horses that provided the main source of nineteenth-century transportation. But the buildings stood along unpaved streets that were muddy in the winter and dusty in the summer. Wagons hauling grain and other freight rutted the streets, and the horses littered them with manure. The manure bred swarms of flies. Besides the constant stench, the manure soiled a lot of shoes and clothes. For years farmers would herd flocks of sheep through Battle Creek to the railroad loading pens. The only way to avoid the mess was along the wooden walks on some streets.

Despite the rapid growth, the people of Battle Creek had many reminders that the village had not always existed. Wild turkeys roamed the surrounding woods, and Indians still came to town to sell the berries they had picked in the countryside.

Half of the group of Adventists from Rochester consisted of the Whites and family helpers. By now James was 34, Ellen almost 28, Henry 8, Edson 6, and Willie 1. Clarisa Bonfoey, 35, and Jennie Fraser, 25, would live with them in a rented house on the south side of Van Buren Street. Stephen and Sarah Belden would now live by themselves, and Warren Bacheller shared quarters with his mother and sister. Uriah Smith and George Amadon, both still single, found lodging with a local family.[3]

ORGANIZING THE PUBLISHING HOUSE

Earlier, in October, the Battle Creek Committee had convened a "general" conference for November 16. It invited delegates from churches in other states to select "those Brethren who shall conduct the Review." Joseph Bates served as chair. The conference adopted White's suggestions and even broadened them. For example, it voted to repay White for what he had personally invested in the publishing program. The session appointed a committee consisting of Henry Lyon, David Hewett, and William Smith to examine the Review's financial status and added Stephen Pierce to the list of corresponding editors. Also it named a committee to hold the publishing house in trust for the Sabbath-believing Adventists and to supervise the Review and Herald. As James White had suggested, the delegates named Uriah Smith as resident editor, leaving White as a corresponding editor as well as to oversee publishing books. And finally, they presented a vote of thanks to White for his sacrificial efforts during the previous six years.[4]

The following year it was proposed that the "book concern be united with the *Review,* as the property of the church, . . . so that no individual shall have any personal interest in the publishing department."[5] Another general conference voted later that year that the publishing committee of the Review take over the Church Book Fund and the Publishing Department and that the church as a whole should erase their debts.

Though now relieved of many management burdens, James was still legally responsible for the publishing house. As far as its creditors were concerned, the Review and Herald was his personal business. After all, he had headed the publishing program for years, and the body of believers had no name or legal corporate existence.

The first publishing house building was a two-story frame structure on West Main and Washington streets. In 1861 it was moved and re-placed by a two-story brick building that provided more space for the growing work.

The move had been good for the Whites. Their health soon improved. With more people to help, James must have felt less pressure.

At first the Whites rented a small cottage on the south side of Van Buren Street, between Cass and Washington streets, almost opposite to the home of David Hewett. Known as the most honest man in town, Hewett had been the first Sabbathkeeping convert in Battle Creek. The rent for the house was $1.50 a week at a time when James received only $4 a week for editing the *Review and Herald.* Among the cottage's many problems, it lacked a woodshed to store the large supply of fuel needed during the harsh Michigan winters. Also, the family had to walk a long distance to obtain water.

A HOUSE FOR THE WHITES

On January 1, 1856, Ellen wrote to Elsa Below, a friend living in Mill Grove, New York, that their fellow Adventists thought Ellen and James ought to build a little house. A week later, January 8, Ellen paid $100 for a lot on the southwest corner of West Michigan and Kendall streets. The couple decided not to live there, however, and Ellen sold the land to John P. Kellogg on May 5, 1856, for $105. Two months later, August 4, James White purchased lots 64 and 65 of Manchester's Addition (named after its developer, Elias C. Manchester) for $230 from Cyrenius Smith, a carpenter. The two pieces of property nearly equaled an acre and a half. At the same time White bought the west part of lot 63, where he built the little house that he sold to his parents in 1859.

James could buy the land because of help from friends. As Ellen wrote later: "From the time we moved to Battle Creek, the Lord began to turn our captivity. We found sympathizing friends in Michigan, who were ready to share our burdens and supply our wants."[6] James would frequently publish requests for help in the pages of the *Review*. (And he could be just as generous in turn.) Help was especially important in buying a house, because people usually had to pay cash (even until well into the twentieth century mortgages, when available, were no longer than five years).

Other friends helped clear the wooded lots, except for a small grove of second-growth oak in the northwest corner. James kept it as a place for meditation and prayer. Noted for the power and fervency of his prayer life, he spent much time in the little grove. In their letters and her diary, he and Ellen would often mention visiting there. The Whites planted a garden and small fruit orchard on the rest of the property. Through the years they put in raspberry and currant bushes and set out strawberry plants. The garden and orchard would be a major food source for the family. A neighbor, later remembering one of the White gardens, commented that she had never seen such corn as Brother White raised. Ellen enjoyed spending a half hour each afternoon in her flower garden, her children working beside her. As they grew older they would raise and sell seeds there.

With their friends' assistance they also built a small six-room house costing about $500.[7] Some gave money, others labor. Cyrenius Smith did much of the construction. The frame of the house consisted of hand-hewn heavy oak timbers, perhaps obtained from Richard Godsmark, of Bedford, Michigan. Godsmark supplied the lumber for the first building of the Review and Herald Publishing Association. One and two-thirds stories high, and facing east on Wood Street, the Whites' new house had a combined parlor and sitting room on the front of the ground floor, a small bedroom on the north, and a kitchen that also served as a dining room on the south end. A 12-foot lean-to room on the south side served as the children's room. Each morning during their years at Wood Street the White family would assemble at 7:00 in the front room for worship. James would read a passage of Scripture, comment on it, then lead the family as they sang a hymn. The most frequently remembered song was:

"Lord, in the morning Thou shalt hear my voice ascending high;
To Thee will I direct my prayer, to Thee lift up mine eye."

After the hymn James would pray. "He did not 'offer a prayer,'" his son Willie later remembered. "He *prayed* with earnestness and solemn reverence. He pleaded for those blessings most needed by himself and his family, and for the prosperity of the cause of God."[8]

In the evenings, if there were no special meetings in the Battle Creek Seventh-day Adventist community, the family would gather at 7:00 or later for another worship. If James was at home, he would read a chapter from the Bible and pray, thanking God for the day's blessings and committing his family to God's care during the night.

A LOVING FATHER

When James was away, he missed his family and frequently wrote to them. "I want to see you and the children very much," he told his wife. "I hope our dear boys will seek to be good and right. Language cannot describe my anxiety for their welfare and future salvation."[9] When their final child, John Herbert, was born September 20, 1860, at their Wood Street home, James and Ellen did not immediately name him. James began to call him "Nameless."[10] "Remember me affectionately to Henry, Edson, Willie, and kiss the babe."[11] James assured her, "I love my family and nothing but a sense of duty can separate me from them."[12]

Sadly, that family would be broken when John Herbert died from erysipelas, an infectious skin disease, on December 14. Ellen would plant pansies from her garden and myrtle and tall moss on his grave in Oak Hill Cemetery. As happens often, James found it easier to deal with his sons while they were young. When they grew into their teens, the relationship would become more strained. But for the present, the years at the Wood Street home were pleasant ones.

Upstairs the front room was about eight feet high in the center and sloped to four feet on the north and south ends. Behind it was a small bedroom. From downstairs one climbed a narrow, steep stairway of 11 steps to a landing and turned left into a small bedroom. Sometime before March of 1862 the Whites converted the bedroom on the south side of the stairway into a "large clothes press [closet]" and a narrow hallway leading to the room on the front of the house.[13] James occupied the back bedroom, Ellen the large front one. During a time when whole families slept in the same room, the Whites had separate bedrooms, perhaps because Ellen often woke up in the middle of the night to write. James, who drove himself constantly, desperately needed his sleep. The two bedrooms allowed him to get his rest and her to record her visions without disturbing him. Diaries and letters indicate that the bedroom pattern continued in at least some of the homes they later owned.

The front upstairs bedroom became Ellen's writing room. In it she would compose *Spiritual Gifts,* volume 1. Published in 1858, it was the first edition of the book Seventh-day Adventists now know as *The Great Controversy.* She started it at the end of a funeral at Lovett's Grove, Ohio (March 14, 1858), after receiving a vision on the theme of the struggle between Christ and Satan. The Whites' new home also had convenient access to a good well. Jonah R. Lewis, their Sabbath-observing neighbor to the south, dug a well close to their joint property line and equipped it with a wooden curb, windlass, and oaken bucket. He also made a path from it to Wood Street—that way, all the neighbors could use the well too.

The Whites moved in by at least November 4, 1856. Eventually James added a lean-to room on the north end. Ellen's parents, Robert and Eunice Harmon, briefly lived in it. James was still uncomfortable with their presence and, as we shall see later, had been planning a new home for them. After the Harmons left, James's parents used it until they moved to their own home across the street.

Because their rental house had not had a woodshed, James made sure that their own did. Fourteen feet in length, it also contained the family outhouse, or privy, with two seats, one a child's and the other for an adult. A cistern collected rainwater. The Whites also had a two-story carriage barn to house their horse and carriage and store hay for the horse. Such carriage barns were common at the time and equivalent to today's garage, though usually larger.

On June 19, 1861, Ellen White wrote to her friend Lucinda Abbey (who would marry William Hall) that the carpenters working adding the new addition were making such a racket that she had retreated to the Review office to write her letter. The addition replaced the small old woodshed and included a good-sized kitchen, a large bedroom, a clothes press (closet), a buttery (pantry), a "meal room" off the buttery (probably to store grain and flour), and a small "stove room" to cook in during the summer and to store firewood during the winter. The "meal room" had a bread board for kneading dough. Then the loaves could be carried into the kitchen for baking. Because of her own busy schedule, Ellen did not spend much time in the kitchen. The family cook, Jennie Frasier, prepared most of the meals. And if a batch of bread dough turned out bad, she would hide it in the tin boiler in the cellar.

JAMES WHITE—GADGET LOVER

During their years on Wood Street James began to indulge interests that would label him today as a lover of gadgets. If it was new, he wanted it. For example, coal oil (kerosene) lamps began to appear in Battle Creek in the mid-1850s, and although many people would continue using candles for many more years, the Whites had adopted the lamps by about 1859. Many homes had cisterns to collect rainwater, but people used it only for washing clothes because it was not safe to drink. At least for his second home in Battle Creek James obtained a Kedzie patent water filter to purify the cistern water. A cone-shaped device, it allowed water to flow through alternate layers of charcoal and wood shavings. He ran ads for it a number of times in his publications.

Later, in *The Health Reformer,* he advertised the Doty Washer and Universal Wringer. A note (possibly written by James himself) described it as "a great labor-saving institution," then commented that "in our own household, a promiscuous [mixed] family washing of one or two hundred pieces is frequently all in the rinsing water before breakfast, by the aid of these labor-saving appliances, instead of being dragged through nearly all day, as formerly. Our 'better half' regards the Doty Washer as next to the sewing machine, in point of economy of time, labor, patience, and household comfort."[14]

As a way of relaxing, Ellen would tear cloth into narrow strips that could be sewn together and wound into balls. The neighborhood women gave her sacks of material. The cloth strips would then be woven into rag rugs. When the Whites moved into their Wood Street home, she decided to carpet the bedrooms with rag carpets. But her practice of tearing the rags into strips and braiding them bothered James. When he brought friends home he didn't want them to see her sitting surrounded by a pile of rags. Family tradition tells how one day he came home from the Review, where he had been working on a new hymnal that for the first time contained the song "No Sorrow There." Seeing his wife tearing strips of cloth and winding them up into balls—and perhaps with the tune still running through his mind—he began to sing:

"In expectation sweet, we will watch, and wait and pray,
Until Christ's triumphant car we meet and see an endless day,
There'll be no rag carpets there, There'll be no rag carpets there,
In heaven above where all is love,
There'll be no rag carpets there—
There'll be no rag carpets there."[15]

Whether her hobby upset him because it did not allow her enough rest (or, as one historian suggests, if he couldn't have Brussels carpets, he would rather have none at all) she caught the hint and stopped making the rag strips, even though the money earned from them had helped James out during emergencies. Later she would sell the rag carpets made for the Wood Street home to help defray the expenses of moving to the country so he could regain his health after a stroke.[16]

In February of 1861 James White purchased lots 4 and 5 of Manchester's Addition (located across the street) from Amable and Domitilde Daigneau, the parents of a French-Canadian neighbor, John M. Daigneau. It apparently had a house on it that he used as a rental property.

On April 15, 1863, the Whites sold the Wood Street house and lots 4 and 5 (totaling five acres) to Robert Sawyer for $1,480.[17] They then moved to the corner of Washington and Champion streets, where they lived until

August 1866. The lot was 84/100 of an acre and cost $1,300. James made improvements to the house and grounds and sold it for $4,500.[18] (Court records and the minutes of the Health Reform Institute indicate that the Whites owned or resided at the property on the corner of Champion and Washington streets between 1873 and 1875 and later about the time they moved to their final home in Battle Creek.) Earlier that June they had purchased a house and two parcels of land totaling 11 acres for $3,250 north of the Health Reform Institute.

When James decided to sell the house on the corner of Champion and Washington, he advertised it in the *Review*.[19] After giving its specifications, he reported that he had spent $1,200 the previous summer in papering, painting, and other expenses, as well as a new barn that had cost $400. The land now had 25 bearing apple trees, 40 peach trees, 40 pear trees, 22 quince bushes, 3,000 strawberry plants, and grapes, blackberries, and raspberries "in abundance." "Battle Creek is fast building up," he declared, "and is one of the most flourishing cities in central Michigan. With a prospect of a new railroad, and other improvements, it holds out great inducements to those who choose city-life, especially to those who are interested in the Health Institute and growing cause of Bible truth.

"Here will be found a large assembly of Sabbathkeepers, soon to be accommodated in their new house of worship, a flourishing Sabbath School, and the interests and advantages of the Publishing Department."[20] He asked either full cash or two-thirds down with good security and promised immediate possession. James explained that he was selling because he wanted a cheaper place.

Perhaps a reason he had wanted to move was that the neighborhood had become less rural (even though he extolled the advantages of city life in his ad in the *Review*). The pastureland to the west of the Wood Street home and the wooded area to the north were disappearing. Manchester's woods had been acquired by the Michigan Fair Association, who built a racetrack a mile in length around it. Trotting horses were trained on it every Sunday, and during the early days of the Civil War it served as a training ground for recruits. The military activities captivated the White boys, and their influence began to concern their parents. Fascinated by military life, Henry Nichols would march along with the soldiers. Also James White apparently thought the house was too far from the Review—

it was five blocks away—and he wanted to move closer. The Health Reform Institute bought it on October 22, 1867, while the Whites were living in Greenville, Michigan.[21]

JAMES WHITE—REAL ESTATE AGENT

His experience with the Wood Street house encouraged White on one of his most successful business sidelines: buying and selling real estate. References to real estate transactions frequently crop up in his letters.[22] Court records at Marshall, Michigan, the county seat for Calhoun County, reveal his extensive real estate dealings. He did, however, get off to a difficult start with one piece of property. On November 4, 1856, he purchased the four-fifths-acre lot 62 for $130. It had a small house on it. Apparently he had already been fixing it up for Ellen's parents so they would not have to continue living with him. He had told them once that if they would give him their life savings—about $500—he would take care of them for the rest of their lives. But they could not make up their minds. And James had already spent money on the project. Somehow he had to recover his investment, so quickly he decided to sell it to someone else. The same day he bought the lot James wrote to a friend of Ellen's, Elsa P. Below of Millgrove, New York, asking if she would be interested in the property.

"I have bought four-fifths of an acre with a building on it, for three hundred dollars,"[23] he told Mrs. Below. "I bought it for Father Harmon. I have cleared it off and cultivated it and fenced it, cost fifty dollars. I have built a front on it; cost two-hundred fifty dollars. The whole stands me six hundred dollars. I think the old folks will not be able to take it.

"I owe them two-hundred-fifty dollars, which I shall have to raise for them unless they take the place. I also owe about one hundred-fifty dollars which I have run in debt building their addition. . . . Here is a description of it, hastily got up.

"The old part is one year old, plaster-sided, etc. It is sixteen feet north and south, fourteen feet east and west. The new part is twelve feet east and west, twenty-one north and south. In the new part below is a room 12 x 12, a bedroom 8 x 9, and a stairway. It has two finished chambers, high and good, one 12 x 12, the other 9 x 12 with stairway out. In the old part is a buttery [pantry]—go downstairs from the buttery, a clothes press in the north-west [sic] corner. Also a kitchen 14 x 12, and quite a storeroom in the chamber of the old part.

"This house is to be painted with two coats outside, and the new part inside, a good eave-trough, and hogshead sink, and a good log barn. The land is *all* fit for the finest garden, with a post and board fence about it. All this for six hundred dollars.

"I think you would be pleased with the place. Our home is about twelve rods from this house I offer you. My boys are getting large enough to run errands, and would be happy to assist Sister Below. I hope the way will open for you and your daughter to come and live near us. But if you cannot, can you lend me three hundred dollars for a year, or for six months? . . . Sister Devereux will write particulars."[24]

James included with his letter a rough sketch of the house and a letter by Melvina E. Devereux, a Review employee, also encouraging Mrs. Below to move to Battle Creek. The way she begins it suggests that White may have been using a little persuasion on her. "Brother White has promised you I would finish this [letter] and so I must. He wrote it late Thursday eve—and expected me to finish it next day. I was up there [at his home?] making her [Mrs. White?] a hood—staid [sic] till next day noon, finished it and then had to go to the [Review] Office."[25] Devereux gives additional information about what White had planned to do with the house as well as about James's skill as a gardener.

"Nothing would give me more pleasure than to have you here. . . . I think from what I heard you say that the place would just suit you. The land is very rich. Such corn as Brother White raised there I never saw before. He planted it late, too, as it had to be grubbed out and fenced before he could plant. The soil is very soft and if you intend to keep on doing your own gardening you could do it a good deal easier here. . . .

"Brother and Sister Harmon did talk of taking the place after she was sick. But now they are hanging off again. Brother White had the addition put up on the supposition that they intended to take it, in fact they moved into the old part as soon as she was able to. But I believe they have about concluded not to buy at all. Brother Harmon's health has been very poor lately. I don't know what does ail him—some kind of a bowel complaint. He is better now, but I should not wonder if he did not live long. He is quite old."[26]

About November James sent a follow-up letter. Not only did he again urge her to move to Battle Creek, he added that if she had any money to lend, banks paid 10 percent interest in Battle Creek and individuals offered 12 to 20 percent. He suggested that if she couldn't sell her home in New York, she should rent it out and move anyway.[27] On March 23, 1857, he wrote to her again, suggesting that Cottrell would look after her place there. White told her about fuel prices and other economic advantages in Battle Creek, then advised her on how to pack for the move.

Fortunately for James, Mrs. Below bought the property on May 8, 1857, for $590. He dropped his asking price $10.

In 1867 when James sought to interest the Health Reform Institute into buying his property north of it, he offered an interesting list of 12 reasons the institute should purchase it, including the idea that the denomination owed it to him and Ellen for their services to the denomination. He argues "(6) Is not the property cheap at $6,000? . . . (8) Is not our condition as to financial matters one that should be relieved by our fellow-laborers and brethren, if they can do so without bringing them into a condition equally bad and unpleasant? (9) As worn pioneers, have we not claims on our brethren to help us, if in doing so they meet with no great loss? . . . (11) Are you aware that the very soul and strength of influence that has called means together is the testimonies of my wife? Would it not be liberal and well to free her from the constant burden she bears in consequence of our condition?"[28]

The Institute did acquire it. Then in 1870 he would negotiate with the San to let him have it back for less than the San board had paid him. Two years later he sold it back to the Institute.[29] Through the years he built or owned homes in Greenville, Michigan; Washington, Iowa; Kansas; Colorado; Oakland, California; and two in Healdsburg, California. The Washington, Iowa, home became a refuge when problems became too stressful in Battle Creek. James would retreat to there and find it relaxing to work around the property. The Healdsburg homes are still valuable properties even though much of their land has been sold off.

Sometimes he was willing to sell a house at a loss, especially if an emergency faced some part of the denomination or he wanted to pay a pledge he had made for some project. When the Oakland, California, church faced the possibility of losing its building, he offered to sell his own home in Oakland to help erase the debt.[30] In 1875 he sold homes in Iowa and Michigan for less than he could have received for them. Part of the proceeds went into $5,000 he donated for various church projects during a two-year period.[31]

On one occasion Ellen wanted the denomination to buy some property to be the site of Battle Creek College. It was a substitute for property on Goguac Lake that was too far from the publishing house and San to be practical. To her disappointment the new property was smaller than she wished. Surprisingly, James White subdivided and sold off half the property. But she was practical and realized that they needed to raise money for the project. After the college started, he wanted to build cottages on the school property and rent them to students and others.[32]

James seems to have bought up property whenever he found it cheap. It also appears that denominational leaders may have employed White's real estate skills. If they wanted someone to come to a certain area, they could turn to James to find a place for the individual to live.[33] Perhaps this might explain the property James White owned in St. Joseph County, Indiana. It was near South Bend, Indiana, in Liberty Township, not far from the site of the Seventh-day Adventist church in the area.[34]

For a time James considered buying property at Grand Ledge, Michigan, and operating there, but he concluded that the railroad connections and mail service to Battle Creek were too poor.[35] Instead he looked for a place around Battle Creek itself, though he would have returned to his Healdsburg home if the church leadership had encouraged him to go to California.[36]

HIS DREAM HOME

The final home he owned was a 16-room, three-story brick Italianate mansion on the road to Goguac Lake about a mile and a half from the center of Battle Creek. The 30-acre estate had woods on 10 acres and an orchard of more than 200 fruit trees. He paid $6,000 for it,[37] but to raise the money, he had to sell his homes in Oakland and Healdsburg, California. White advertised the Healdsburg property (as well as Willie's Oakland house) in the *Signs of the Times*.[38] Several times he wrote to Willie pleading that his son sell the houses as quickly as possible.[39] Reading between the lines, one could get the impression that Ellen was urging Willie *not* to sell them. She preferred to live in California. But at last James was able to buy the Battle Creek house. If uncomfortable with the mansion, she did not let her feelings prevent them from sharing it together until his death.

White had spent many years in poverty, dependent on others for a place for him and his family to live. He had struggled hard to support his family and keep the Review and Herald publishing house and other denominational institutions afloat. At the same time James had unceasingly given to others. Now he had his dream home, and he lovingly alluded to it in his letters. "O dear," he wrote to Ellen as he traveled, "I hope you can be made happy at our good home."[40]

Not only could he relax and enjoy the home; he could share it with others. The Whites enjoyed inviting guests. On April 24, 1881, James performed the wedding of Dudley M. Canright to his second wife, Lucy, in the large parlor. It would be the last such ceremony listed in his handwritten record book. Afterward Lucy sent a thank-you letter to say that she and her husband wanted to invite the Whites to her home, although it could not compare with theirs. She told James that she and Dudley would "always remember with pleasure our visit at your romantic home, and also the fine ride to the city you and I took together. I used to be somewhat afraid of Bro. White, but since our wedding and especially that ride, instead of feeling that way, you seem almost like my father. Indeed, [I] shall love you for making our wedding go off so pleasantly.

"Dudley and I often speak of it and wonder if there ever was a nicer wedding; of course we think not."[41]

White loved his house, but if past history is any indication, at least some in the Battle Creek Adventist community would have resented it. And Ellen, with her frugal Maine heritage, may have been uncomfortable with its elegance. As for James himself, he lived in it only about seven months before his death. She then sold it, and it later burned down.

---

[1] For background on early Battle Creek, see Ron Graybill, "The Whites Come to Battle Creek: A Turning Point in Adventist History," *Adventist Heritage,* Fall 1992, p. 25; Gerald G. Herdman, "Glimpses of Early Battle Creek," *Adventist Heritage,* January 1974, pp. 17, 18.

[2] *The Health Reformer,* June 1871, p. 298.

[3] Ron Graybill, "The Whites Come to Battle Creek," pp. 25, 26.

[4] *Review and Herald,* Dec. 4, 1855.

[5] *Review and Herald,* Feb. 21, 1856.

[6] Ellen G. White, *Life Sketches,* p. 159.

[7] The Adventist Heritage Ministry has restored the house to its original condition. Study by the restorers and archaeological excavations conducted by Western Michigan University have corrected some mistakes about the house made in Willie White's memoirs of growing up in the Wood Street residence.

[8] William C. White, in *Review and Herald,* Feb. 13, 1936.

[9] JW to EGW, Oct. 29, 1860.

[10] JW to EGW, Nov. 4, 1860 [date uncertain].

[11] JW to EGW, Oct. 31, 1860.

[12] JW to EGW, Nov. 1, 1860.

[13] EGW to "Friends at Home" (letter 4, 1862), Mar. 5, 1862.

[14] *The Health Reformer,* October 1870, p. 80.

[15] Arthur L. White to H. J. Thompson, May 25, 1944.

[16] EGW manuscript 50, 1902.

[17] See Deed Book at the Calhoun County seat, vol. 53, pp. 445, 446.

[18] Deed Book, vol. 72, p. 194.

[19] See, for example, *Review and Herald,* Mar. 19, 1867.

[20] *Ibid.*

[21] See Deed Book, vol. 66, pp. 272, 273.

[22] Examples include JW to WCW, May 22, 1877; JW to WCW, June 10, 1877.

[23] The deed records a purchase price of $130, while White states that he paid $300 for it. Was this his markup for profit, or had he already invested more in the place than he indicates in his letter?

[24] JW to Elsa P. Below, Nov. 4, 1856.

[25] Melvina E. Devereux to Elsa P. Below, Nov. 4, 1856. Devereux added, "From what I can see, Brother White is well-pleased with my work in the Office. He appears to be—and I think he generally shows out his true feelings." Did she expect him to read this?

[26] *Ibid.*

[27] JW to Elsa P. Below, c. November 1856.

[28] James White to Brethren—Directors of the Health Institute, August 1867. See also JW to "Dear Brethren," September 1867, in which James and Ellen argue that the institute should buy their home instead of putting up a large and expensive brick building. They signed themselves as "Servants of the Church." Additional details of the negotiations appear in the board minutes of the institute.

[29] See Deed Book, vol. 71, p. 717, and vol. 75, p. 750.

[30] Harold Oliver McCumber, *Pioneering the Message in the Golden West* (Mountain View, Calif.: Pacific Press Pub. Assn., 1946), pp. 141, 142; cf. JW to WCW, June 2, 1875.

[31] *An Earnest Appeal From the General Conference Committee Relative to the Dangers and Duties of Our Time* (Oakland, Calif.: Pacific Press, 1876), p. 42.

[32] JW to WCW, May 7, 1876.

[33] Observation by Jean Davis. We may see something similar when the California

Conference voted to establish a publishing house in Oakland, California, and purchased two building lots. James White and John Morrison titled them in their names, with the understanding that they would turn over part or all of them when it came time to construct the printing plant. See Arthur W. Spalding, *Origin and History of Seventh-day Adventists* (Washington, D.C.: Review and Herald Pub. Assn., 1962), vol. 2, p. 158.

[34] Source: Jean Davis.

[35] JW to WCW, Oct. 14, 1880.

[36] JW to WCW, Nov. 13, 1880.

[37] JW to WCW, Nov. 3, 1880. In an October 31, 1880, letter White said it was 35 acres and costing $7,000. Did he sell off part of the estate?

[38] *Signs of the Times,* Sept. 12, 1878.

[39] JW to WCW, Oct. 14, 1880; JW to WCW, Oct. 31, 1880; JW to WCW, Nov. 7, 1880; JW to WCW, Nov. 21, 1880.

[40] JW to EGW, Feb. 11, 1881.

[41] Lucy Canright to JW, May 17, 1881.

CHAPTER VIII

THE LINGERING PAIN OF PARIS, MAINE

MANY farmers of Maine, tired of the struggle to wrest a living from the glacial hillside farms, abandoned them to be reclaimed by nature, and moved to the deep soil of the Midwest or found employment in the state's developing factories.[1] The Edward Andrews and Cyprian Smith families chose the former and moved to the extreme northeastern corner of Iowa in November 1855. Andrews obtained a farm on the flat prairie three and a half miles directly south of the little town of Waukon. Soon other Sabbatarian Adventists began to settle in Allamakee County. The George I. Butler family settled there from Vermont. In 1856 J. N. Loughborough moved from Rochester, New York, along with his next-door neighbors, Jonathan and Caroline Orton. Drusilla and Bradley Lamson, their daughter and son-in-law, soon followed.

John Nevins Andrews married Angeline Stevens on October 29, 1856, and they moved in with her parents. He and Loughborough now abandoned evangelism and turned to farming, including raising pigs (health reform was yet to come). Their departure from the ministry was a great loss to the growth of Sabbatarian Adventism.

Two months after the marriage of John to Angeline Stevens, the Whites attended a meeting at Round Grove, Illinois. Ellen had a vision that convinced her that they must go to Waukon. Not only must they attempt to convince Andrews and Loughborough to return to the ministry, they had to deal with the increasing alienation of the Waukon Adventists toward the Whites and the rest of the Sabbatarian Adventist movement. If the Whites did not reach them soon, the Iowa group could split into an independent faction and be lost, perhaps forever. But it was December, and they would have to travel through 200 miles of ice and snow in an open sleigh to reach Iowa. Just as they prepared to leave, it rained for an entire day, but Ellen felt they must proceed, regardless. With Josiah Hart, the sleigh's owner, they began. Rain alternated with snow. Once they had to spend seven days in an inn until the weather cleared.

When they reached the Mississippi River, they discovered that though it had frozen over, a foot of water now covered the ice. As they crossed the river they could occasionally hear the ice cracking beneath them. Once they reached the Iowa shore the temperature began turning bitter. They had to rub their faces constantly to restore circulation during the 18-mile drive from the Mississippi across the windswept prairie. Finally they reached snowbound Waukon.

The Whites found the situation in the community of Sabbatarian Adventists most discouraging. It especially bothered them that the believers were doing little to "set the truth before others" or to witness to their neighbors. Instead, they were "almost wholly occupied with the things of this life."[2] The Whites suggested that the Laodicean message of Revelation 3:14-22 also applied to Sabbatarian Adventists (many Adventists felt at the time that they represented the Philadelphia church of Revelation 3:7-13). Naturally the Waukon believers rejected the idea. James noted that at best they received him and Ellen only with "Christian courtesy."

In time he learned that one of the strongest grudges the Waukon believers held against him was that he had moved the Review from Rochester to Battle Creek.[3] But it was not the only problem. The bitterness and hostility that had erupted in Paris, Maine, was still lurking beneath the surface.

When James carefully explained why he had transferred the publishing entity from New York to Michigan, the alienation began to ease. J. N. Loughborough accompanied him back to Battle Creek and resumed his ministerial activities. John Nevins Andrews began conducting meetings in the Waukon area. Then, on September 6, 1858, Angeline Andrews' father, Cyprian Stevens, died in agony five days after being bitten by a rattlesnake. The following June John Andrews attended a conference in Battle Creek that voted that he should work with Loughborough in holding evangelistic meetings in the tent Michigan believers had purchased. George Amadon came to Waukon to take John's place on the family farm, and Hiram Edson covered Amadon's wages.

SIMMERING RESENTMENT

Andrews was again in full-time evangelism, but the feelings his father and in-laws held against the Whites were still at work. Both he and Uriah and Harriet Smith—his brother and sister-in-law—still rankled over the incidents in Maine. Their feelings stirred up doubts and questions about the Whites, doubts that appear in Angeline Andrews' diary. Once, when visiting a couple named Thomas and Mary Mead in 1860, she began telling them how she felt about what had happened so many years before and how it raised questions about the Whites in her mind. That night she confided in her diary, "I have great confidence in Bro. and Sr. Mead [but] I cannot yet take just the position in regard to Sr. W.'s visions they [the Meads] do—they fully believe them to be all right from God, consequently of equal authority with the Bible."[4]

When the subject of Ellen White's role came up in a Sabbath meeting later that month, Angeline wrote that "there is some difference of views as to the place [the visions] should occupy in the church. . . . Some hold them as equal authority with the Bible and are designed to correct and guide the church. . . . Others believe [the] Bible does not sanction such use of them. Oh, that we might understand just the right position to take in regard to them."[5]

Angeline's doubts were not just intellectual. In large part they sprang from the Andrews/Stevens sense of hurt over how James White had dealt with them years earlier in Paris, Maine. Ellen White had recognized this problem when she had a few weeks previously written letters to Harriet Smith and John Andrews.

Mrs. White told Uriah Smith's wife that "those who fall into an agony, as you have, at the least censure or reproof do not realize that they are perfectly controlled by the enemy. . . . You may call your feelings grief, but you have not realized them as they were. It has been anger, and you have been selfish. . . . How much faith do you have in the visions? They do not bear a feather's weight on your mind."[6]

Ellen also wrote that "when everything moves on smoothly, then past dissatisfactions and difficulties in Paris lie dormant, but when a reproof or rebuke is given, the same dissatisfaction arises. 'Brother White was wrong back there; he was too severe and he is too severe now.' Then jealous, hard feelings arise. As he is in union with the visions given, as the visions and his testimony agree, the visions are doubted, and Satan is working secretly to affect and overthrow the work of God."[7]

She had to confront Harriet because of her influence on her husband, Uriah, and through her sister, Angeline, she encouraged John Andrews to deal with the feelings that he had picked up from his father, Edward Andrews. Ellen told Harriet that the resentment toward James White, which also prompted doubts about his wife's role as prophet, had been "brought down from Paris to Rochester, and from Rochester to Waukon, and from Waukon" to Battle Creek.[8] The Andrews and Stevens families had poisoned the minds of many families at Waukon and elsewhere. "Brother John must yet see all the past and realize what influence he has exerted; that his influence told on the side of the enemy's ranks and his family do not stand clear. . . . They will not stand in the light until they wipe out the past by confessing their wrong course in opposing the testimonies given them of God. . . . Either their feelings must be yielded, if it tears them all to pieces, or the visions must be given up. There will either be full union or a division. The crisis has come."[9] People could not separate the roles of James and Ellen White, and when they attacked one, they at the same time undercut the influence and credibility of the other. Thus Ellen was not just defending herself, but her husband as well.

JAMES WHITE DEFENDS HIMSELF

As Edward Andrews agitated his grievances, the Whites knew that they had to deal with the situation, both in Waukon and among Sabbatarian Adventists in general. James composed a lengthy letter about the situation to E. P. Butler, father of future General Conference president George I. Butler. It summarizes from White's perspective the issues Edward Andrews had raised in the years since the Whites had left Paris, Maine, and the relationship James had had with his son, John Nevins. Although it is a long letter, we will quote most of it, since it provides background to a little-known issue.

"I am sorry to trouble you again with matters pertaining to the Andrews' difficulty," he told Butler. "But the enclosed [document] seems to demand some notice, and judging from the past, I have no hope of receiving justice in this matter, made more or less public among you by addressing a reply to the writer of the enclosed note. This is my apology for troubling you.

"It must appear strange to you that this matter should continue eleven years, when you consider the close relation I have sustained in the message to the writer's son and the accuser has had so many opportunities to talk the matter over. First when we visited Paris, Maine; second, when making us apparently a pleasant visit at Battle Creek on their way to Waukon; third, when we visited Waukon, and the Lord met with us. But the thing has been salted down eleven years, or talked out in my absence to prejudice and distrust those who are ignorant of all the facts. And now, when I have become gray and bald, and through the multitude of cares during the lapse of time, I have nearly lost sight of the matter, a letter discussion of the subject is introduced.

"But I shall not engage in a full discussion by letter. I would be happy to be at Waukon and answer to charges brought against me, as I have had the privilege four or five years since. I will, however, make a few statements relative to the enclosed letter.

"1. The contract spoken of was not, I think, put in writing; therefore there is quite a chance in eleven years to forget whether I was to pay at the rate of $20.00 per year, or $20.00 whether I staid one month or longer.

"2. We were then paying $1.00 per week for board, but found our own wood and lights and two-fifths of the rent of the whole house. This pay for board seems small, but Mr. Millett, the leading man in the Oxford Journal Office paid but $1.50 at a good tavern, which was worth more than twice what we two dyspeptics got selecting the plainest from a farmer's table. I seldom ate anything beside potatoes and salt with a few spoonfuls of milk on them and corn bread. And when I undertook to keep house [that is, set up his own living arrangements] to prevent utter starvation, the difficulty assisted by the Steven's family commenced in good earnest. At the rates of good board, ours, all found, could not be worth more than $1.00 per week.

"I have not the least idea that I changed the terms of the aforesaid contract to cheat a poor man out of $8.00. Neither does any other man who knows my course believe this base suggestion.

"Edward Andrews does not really believe this. He cannot. He knows I gave his son John a pair of boots and gave him woolen flannels, that I and wife did most to get William [John's brother] a coat and pair of boots, when I suffered for many of the comforts of life. That I gave up my horse to John [Andrews] and Brother Rhodes and suffered greatly on my tour to Vermont in consequence. After receiving from my hand numerous presents for himself and family, Edward Andrews is the last man that walks the sod to make the base suggestion that I altered a verbal contract to cheat him of $8.00. I have no doubt [that] he makes this statement in his ingratitude to try to sustain his unbelief in the visions [of Mrs. White] which have reproved him and his family.

"Suppose I had injured Edward Andrews eleven years since. Can he not see any redeeming features in my course toward his son since that time? When I last visited Paris, Me., I gave John "$50.00 in clean money. And in all his travels east to search historical facts [for his book on the history of Sabbath and Sunday], my letters have followed him at every point to the brethren to do liberally by him. His first edition of Hist. Sab. was worth to him $125.00 at my suggestion alone, to say nothing of the frequent donations from my own purse or articles of clothing. I have helped him $60.00 in books and a stove in the S.D.A.P.A. [Seventh-day Adventist Publishing Association] this last fall.

"J. N. Andrews' lack of taking a firm position, discouraged me utterly in regard to him near a year since, yet I tried to follow him in Minn. last summer with a few small [money] drafts. Had he stood by me as I have tried to stand by him, I could have had courage to have seen him fully sustained. But I had no faith that God would bless his labors, and as I was not in the least consulted as to that mission, I could not feel it duty to do anything, [but] still did what I did, out of regard for his evident sincerity in laboring for the good of the cause in the past.

"Cannot Edward Andrews see something in all this to lead him to think that possibly he is mistaken? Or will he in view of these things persist in the contemptible charge that according to his certain memory I changed a contract to cheat him out of the sum of $8.00."[10]

Commenting on the marriage between John and Angeline, White felt that "if the two families [Andrews and Stevens] had believed and acted upon the visions when they professed to believe them, poor Brother John might have been saved the dreadful trials he has suffered. When we left Paris, [my] wife saw that there was an unholy union between the two families which must be broken. They were then living some distance apart, but very soon moved into one house, and all the evidences show that that union increased. Also, [my] wife, in almost every vision for Brother John, which were, I think, as frequent as once a year, addressed him like this— 'Paris is no place for you. There is an influence there that would get you down from the work.' These warnings were timely, and sufficient had all the professed faith in them been lived out.

"These charges are of the same unreasonable character of that in which I was blamed for moving the office to Michigan which I proved groundless when at Waukon. I may be favored with the privilege of speaking for myself before my accuser, and those whose minds have been poisoned by him. However, that may be, I am ready to meet all charges against me before those who keep the seventh-day, at any proper time and place, but shall not spend further time in this matter with ink and paper. I still have a high regard for Brother John Andrews, and pity him from the bottom of my heart. If the two families had heeded the visions given them in 1850, doubtless his union with his wife would have been formed under circumstances free from their present trials. The cause would have been saved dreadful injuries, and we saved from premature old age, despondency and anguish of spirit. Or if John had been of a different temperament, so as to stand out free from the influence of the rebellious at Paris, he might have been saved from most of his trials. I have said it in public and private that I regarded J. N. Andrews and Uriah Smith as two splendid young men and sincere Christians, possessing sweetness of temper and fine feelings beyond any two men of their mind and talent I ever saw. They are coming out like gold, seven times purified. But O, the unnecessary anguish of spirit these two men have suffered in consequence of the stubborn rebellion at Paris. It has well nigh ruined them both, and resulted in tearing them down from responsible stations.

"Thank God, it is not too late for wrongs to be righted. Let the living shake and manifest character! God is righting up all who will be helped. Amen."[11]

CONFESSION AND RECONCILIATION

Besides explaining the situation to prominent church members, the Whites also dealt directly with the believers in Waukon during 1861. Their letters began to have some impact. In November John Andrews sent a confession about his wrong attitude. As more messages would come from the Whites, Andrews would personally read them to the Waukon congregation. Then early in 1862 in a letter also signed by his wife, John declared, "My heart is pained in view of my past course and the position which I have occupied relative to the visions. Oh, why have I stood out in rebelling against them as I have? How dark has been my mind and how little have I realized of the exceeding sinfulness of my course. . . . Dear Brother and Sister [White], how many and heavy have been the burdens you have borne on my account and others of us at Paris. . . . I know I can never make amends for the past, but I am resolved to do what I can. . . . My influence against the visions has not been from a multiplicity of words against them. . . . But I confess I have not stood up for them and borne testimony in their favor."[12]

In another letter sent the same day, Andrews added, "I have lacked to some extent that living faith in the visions that God alone will accept. Not that I have knowingly gone contrary to their testimony, but they have seemed to be a source of terror and distress so that I could not make that use of them that is such a blessing to others."[13]

Angeline Andrews, her mother, Almira, and her sister Pauline, also sent similar letters of confession and reconciliation to the Whites.[14] But Edward Andrews could not admit his problems as easily. Another year would pass before he finally confessed his errors.[15] It was only after Edward's death that his son began to write articles defending James's leadership and Ellen's prophetic gift.

From the evidence, it is apparent that James White's personality aggravated the problem. The believers in Paris, Maine, had been fanatical and extreme, but James's dealing with the situation had made it more difficult for them to acknowledge their problems. Harriet Smith described White as "cutting and slashing," while John Andrews put it politely, "No one is so faithful in plainness of speech."[16]

In June of 1862 John Andrews began to do evangelism with the New York believers' tent. That November Ellen White wrote him "that God has accepted your efforts. Your testimony in New York has been acceptable to him. . . . He has wrought for your wife and she has been learning to submit her will and way to God. . . . There has been a work, a good work, with some in Waukon."[17] But the damage would linger, especially with Uriah Smith, and Andrews would struggle with other problems. Mrs.

White would have to write him stern letters about those, especially his obsession with scholarly study.[18]

[1] Diane and Jack Barnes, comp., *The Oxford Hills: Greenwood, Norway, Oxford, Paris, West Paris and Woodstock*, p. 140.

[2] *Review and Herald,* Jan. 15, 1857.

[3] JW to E. P. Butler, Dec. 12, 1861.

[4] Angeline Andrews diary, July 19, 1860.

[5] *Ibid.,* July 28, 1860.

[6] EGW to Harriet Smith (letter 7, 1860), June 1860.

[7] *Ibid.*

[8] *Ibid.*

[9] *Ibid.*

[10] JW to E. P. Butler, Dec. 12, 1861.

[11] *Ibid.*

[12] J. N. Andrews to EGW, Feb. 2, 1862.

[13] J. N. Andrews to EGW, Feb. 2, 1862.

[14] A. S. Andrews to JW and EGW, Jan. 30, 1862; Almira Stevens to JW and EGW, Jan. 23, 1862; P. R. Stevens to EGW, Jan. 27, 1862.

[15] Edward Andrews to JW and EGW, Jan. 25, 1863.

[16] EGW to Harriet Smith (letter 13, 1869), Sept. 24, 1869; *Review and Herald,* Mar. 3, 1868.

[17] EGW to J. N. Andrews (letter 11, 1862), Nov. 9, 1862.

[18] EGW to J. N. Andrews, (letter 31, 1872) 1872.

Chapter IX

EVERYWHERE FOR THE LORD

THE expanding railroad system in the northern United States enabled James White to travel even more extensively as he sought to advance and encourage the growing body of Sabbatarian Adventists. Travel reports became a major part of the contents of the *Review and Herald*. One he sent to Uriah Smith printed in the August 5, 1858, issue illustrates his unrelenting schedule, during which he tried to utilize every available moment.

"Bro. Smith: Here we are in Iowa City, Iowa, and while Bro. M. Hull is preaching, we [White loved to use the editorial "we" for everything] are writing. . . .

"We wish to say to the many dear friends who have addressed us by letter for the past two months, that we have not had time to answer their kind letters; neither have we had time to attend to all the business contained in those letters. To give our friends some idea of how our time is occupied, and how little spare time we have, we will give a brief statement concerning the last few weeks.

"July 8th. At 2 P.M., we took the [railroad] cars at Battle Creek for Jackson; at 2 A.M., the 9th, took the cars for Detroit; at 7 A.M. For Pontiac; at 9 A.M. Took the stage for Orion; that evening preached in the Michigan Tent; Sabbath, the 10th, preached twice; First-day [the early Adventist term for Sunday], 11th, preached once; 12th, took the stage and cars for Detroit; 13th, rode on the cars to Rochester, and after 9 P.M. Walked a mile to Bro. Orton's; 14th and 15th bought a tent, and was attending to other business until the cars left for the West at 7 P.M.; rode on the cars all night; reached Green Spring, Ohio, the 16th, at 10 A.M.; rode in a wagon to Milan; Sabbath, the 17th, preached at Bro. Tilliotson's; 18th, rode 12 miles, preached once in the Ohio Tent, and after Bro. Loughborough closed his discourse at half past 9 P.M., rode 12 miles; got to rest at 1 A.M., and was waked up at 5 to take the cars for home; reached Jackson at 6 P.M., the 20th; took the cars that night, reached home at 1 A.M.; went to the [Review] Office the 21st, and found a multitude of letters, and more business than we could attend to. At 2 P.M. Received a letter urging us to visit Crane's Grove, Ills., by the 23d. This gave us two days to prepare 100 pages of MS. for the printers, read 40 pages of proof-sheet, and hastily attend to a week's work of other business. At 11 P.M., the 22d, took the cars; reached Crane's Grove the 23d at 6 P.M.; Sabbath, the 24th, met with the brethren in the forenoon at Bro. Berry's; in the afternoon preached in the school-house; the 25th, preached twice; the 26th, rode in a lumber wagon to Bro. Sanborn's in Wis.; the 27th, rode in the same way back to Crane's Grove; the 28th, took the cars to Morrison; at 4:00 A.M., the 29th, took the cars for Iowa; rode thirty miles in a western stage; the 30th, rode horse-back to this place, 20 miles, swam the pony after a small boat one half mile; Sabbath, 31st, preached twice, and to-day once. And now, thank the Lord, we are well, free and happy. Health is better than for twelve years. We give this sketch that our friends may know where we are, what we have been doing, and why we do not answer their numerous letters. August 1st, 1858 J. W."[1]

THE WILLIAM J. HARDY FAMILY[2]

During one of their tours to meet with scattered believers, the Whites met the Hardy family. William J. Hardy was an African-American who had been born January 9, 1823, in Seneca County, New York. His parents moved to Washtenaw County in Michigan in 1827, the year New York freed its slaves, though it is not known if they themselves had been slaves or free Blacks. Soon after their arrival the father died and the boy was sent to work for a farmer near Ann Arbor. In 1844 he married Eliza Wats and settled in the township of Gaines in Kent County, where he eventually bought a 160-acre farm. There he worshiped with the Freewill Baptists.

His personality and hard work earned the respect of his fellow townspeople, who elected him to a number of public positions, including county supervisor for Gaines Township in 1872. He was the first African-American to hold office in Michigan, and frequently went as a delegate to Republican county conventions. One of his sons was the first African-American to graduate from high school in the state.

Sometime during the summer of 1857 Eliza Hardy accepted the Sabbath through the evangelistic preaching of Joseph Birchard Frisbie. Shortly afterward William also joined the Sabbatarian Adventists. He would become active in the local congregation. Records indicate that he served as church clerk for the Caledonia, Michigan, Seventh-day Adventist Church and probably held other positions. During the 1870s the *Review and Herald* reported that the "burden of the work . . . [in Gaines, Michigan] now rests almost wholly on Br. W. J. Hardy."[3]

Adventist leaders soon began to visit the family after Eliza became a Sabbatarian Adventist. John Byington, who would serve as the first General Conference president, stayed with them in late 1857. The Whites soon heard good things about the family and decided to meet them. Unfortunately, James did not get to go on the trip. He had to wait in Battle Creek to meet J. N. Andrews, who was arriving for a special meeting. Accompanied by John Loughborough, Ellen started out on January 25, 1859, on the 14-mile journey from Grand Rapids. Unfortunately, the directions they had received from a church member named Cramer were wrong, and they went four miles out of their way in a heavy snowstorm.

Finally they arrived at noon. The Hardys welcomed them and quickly prepared a meal. Impressed by the family, Ellen wrote in her diary: "The children are well-behaved, intelligent, and interesting. May I yet have a better acquaintance with this dear family."[4]

---

[1] *Review and Herald*, Aug. 5, 1858.

[2] Sources about this family are contained in Historic Adventist Village document "Section 15: William J. Hardy Home."

[3] H. M. Kenyon letter, *Review and Herald*, Mar. 7, 1878.

[4] Arthur L. White, *Ellen G. White: The Early Years*, p. 398.

CHAPTER X

ORGANIZING A CHURCH[1]

THE publishing house continued to be a major problem. It needed some kind of legal organization, and the difficulties resulting from this lack would be one of the factors that prompted White and others to seek a larger organizational structure. Modern Adventists are so used to church structure that they cannot imagine a time without it. But the denomination had to go through a long and difficult struggle to achieve such organization. James White was the architect of the Seventh-day Adventist Church and its structure. The modern church member cannot appreciate what he accomplished without understanding something of the long and difficult struggle to organize the highly independent Sabbatarian Adventist believers into a united body. It was a discussion of intense passion and controversy. Church organization is such a fundamental of Adventism today that it is hard to realize the determined resistance it met.

Somebody had to legally own the publishing house building and equipment and bear legal, financial, and administrative responsibility. So far Sabbatarian Adventists had no legal body to control the publishing company, and until the state of Michigan established laws recognizing religious and other nonprofit entities, either an individual or a group of business owners would have to have legal responsibility for the publishing house.

The fact that the law considered White as the legal owner of the Review and Herald placed him in an awkward position. Besides making him vulnerable to the charge that he was operating it for personal gain, if it went bankrupt, he was responsible for its debts.

In 1860 James White invested about $30,000 of publishing house stock funds with two local brokers. Although the incident occurred after the Adventist believers had begun to legally incorporate the Review and Herald, it shows one kind of danger White had constantly faced as sole owner. Sometime later he dreamed that the two men were selling shoes in a dilapidated store. White interpreted the dream to mean that the men had to take up a menial business after losing their money.

After he discussed the dream with the Review staff, they decided to withdraw most of the money immediately and purchase construction materials for the new brick publishing house building planned for the spring of 1861. Then on July 1, 1861, White asked for the remaining balance. A few days later the brokers' business collapsed. People in Battle Creek lost a total of $50,000.[2] If such an incident had happened earlier and James had not retrieved his money, others would have considered him personally responsible for losing it.

With White as sole legal owner, his fellow Adventists would have less of a sense of the publishing house as belonging to the body of believers. If James were sued, went bankrupt, or apostatized, the church members could lose the institution. Also, the fact that he alone was responsible for the institution placed an even greater administrative burden on him. James was heavily involved in all the decisions and shouldered all the blame when anything went wrong. With one person responsible for every decision, the publishing house would have become little more than a reflection of that individual. Leadership needed to be shared by a larger body. Although as far back as Rochester days White had begged the three-person publishing committee to assume greater responsibility, neither it nor the believers as a whole were ready to take the step.

ADVENTIST FEAR OF ORGANIZATION

For Sabbatarian Adventists to create any kind of administrative structure, they would have to overcome a strong heritage that rejected all attempts at organization above the local congregation.

In an earlier chapter we saw the philosophical reluctance of the Christian Connexion to form anything other than individual churches. Yet as George Knight has pointed out, the Millerite movement drew so many members away from the loosely knit denomination that it felt compelled to develop a more structured organization just to protect itself from "bigoted schismatics."[3] The Christian Connexion movement experimented with state conference organizations, but they lacked any authority and would not even at times print the minutes of their meetings. The main way the Connexion held itself together was through its periodicals.[4] Their radical call for "Christian liberty" would linger among the many Sabbatarian Adventists with Christian Connexion backgrounds. On the other hand, James White, a former minister in the denomination, would know the inherent weaknesses of the Christian Connexion's approach to organization and what Sabbatarian Adventists must do to avoid them.

But the greatest resistance to the concept of organization came from memories about the hostility the Millerite movement had endured from organized mainline churches. It was one thing to discuss Christ's return as a theoretical possibility, but quite another when the idea began to divide congregations as the expected date loomed. When some ministers tried to stop the agitation, the Millerites felt it their sacred duty to push the issue anyway. As a result, by the summer of 1842 many local congregations refused to allow Millerites to hold meetings in their buildings, ordered members not to discuss the Second Advent, and removed ministers who preached on the topic.

In reaction Millerites organized Second Advent associations to collect funds for evangelism and to rent halls for Sunday afternoon meetings. Some local Millerite groups built their own meeting places. But the most influential Millerite response to their increasing isolation from the mainline churches was to preach the "Babylon has fallen" message. Charles Fitch in July 1843 published one of the most famous Millerite sermons. Calling it "Come Out of Her My People," Fitch based it on Revelation 14:8 and 18:1-5. The two passages summon God's people to leave spiritual Babylon (the Old Testament city had become the New Testament symbol of God's enemies). Fitch regarded Babylon as any Christian church that "opposed . . . the PERSONAL REIGN of Jesus Christ over the world on David's throne."[5] Their resistance to the Millerite message made them "ANTICHRIST."[6] Because of this, Fitch urged his readers, "If you are a Christian, *come out of Babylon!* If you intend to be found a Christian when Christ appears, *come out of Babylon,* and come out NOW! . . . Dare to believe the Bible. . . . Come out of Babylon or perish."[7]

Another prominent Millerite, George Storrs, declared that Babylon "is the *old mother* [the Roman Catholic Church] and all her children [the various Protestant denominations]; who are known by the family likeness, a domineering, lordly spirit; a spirit to suppress a free search after truth, and a free expression of our conviction of what is truth."[8] God's true people must leave all the other churches because "we have no right to let any man, or body of men, thus lord it over us. And to remain in such an organized body . . . is to remain in Babylon."[9] Organized religion, he believed, has been a continuous litany of bigotry and persecution. God's people, therefore, should reject all visible organized churches and consider themselves only as part of His invisible church that He has organized along bonds of love. Storrs firmly believed that "no church can be organized by man's invention but what it becomes Babylon *the moment it is organized.*"[10] Such an appeal was guaranteed to produce an even stronger resistance from most denominations with a strong organizational structure.

UNITED BY NEW TRUTH

Besides the philosophical wariness of church structures and the painful memories of persecution by organized religion, those who would become Sabbatarian Adventists had still another reason for ignoring ecclesiastical organization—they no longer saw any need for it. Religion was now just a matter of waiting until Jesus returned. Everyone's fate was already settled, so Adventists had nothing to do that required any kind of church structure except that needed to conduct local worship. They had no clergy to supervise or institutions to manage. But as time passed some Adventists came to new understandings, such as the seventh-day Sabbath, the heavenly sanctuary, and the nonimmortality of the soul. Many had abandoned their belief in the Second Coming, and those who adhered to it did not know what to make of the 1844 experience. The doctrine of Christ's two-phase ministry in heaven especially helped them make sense of what they had gone through and to validate it as genuine and from God. Ellen White's visions also brought new insights. Soon the Sabbatarian Adventists began to want to share what they had learned with fellow ex-Millerites. One of the first attempts was when James and Ellen White and Joseph Bates printed a collection of articles in a publication called *A Word to the "Little Flock."* By 1848 Sabbatarian Adventists had begun a strong drive to enlighten former Millerites about the new teachings. Fragments of the shattered Millerite movement began to coalesce into a Sabbatarian Adventist movement.

James White wrote in November 1849 that "the scattering time we have had; it is in the past, and now the time for the saints to be gathered into the unity of the faith, and be sealed by one holy, uniting truth *has come*. Yes, Brother, *it has come*. It is true that the work moves slowly, but it moves sure, and it gathers strength at every step. . . . Our past Advent experience, and present position and future work is marked out in Rev. 14 Chap. as plain as the prophetic pencil could write it. Thank God that we see it. . . . I believe that the Sabbath truth is yet to ring through the land, as the Advent never has. . . . Jesus is coming to gather the poor outcasts *home,* HOME, HOME." [11]

THE SABBATH CONFERENCES

One major means to bring the dispersed Millerites into a new and stronger unity was the Sabbath conferences that started in the spring of 1848. Six well-known and one lesser-known conference met that year, six in 1849, and 10 in 1850. Seventh-day Adventist tradition has thought of them as hammering out doctrine, but James White saw them more as platforms to present what he and Bates had discovered. He described the Thursday, April 20, 1848, session: "We had a meeting that evening of about fifteen in all. Friday morning the brethren came in until we numbered about fifty. They were not all fully in the truth. Our meeting that day was very interesting. Bro. Bates presented the commandments in a clear light, and their importance was urged home by powerful testimonies. The word had effect to establish those already in the truth and to awaken those who were not fully decided." [12] James White came to present truth, not to learn it.

Ellen White depicted the second Sabbath conference: "There were about thirty-five present, all that could be collected in that part of the State. There were hardly two agreed. Each was strenuous for his views, declaring that they were according to the Bible. All were anxious for an opportunity to advance their sentiments, or to preach to us." [13] Then she clearly explains what she and her husband saw as the meetings' reason for existence— "They were told that we had not come so great a distance to hear them, but had come to teach them the truth." [14] The delegates were there to learn from the Whites and Bates, not to debate. The strong Christian Connexion tradition of individual interpretation had to be restrained if the believers were to arrive at a consensus. And that would require forceful leadership.

James White would be at the forefront of the struggle to forge a group of believers who shared a common body of doctrine.

As did the Christian Connexion believers, Sabbatarian Adventists began to publish periodicals to teach the scattered believers and draw them together. Besides religious articles, the publications printed notices and resolutions from the Sabbath conferences and news about individual groups and members, who might otherwise go for months without hearing a Sabbatarian Adventist speaker. The magazines both presented doctrine and created a sense of community, the latter vital before any significant kind of organization could ever evolve. The Sabbath school lessons also brought Sabbatarian Adventists together. As the whole movement studied the same material, it created an even stronger sense of unity.

By now Sabbatarian Adventists had replicated the Christian Connexion pattern of periodicals and general meetings ("conferences") of believers. But new problems would force them to go further. The difficulties included issues of church discipline, regulating who was qualified to serve as a minister, how to pay for the clergy, doctrinal controversies, and the continual question of what to do about the publishing house. In September 1849 James White wrote about both the need to discipline church members and to find some way to support traveling ministers.[15] (Congregations did not have resident ministers assigned to them. Local elders took care of each church.)

He observed that "it does seem to me that those whom God has called to travel and labor in His cause should first be supported before those who have no calling from God are encouraged to go from place to place."[16] For example, Joseph Bates, despite White's protests, had endorsed the visit of a woman named Lawrence to believers in Connecticut. Unfortunately, she turned out to be "a trial to herself and others and suffered much."[17] In his letters he mentions a number of other individuals that he wished were not wandering from one group of believers to another. He felt that to support them was worse than throwing money away. Such people could be dangerous, as when several of them influenced a meeting at Fairhaven that the Whites did not have the money to attend. James complained that good ministers had to work for a living while troublemakers received money from believers.[18]

A SEARCH FOR GOSPEL ORDER

Some months later he expressed concern about someone whom he felt should not be a traveling preacher, commenting that the Sabbatarian Adventist believers needed to move in "gospel order,"[19] a phrase that would become prominent in the search for organization.

Problems of all kinds would increase as the number of Sabbatarian Adventists continued to grow, perhaps reaching 2,000 in 1852. More members and congregations brought more difficulties. Many new congregations had no or little structure or organization. The members would often not know what to do to conduct Sabbath school or worship. Fanatics and self-appointed preachers began to prey on isolated congregations. Beginning in 1851 James and Ellen White began to tour congregations in order to deal personally with problems. They recorded their experiences in the *Review and Herald* as examples of what must be done.

Fanaticism and chaos at the local congregational level was the most immediate threat. James White reported that an 1851 conference in Medford, Massachusetts, had to point out the errors of two individuals and disfellowship others. He used the expression "church order."[20] Elsewhere he described the disfellowshipping of a church member who had gotten involved in spiritualism at the Washington, New Hampshire, church. White spoke of the need for unity and "gospel order" in various congregations.

A nascent organizational structure on the local level was now being seen. In July 1851 Sabbatarian Adventists reported their first ordination, that of Washington Morse. It allowed him to conduct Communion services.[21] The Washington, New Hampshire, church, following the example of Acts 6, appointed a committee of seven to aid poor members.

Something especially had to be done about impostors and charlatans usurping Sabbatarian pulpits. The church needed some kind of screening system. In 1853 certain prominent Sabbatarian Adventist ministers began giving recognized speakers an identification card "recommending them to the fellowship of the Lord's people everywhere, simply stating that they were approved in the work of the gospel ministry."[22] For example, James White and Joseph Bates signed the one carried by John Loughborough. Also by late 1853 Sabbatarians ordained traveling preachers and local deacons.

In December 1853 White published four articles entitled "Gospel

Order." His December 6 article hit head-on the old objection of organization as "Babylon." "It is a lamentable fact," he commented, "that many of our Advent brethren who made a timely escape from the bondage of the different churches . . . have since been in a more perfect Babylon than ever before. Gospel order has been too much overlooked by them. . . . Many in their zeal to come out of Babylon, partook of a rash, disorderly spirit, and were soon found in a perfect Babylon of confusion. . . . To suppose that the church of Christ is free from restraint and discipline, is the wildest fanaticism."[23]

Additional articles in the series called for churches to follow the Bible as a "perfect rule of faith and practice;"[24] set out the calling, qualifications, and ordination of ministers;[25] and advocated the support of the ministry through prayer and finances.[26] At the same time Ellen wrote an article based on a vision she had received during the fall of 1852, declaring that just as order exists in heaven, so it must govern God's people on earth. She stated that "the Lord has shown that gospel order has been too much feared and neglected. Formality should be shunned; but, in so doing, order should not be neglected. There is order in heaven. There was order in the church when Christ was upon the earth, and after His departure order was strictly observed among His apostles. And now in these last days, while God is bringing His children into the unity of the faith, there is more real need of order than ever before."[27] Like her husband, she discussed ministerial criteria and called for the ordination of those recognized as worthy by "brethren of experience and of sound minds."[28]

James concluded that Sabbatarian Adventists must have, along with more spirituality, a greater degree of organization if they were to continue to grow. In 1854 he declared that God "is waiting for his people to get right, and in gospel order, and hold the standard of piety high, before he adds many more to our numbers."[29] But growth was not the only thing driving the need for order. Sabbatarian Adventists were also struggling with schisms. Early in 1854 two ministers, H. S. Case and C. P. Russell, began to oppose the Whites, attacking James's financial operation of the publishing house and questioning Ellen's visions. That fall they launched the *Messenger of Truth* publication as a rival to the *Review and Herald*. Another faction arose when two ministers (out of a total of four!) in Wisconsin began to teach a temporal millennium and an age-to-come view that held out a second chance for conversion during the millennium itself. Soon the men—J. M. Stephenson and D. P. Hall—joined ranks with the *Messenger of Truth* party. With such groups fragmenting Sabbatarian ranks, the need for unity and organization was increasingly obvious.

WHAT KIND OF ORGANIZATION?

A new voice added to the call for organization when fellow former Christian Connexionist minister Joseph Bates began to advocate order. Reflecting his Restorationist heritage, Bates argued that God's people must bring biblical church order back to Christianity before the Savior returns. He claimed that the medieval church had "deranged" biblical church order along with the Sabbath. Since under God's guidance Sabbatarian Adventists had drawn Christianity's attention to the Sabbath, it seemed "perfectly clear" to Bates "that God will employ law-keepers as instruments to restore . . . a 'glorious Church,' not having spot or wrinkle. . . . This unity of the faith, and perfect church order, never has existed since the days of the apostles. It is very clear that it must exist prior to the second advent of Jesus, and be completed by the refreshing from the presence of the Lord, in resolution of all things, &c."[30] But while Bates believed that Christianity must reestablish the apostolic order, he would reject any structure or organization not specifically mentioned in the New Testament.

For a time James White echoed the same limitation. In his mind, "by gospel, or church order we mean that order in church association and discipline taught in the gospel of Jesus Christ by the writers of the New Testament."[31] In 1855 he wrote of the "perfect system of order, set forth in the New Testament by inspiration of God. . . . The Scriptures present a perfect system, which, if carried out, would save the Church from imposters" as well as enable the ministry to do their work.[32]

Joseph Birchard Frisbie, who would lead James and Ellen's friends the Hardys into Sabbatarian Adventism, also wrote much on church order. He shared the belief of both Bates and White that Sabbatarians must use only those features of church organization explicitly mentioned in the Bible. This, he felt, especially applied to the question of a church name. One could use only biblical terminology. Thus "THE CHURCH OF GOD . . . is the only name that God has seen fit to give His church." Citing such passages as 2 Corinthians 1:1 ("the church of God which is at Corinth") he argued that "it is very evident that God never designed that His church should be called by any other name than the one He has given."[33] Any denominational name "savors more of Babylon, confusion, mixture, than it does" of God's church. Employing the same kind of reasoning, he believed that one should not keep membership lists. After all, God records the names of His children in the books of heaven.[34]

The next month Frisbie began to discuss the office of elder, noting that the New Testament church had two classes of elders—"traveling elders" and local ones. Traveling elders supervised several churches; local elders "had the pastoral care and oversight of one church." Local congregations should have both elders and deacons. The first position "had the oversight of the spiritual, the other the temporal affairs of the church."[35] By the end of 1855 Sabbatarian Adventists ordained both local elders as well as deacons and pastors.[36]

The local congregation, with its elders and deacons, was now acquiring a much more organized structure. But it was difficult for Sabbatarian Adventists to think beyond the individual congregation. We can see this mentality at work when Joseph Bates began a lengthy article on church order by defining "church" as "a particular congregation of believers in Christ, united together in the order of the gospel."[37] Sabbatarians would have to visualize the meaning of unity at a higher and broader level. It would require dealing with at least four issues.

ORGANIZATIONAL ISSUES FACING ADVENTISM

The first involved the legal ownership of property. Long aware of the problem because of his management of the publishing house, James White (in 1855) resigned as editor of the *Review* in order to avoid having the publishing house in his name only. He suggested that a committee own the Review and that a financial committee conduct its business operations.[38] Local congregations had to wrestle with who owned their church buildings, and some suggested committees to hold the individual church edifices. Otherwise, the law recognized a church building as the property of whoever owned the land it sat on.

The second problem facing Sabbatarians was how to pay their ministry. Many clergy worked at farming or crafts. Those who farmed, such as John Byington, tilled their farms during spring and summer while pastoring those groups within horse and buggy driving distance. Other areas might have a visiting preacher only during winter. Those who did preach more extensively earned little pay and sometimes were compensated only in kind (food and other supplies). Ministers often had to walk from place to place and could easily be recognized by their shabby or worn-out clothing. And they were few in number. At the time the Seventh-day Adventist Church officially organized it had about 30 ministers for a membership of about 3,500, and several of those held administrative and editorial positions in Battle Creek.

One of the reasons the Whites made their midwinter trip to Waukon, Iowa, had been to persuade John Nevins Andrews and John N. Loughborough to return to the ministry. Exhaustion and starvation wages had forced Andrews to leave preaching in his mid-20s to take a job as a clerk in his uncle's store. Loughborough had, as he dramatically understated it, become "somewhat discouraged as to finances."[39] Although the Whites convinced the two men to resume their ministerial duties, their financial problems remained. Loughborough, for example, during his first three months after leaving Waukon received only room and board, a buffalo-skin coat worth about $10, and $10 in cash. The next year (1857) he received for a winter's service in Michigan three 10-pound cakes of maple sugar, a peck of beans, one ham, half a hog, and $4 in cash.

Besides no structure to pay ministerial salaries, Sabbatarian Adventists also lacked any system to take care of other expenses, even such minor ones as postage. People would send White letters about church-related matters without paying the postage, and he would have to pay it when the mail arrived (having the recipient pay the postage was a common practice at the time).[40]

To deal with the situation, during the spring of 1859 the influential Battle Creek, Michigan, congregation formed a group under the leadership of John Nevins Andrews to study the Bible in order to find a plan to pay the ministry. (It was these meetings that prevented James from accompaning Ellen and the Loughboroughs to the William Hardy home.) The committee submitted its report early the next year. Its plan—termed Systematic Benevolence (some nicknamed it "Sister Betsy")—encouraged men to contribute 5 to 25 cents per week, and women 2 to 10 cents. Beyond that, the plan assessed both men and women 1 to 5 cents per week for each $100 of property they might own.

Both James and Ellen White were enthusiastic about the concept. But it worked better in theory than practice. Because ministers were constantly traveling, how could the local congregation collect the money and then pay it to the minister, especially if he had already gone elsewhere? The *Review and Herald* then advised each group of believers to appoint a treasurer who would keep $5 of the money raised on hand for any itinerant minister who might come through (the rest would go to the state's tent evangelists to cover their expenses). But at best, even this measure was only a stopgap. (It would last until 1878 when the General Conference Committee recommended that, starting with the first week of 1879, believers pay one-tenth of their increase to finance the ministry.) Any plan to support the ministry required an organizational level above the individual congregation to receive and distribute the funds.

The third difficulty, which required some form of broad organization to solve, was the question of how to allocate or assign ministers. In 1859 James White commented that while Battle Creek might have several preachers in residence, other congregations were "destitute, not having heard a discourse for three months."[41] White did not want all the money going to just a few ministers in already-existing Adventist centers. The church must expand to new areas. "We solemnly protest against supporting men on the old ground, doing little or nothing, and neglecting brethren, and letting them suffer, who are raising up churches, breaking into new fields, with poverty and destitution all around them, and sometimes thankful for 'Johnny-cake and string beans!'"[42] He suggested that Sabbatarians needed both to locate preachers' families near where the ministers worked, and that a system must be in place to pay them. James urged congregations and groups to send their requests for clergy to him, personally.[43] Soon he found himself assigning and paying ministers, but without any official structure to do it through. Besides being awkward, the practice left him vulnerable to criticism over mismanagement and misappropriation of funds. He could not escape the obvious fact—Sabbatarians needed a more comprehensive system of organization.

The fourth issue demanding a more widespread church structure concerned the transference of church memberships. It especially became a problem when a person disfellowshipped by one congregation sought membership in another. Sabbatarian Adventists had to decide how to handle transfers between individual churches as well as the larger question of how each independent congregation related to all the others.[44]

JAMES WHITE AND THE PUSH FOR ORGANIZATION

By the middle of 1859, James White was prepared to push the issue of a formal denominational structure. During a conference in Battle Creek he delivered a major presentation on Systematic Benevolence, believing that "the shortness of time and the vast importance of the truth calls upon us in the most imperative manner to extend missionary labor." After he declared that the way Sabbatarians paid its ministers was a "blot on the cause," the delegates "unanimously carried" his proposal for financially supporting the Adventist ministry.[45]

White was dealing with a religious movement largely composed of fiercely independent people of New England heritage (including those areas of the Midwest settled by immigrants from New England) who valued private interpretation above everything else—in this case almost to the point of anarchy. If it were to survive, the Sabbatarian Adventist movement had to come to a consensus and unity that could cope with its continued growth. The fledgling denomination (especially James White) was gradually realizing that it had a mission far larger than previously conceived. It was slowly sensing that its divine purpose was to evangelize the whole world (though that understanding would take decades to mature fully). James White had already stopped being uncomfortable about the idea of converting others to Adventism as he had in earlier years.[46] A church that targeted the whole world could not be a loosely knit cluster of weak and squabbling congregations. An effective church had to have careful organization. James White later remarked that God's purpose for "bringing [Sabbatarian Adventists] out from the churches was to discipline and unite them for the last great battle of truth under the third [angel's] message. It was not ambition to build up a denomination that suggested organization, but the sheer necessities of the case."[47] To achieve such organization would require a strong and forceful leader who would not give up easily—and James White was exactly that kind of person.

By now he had decided that he had to meet the issue head-on. *"We lack system,"* he proclaimed. "Many of our brethren are in a scattered state. They observe the Sabbath, read with some interest the REVIEW: but beyond this

they are doing but little or nothing for want of some method of united action among them."[48] He urged Sabbatarian Adventists in each state to meet
one to four or five times a year. Such sessions would guide the churches'
activities in each area.

"We are aware that these suggestions will not meet the minds of all,"
he spoke from bitter experience. "Bro. Overcautious will be frightened,
and will be ready to warn his brethren to be careful and not venture out
too far; while Bro. Confusion will cry out, 'O, this looks just like Babylon!
Following the fallen church!' Bro. Do-little will say, 'The cause is the
Lord's, and we had better leave it in His hands, He will take care of it.'
'Amen,' says Love-this-world, Slothful, Selfish, and Stingy, 'if God calls
men to preach, let them go out and preach, he will take care of them, and
those who believe their message'; while Korah, Dathan and Abiram are
ready to rebel against those who feel the weight of the cause and who
watch for souls as those who must give account, and raise the cry, 'You
take too much upon you.'"[49] Clearly he had himself in mind as the target
of such problem people.

His combative spirit aroused, James declared, "Bro. Confusion makes
a most egregious blunder in calling system, which is in harmony with the
Bible and good sense, Babylon. As Babylon signifies confusion, our erring
brother has the very word stamped upon his own forehead. And we venture to say that there is not another people under heaven more worthy of
the brand of Babylon than those professing the Advent faith who reject
Bible order. Is it not high time that we as a people heartily embrace everything that is good and right in the churches? Is it not blind folly to start
back at the idea of system, found everywhere in the Bible, simply because
it is observed in the fallen churches?"[50]

Long experience had given him some idea of what needed to be done.
Using a railroad analogy, he said that guiding God's cause involved more
than "to use the brake well."[51] It needed a powerful engine to propel it,
and that engine was careful organization.

His lengthy and varied involvement in all aspects of the Sabbatarian
Adventist movement gave James White a greater understanding of its
needs than perhaps any other leader. As a result he began to see things in
new ways. Denominational historian George Knight considers three particular shifts in viewpoint as especially important. First, White dropped

the idea that the church could not use a specific form of organization if it did not appear fully outlined in Scripture. James declared in his 1859 article that Sabbatarians "should not be afraid of that system which is not opposed by the Bible, and is approved by common sense."[52] His comment represents a new hermeneutic or way of interpreting Scripture. *"He had moved from a principle of Bible interpretation that held that the only things Scripture allowed were those things it explicitly approved to a hermeneutic that approved of anything that did not contradict the Bible."*[53]

But by moving away from a strictly literalistic approach to Scripture, James went beyond the comfort zone of many. Leaders such as Frisbie and Cottrell felt that Sabbatarians could use only what the early Christians did and only in the form and at the level that the Bible presented it. White, however, emphasized that his fellow believers had already gone beyond that point. For example, they had a weekly periodical printed on a steam-operated press, constructed church buildings instead of meeting in private homes, and published books—things not mentioned in the New Testament. Because they already had and must continue to go beyond the sketchy organization of the Bible, they must do so with common sense guided by prayer.[54]

Second, Knight suggests that White redefined "Babylon." Millerites and early Sabbatarian Adventists had seen it primarily as an issue of persecution or oppression. To them Babylon represented the hostility of other religious groups. But White expanded it to include the biblical tradition of Babylon as confusion. Thus even Sabbatarian Adventism could become Babylon if it allowed confusion to reign in its ranks.[55] And third, James reminded Sabbatarians that they had a mission: to preach the three angels' messages of Revelation 14.[56]

"Thus between 1856 and 1859," Knight observes, "White had shifted from a literalistic perspective to one much more pragmatic. Why, we might ask, did he make such a move while others among the Sabbatarian ministers remained rooted in their biblical (or, more accurately, unbiblical) literalism? I would suggest that the difference had to do with the fact that he was the one who felt the bulk of the responsibility for the Sabbatarian movement. Seeing the issues in the framework of a larger context forced him to think big and creatively. His compatriots could afford their doctrinaire opinions because they had no vision. They were willing to spend their time thinking good Adventist thoughts and communicating with other Adventists through the pages of the *Review*. One gets the impression that they would have been content to remain in a state of more-or-less isolated purity until the Advent. But James White by this time had come to recognize that pragmatics would have to come into play if the Advent movement was to get moving adequately. He refused to think small, felt impelled to move on, and would in the next three years take aggressive steps to put Adventism on a firm organizational base in harmony with Bible principles and commensurate with its mission in the world."[57]

Perhaps the most immediate problem White saw—for both himself and Sabbatarians as a whole facing—was that of owning property. But legally owned property had to be held in the name of someone or some organization. This raised another challenge: if individuals were not to assume responsibility for every church building or other piece of property, it had to be possessed by some kind of legal entity—and that entity had to have a name.

White recognized, finally, that the only practical solution was an organizational body. He forced the issue by declaring, in February 1860, that he would not sign notes of responsibility for individuals who wanted to lend funds to the publishing house. Not only did he not want to bear such a legal and financial burden, but he also believed that it would be better in the long run to have proper legal structures. It was simply too dangerous to put the church's resources in the unregulated control of individuals. Sabbatarian Adventists must make the necessary legal arrangements to hold church possessions in a "proper manner."[58]

White's ideas would, of course, meet resistance. Responding to the notion of a name, Roswell F. Cottrell charged that "it would be wrong to 'make us a name,' since that lies at the foundation of Babylon."[59] It would be better for the church to place its confidence in God, not legal structure. Should Adventists suffer any losses at the hands of others, the Lord would repay them when He returned. "If any man proves a Judas, we can still bear the loss and trust the Lord."[60]

White countered Cottrell's objections in the next *Review*. Stating himself "not a little surprised" at Cottrell's article, James reminded his readers that the publishing house itself had thousands of dollars invested in it without a single legal owner. The devil could use such a precarious situation to

JAMES WHITE'S
WORLD

Above: James White

Top Right: Elizabeth White, James White's mother

Bottom Right: Deacon John White, James White's father

Above: James and Ellen White about 1868

Left: James and Ellen White with Edson (top). Willie, and Adelia Patten. 1864. Miss Patten took care of the boys while their parents traveled.

The effects
of hard
work and
ill health
on James
through the
years

James with evangelistic chart

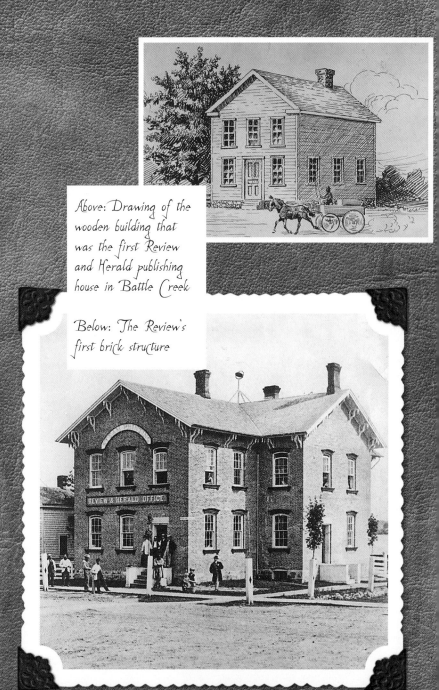

Above: Drawing of the wooden building that was the first Review and Herald publishing house in Battle Creek

Below: The Review's first brick structure

After his first stroke James White attempted to regain his health at Dr. J. C. Jackson's water cure establishment, "Our Home on the Hillside," in Dansville, New York.

In 1879 James White led across Indian Territory a wagon train of convalescent church members, along with a herd of mules to sell in Colorado to pay for the trip. Here the wagons arrive in Boulder.

Above: James White
preached in Battle
Creek's Dime
Tabernacle, and his
funeral was held there.

Right: The restored
Wood Street house, the
first home the Whites
ever owned.

James White founded not only the Review and Herald Publishing Association but also Pacific Press Publishing Association in California.

Although he had only a couple of years of formal education, White helped start Battle Creek College and served as its titular president from 1874 to 1880.

James and Ellen White on the speaker's platform at the Eagle Lake, Minnesota, camp meeting in 1875.

The White family spent many summers during the 1870's in this mountain cabin.

close the publishing house.[61] James considered "it dangerous to leave with the Lord what He has left with us, and thus sit down upon the stool of do little, or nothing. Now it is perfectly right to leave the sun, moon and stars with the Lord; also the earth with its revolutions, the ebbing and flowing of the tides. . . . But if God in His everlasting word calls on us to act the part of faithful stewards of his goods, we had better attend to these matters in a legal manner—the only way we can handle real estate in this world."[62] (Cottrell would eventually write back that he did not want to be out of step with the rest of the church.[63] Though he accepted the decision to organize, others did not, and they would eventually leave Adventism.)

In April White responded, in more detail, to Cottrell's arguments. He declared that since "we are stewards of our Lord's goods here in the land of the enemy, it is our duty to conform to the laws of the land necessary to the faithful performance of our stewardship, as long as human laws do not oppose the divine law."[64] He repeated his 1859 argument that Sabbatarian Adventists were already doing many things not specifically mentioned in Scripture. Referring to Christ's injunction for His followers to let their light shine before the world, he reminded his readers that Jesus did not give many details of how to do it. But "we believe it safe to be governed by the following RULE. All means which, according to sound judgment, will advance the cause of truth, and are not forbidden by plain scripture declarations, should be employed."[65]

Ellen White endorsed her husband's pragmatic approach to church organization when she wrote that Cottrell had taken a wrong position and that "his articles were perfectly calculated to have a scattering influence, to lead minds to wrong conclusions."[66] Echoing her husband's concern about not allowing the devil to disrupt things, she said she wanted "to place the matters of the church in a more secure position, where Satan cannot come in and take advantage."[67]

Simultaneously with the discussion of the topic in the *Review and Herald,* some individual congregations began to organize legally to protect their physical property. James White provided them a strong motivation to do so when he reminded Sabbatarian Adventists what had happened to the church buildings of some Millerite predecessors. He wrote of the Millerite group in Ohio that had constructed a meetinghouse on a lot owned by a member. Eventually he locked them out and turned the structure into a vinegar factory. When the Millerites erected a second chapel on the property of another member (whom they were sure they could trust) he too took over the building.[68]

To avoid the same kind of problem, a number of Sabbatarian congregations began during mid-1860 to experiment with legal organizations. In May of that year, the Parkville, Michigan, church adopted articles of association under the name Parkville Church of Christ's Second Advent. The Fairfield, Iowa, Sabbatarian group a few weeks later named itself "The Church of the Living God."[69]

Perhaps deciding to bring things to a head—at least for the publishing house, White announced in May 1860, "Now is the time for those who oppose legal organization, insurance, &c., to come to the rescue of the Publishing Department."[70] The first steps toward legally incorporating the publishing organization took place at a conference in Battle Creek, which lasted from September 29 to October 2, 1860. Joseph Bates chaired the session and Uriah Smith served as secretary. Delegates from at least five states explored the various problems and suggested possible solutions. All agreed that whatever they did should be biblical but differed over whether they could do only what Scripture specifically outlined. James White repeated his refrain that "every Christian duty is not given in the Scriptures."[71] Eventually the majority accepted his viewpoint.

First, the conference voted a publishing house constitution on October 1, though the incorporation would not be official until the next year. Its first article stated: "This Association shall be denominated *The Advent Review Publishing Association,* the object of which shall be the publication of periodicals, books, and tracts, calculated to convey instruction on Bible truth, especially the fulfillment of prophecy, the commandments of God and the faith of Jesus."[72] The denominational leaders chose as the corporation's name "Seventh-day Adventist Publishing Association," though most would refer to the publishing house as the Review and Herald. It was a share-holding body. One could become a member by purchasing a $10 share.[73] Voting privileges were in proportion to the number of shares held, each $10 share representing one vote. Shareholders could vote by proxy if they wished. Instead of paying dividends, profits from the shares went toward publications to be used in new areas the denomination wanted to enter.

On May 23, 1861, the corporation elected its first officers: James White, president; George W. Amadon, vice president; E. S. Walker, secretary; Uriah Smith, treasurer; and J. N. Loughborough, auditor. Except for the years 1865-1868, when he was severely ill, James White would serve as president of the Seventh-day Adventist Publishing Association as long as he lived.

Second, the October 1860 conference decided that individual congregations should organize in a way that allowed them to legally own their buildings or other property. For a time many of the delegates resisted the concept. Twice White challenged those opposed to incorporation to find a single text rejecting the idea. Unable to find such a passage or refute his logic, they passed a motion in favor of letting local churches legally organize.[74]

SEARCHING FOR A NAME

Third, the October session selected a denominational name, a prerequisite for any further organization. Both those within and outside Sabbatarian Adventism had to call the movement by some name. Through the years Sabbatarians had been referred to by a number of terms, ranging from "Seventh day people," "Sabbathkeeping Advent Believers," "Sabbathkeeping Adventists," "Seventh-day Brethren," "Advent Sabbathkeepers," "Church of God," "Seven Day Evangelists," "Sabbathkeeping Remnant of Adventists," and two names emphasizing the early shut-door teaching, "Seventh-day Doorshutters" and "Shut-door Seventh-day Sabbath and Annihilationists" (the latter term an allusion to the movement's doctrine on the state of the dead).[75]

Until the October meeting, James White, future General Conference president John Byington, J. B. Frisbie, and a number of *Review and Herald* staff supported the name Church of God. In fact, the *Review* had for several years employed the term in its pages[76] and the previous June White had written: "We now suggest that we unanimously adopt the name *Church of God* as a scriptural and appropriate name by which to be known."[77] But a number of other denominations already went by Church of God, and many felt that it was too generic. Ellen White also had reservations about it, writing a year later, "I was shown that almost every fanatic who has arisen, who wishes to hide his sentiments that he may lead away others, claims to belong to the church of God. Such a name would at once excite suspicion; for it is employed to conceal the most absurd errors. The name is too indefinite for the remnant people of God. It would lead to the supposition that we had a faith which we wished to cover up."[78]

The October meeting appointed a committee to recommend a name, but every suggestion met strong resistance. Finally, on the morning of the fourth session of the conference (October 1), delegate Ezra Brackett moved that it should choose a name. When another delegate objected that selecting any name would make the Sabbatarian movement just another denomination, James White replied that "it is objected that we shall be classed among the denominations. We are classed with them already, and I do not know that we can prevent it, unless we disband and scatter, and give up the thing altogether."[79]

That afternoon White commented that he too had once hesitated to adopt a name. But, he continued, while no need existed in the early days of the Sabbatarian movement for an official designation, now "large bodies of intelligent brethren are being raised up, and without some regulation of this kind will be thrown into confusion."[80] He recounted how some had opposed pamphlets, an office for the publishing house, a power press, the publishing of the *Review and Herald,* or any kind of church order. But such things were necessary if Sabbatarian Adventism were to advance at all. A name was essential.

A motion asking "Shall we adopt a name?" passed without dissent (though several abstained). The first suggestion was the popular "Church of God," but many raised objections. James White commented that whatever name they adopted, it should not be objectionable to the world at large or seem presumptuous. Finally, David Hewitt took the floor and moved: "*Resolved,* That we take the name of Seventh-day Adventists." After some discussion the motion was withdrawn and replaced with: "*Resolved,* That we call ourselves Seventh-day Adventists." A delegate from Ohio, T. J. Butler, adamant for Church of God, voted against it—and four (including J. N. Andrews) abstained. After more discussion and explanation Andrews supported the motion and the session recommended it "to the churches generally."[81]

The name was not a new one. A letter to the *Review* in 1853 from Seventh Day Baptists referred to Seventh-day Advent people, as well as an 1856 handbill for some meetings in Hillsdale, Michigan. Others were using Seventh-day Adventist at least 14 months before its official adoption.[82] Ellen G. White, who apparently did not participate in the October meetings, was enthusiastic about the name,[83] and it began to appear in the pages of the *Review and Herald.*

THE 1861 ORGANIZATIONAL MEETING

The next year Adventist leaders convened another conference on denominational organization. The meeting—extending from April 26 to 29, 1861—dealt with two particular issues. The first involved the final steps to legally charter the publishing house. The incorporation of the Seventh-day Adventist Publishing Association became official on May 3, after the state of Michigan passed a law that would recognize nonprofit entities. White no longer had to carry the burden of responsibility for the physical property and financial assets and obligations of the publishing institution. He gave the publishing association all the assets he had developed, including the subscription lists and publishing rights to all the books and tracts he had created.

In addition to incorporating the publishing house, the conference responded to John Loughborough's call for a more thorough church organization. He felt that Adventists had reached the "point where the cause of God demanded organization, not that organization which constituted Babylon, but such as would insure order in the church." The delegates voted that a nine-member committee of ministers should draw up a document on possible church organization.[84]

Appearing in the June 11 issue of the *Review,* the report focused on three vital points. First, it acknowledged that general meetings in the past had not always represented the church membership as a whole. Often the delegates would consist largely of those who lived in the immediate area of the meetings. The emerging church needed to make sure that future meetings more accurately reflected all geographical regions and congregations.

Second, the church should form state or district organizational units. Such conferences would not only issue credentials to ministers, thus regulating who was qualified to preach, but also would "be a great benefit by supplying the church in every part of the field with the means of coming together in their several States or districts for social and public worship, and for the building of each other up in the word of the Lord." Such state conferences would make official decisions through a representational system of delegates from member churches.[85]

Third, the local congregations needed additional structure. They should have up-to-date membership lists, establish a mechanism to transfer members from one congregation to another, and keep records of their business meetings and disciplinary actions. This would prevent individuals who got into trouble in one congregation from joining another church without the congregation being aware of the new members' background.[86]

The committee's report met with a strongly mixed reaction. The members in the American Midwest were more favorable to it, perhaps for two reasons. First, White's influence was stronger there as a result of his personal presence. He had visited many of the churches recently. Members knew and trusted him. Second, a larger percentage of the Midwestern Adventists were newer converts, and thus less steeped in the older notion that organization was Babylon. But having lived a number of years now in Michigan, James had less contact with believers in the Eastern states despite his annual tours of the region. The negative response there stunned him. Many in the northeastern United States regarded White and the Midwestern Adventists as apostates in the matter of church structure. For example, after visiting New York, he left "stung with the thought that the balance of influence is either against, or silent upon, the subject of organization."[87]

White did not mince words. He declared that during his tour of the Eastern states "thus far we seem to be wading through the influence of a stupid uncertainty upon the subject of organization," a situation he blamed on the articles that Roswell F. Cottrell had written the year before.[88] Although Cottrell himself had changed his mind, the "poison of anti-organization" still infected the minds of many. The failure of some influential members to support organization had not helped either. Although many approved of the idea, they had remained silent on the topic. Because they did not endorse organization, "instead of our being a united people, growing stronger, we are in many places but little better than broken fragments, still scattering and growing weaker."[89] How long, he wondered, would the church have to wait before the situation changed?

Ellen White added her voice. A vision on August 3, 1861, showed her "that some have feared that our churches would become Babylon if they should organize; but those in central New York have been perfect

Babylon, confusion. And now unless the churches are so organized that they can carry out and enforce order, they have nothing to hope for in the future; they must scatter into fragments."[90] She echoed James's protests about the lack of moral courage and the "cowardly silence" of those ministers who believed in organization but didn't speak out.[91]

James's comments about his travels among the Eastern churches began to bring results as more and more believers publicly backed organization. The growing support allowed White and other Adventist leaders to summon a general meeting on organization in Battle Creek, October 4-6, 1861. Its first item to consider was "the proper manner of organizing churches." James White urged the members of each local congregation to organize by signing the following church covenant: "We, the undersigned, hereby associate ourselves together, as a church, taking the name, Seventh-day Adventists, covenanting to keep the commandments of God, and the faith of Jesus Christ."[92] The session also established a committee to work out a procedure for organizing local congregations and appointing church officers.

THE FIRST STATE CONFERENCE OF SEVENTH-DAY ADVENTISTS

The proposed covenant became a topic of major discussion as the delegates attempted to distinguish between it and a creed. The old Christian Connexion hostility toward a creed had become a powerful element of Sabbatarian Adventism. But eventually the delegates concluded that it was biblically acceptable to sign such a covenant, and the session moved on to other items. The most important one was a recommendation "to the churches in the State of Michigan to unite in one Conference, with the name of the Michigan Conference of Seventh-day Adventists." The resolution passed, along with a simple organizational structure consisting of a president, a conference clerk, and a three-member conference committee. Joseph Bates and Uriah Smith would serve as president and clerk for the first year.[93] The new conference's first annual meeting elected layperson William S. Higley as president and voted both to pay its ministers a regular salary and to require periodic reports of their activities. It also developed a plan to supervise those ministers it provided for other areas.

The next year (1862) would see the formation of a number of conferences: Southern Iowa, Northern Iowa, Vermont, Illinois, Wisconsin,

Minnesota, and New York. Laypersons often prodded the members into action. Joseph Clarke of Ohio, for example, commented on the reluctance of some to organize. "Why don't you come up, to a man, in this business?" he asked in the *Review*. "When I think, after all that has been said and done on this matter, how Bro. White is tantalized, how the testimony is trampled on, how the church is trammeled, how the good Spirit is slighted, oh, it is provoking, it is sickening, it is discouraging, it is positively flat, nauseous as the lukewarm water from the stagnant pool."[94] With the exception of Vermont, New England resisted organization. A state conference did not appear in Maine until 1867, and the rest of New England waited until 1870.

On October 15, 1861, the *Review* printed the important report of the session's committee on church organizing. It especially concentrated on church officers. The document recognized two categories. The first, traveling preachers, not only did evangelism but organized new congregations and ordained their officers. The second consisted of local elders and deacons. The elders had charge of spiritual aspects while the deacons took care of such things as finances and preparation for the Communion service. (The terms "pastor" and "local elder" seem to be used interchangeably.) The committee report outlined how to organize a new church by covenant, how to elect local church officers, and how to receive new members by letter of transfer.[95]

James White immediately praised the new steps. "We are glad to see our people awake to this subject," he wrote. "To us it is a sign of better days."[96] At the beginning of 1862 he observed wryly, "Then [in the past] we stood nearly alone. The battle went hard, and we needed help; but many of our very prudent men saved their ammunition to fire away upon the subject of organization [until] now when the battle is fought and the victory won. Almost every day we receive a communication from some good brother upon the subject of organization. A few only of these have found place in the *Review*." If only those same individuals had written when such articles "were needed, and not after the battle is fought."[97] Instead, to his disappointment, they did not speak out until the organizational concept had become reality.

ORGANIZING A GENERAL CONFERENCE
But even the state conferences still left many problems unsolved. For example, how was anyone to assign ministers across state conference

boundaries? "I do not believe that we shall ever fully realize the benefits of organization till this matter [of an umbrella structure to coordinate the individual conferences] is acted upon," Joseph H. Waggoner commented in a *Review* article. He suggested that Seventh-day Adventists hold a general conference each year in connection with the publishing association's annual meeting. Each individual local conference should "send a delegate or delegates to the General Conference; and that a General Conference Committee be appointed, with whom the State conferences may correspond, and *through* whom they shall present their requests for laborers."[98]

John N. Andrews responded to Waggoner's article by observing that without such a broad-based organization, "we shall be thrown into confusion every time that concert of action is especially necessary. The work of organization, wherever it has been entered into in a proper manner, has borne good fruit; and hence I desire to see it completed in such a manner as shall secure its full benefit, not only to each church, but to the whole body of the brethren and to the cause of truth, so dear to all."[99]

A week later B. F. Snook also concurred. "Next in order to complete the organization, we need a general conference, in which the ministers or delegates of all the State conferences can meet and confer together on such matters as pertain to the good of the cause."[100] He noticed an emerging problem that still afflicts the church today: sectional or regional feelings. Snook believed that the only way to foster unity was through a general conference. "The times and the cause demand an immediate action on the subject."[101]

Such affirmations sounded good to James White. He was especially concerned to protect the church from "self-called, tobacco-eating, [prophetic] gift-hating preachers" who preyed on Adventists.[102] James had especially felt the sting of those who attacked his wife and her prophetic role.

But although Snook had called for immediate action, a church composed of such independent-minded individuals could advance only slowly. It could move only as fast as the majority was willing to go. James White continued to urge action, but even he could push Adventists only so fast.

As we have already noted, the October 1862 session of the Michigan Conference established a number of operating procedures that would serve as models for other conferences. Perhaps, just as important, it passed a resolution inviting other state conferences to meet with Michigan "in general conference" at its 1863 annual convocation.[103]

White decided to take advantage of the opportunity and persuaded Michigan's leaders to move the meeting from October 1863 to May 1863. In late April 1863 he announced that the upcoming session would be "the most important meeting ever held by the Seventh-day Adventists,"[104] because he wanted to use it to establish an umbrella organization for the growing number of state conferences. Such a General Conference would act as "the great regulator" of the local conferences, thus leading to "united, systematic action in the entire body" of Seventh-day Adventists. The proposed organization would "mark out the general course to be pursued by State Conferences," producing greater unity and effectiveness.[105]

In his mind the General Conference had to be a higher authority than the state conferences, or it would have little use. He focused his argument for such an entity on the obvious need for a more efficient system of allocating ministers. At the moment Michigan and Vermont had more than they needed. Elsewhere, in contrast, the infant denomination was "almost destitute" of them. The church had been working on a plan of systematic benevolence to pay its clergy. In turn, it had a right to expect "systematic labor" from its ministers.[106]

From May 20 to 23, 1863, 19 official delegates worked out the details of the new General Conference of Seventh-day Adventists. Although 10 came from the Michigan Conference, the others represented the New York, Iowa, Wisconsin, and Minnesota conferences, and the about-to-be-formed Ohio Conference. "For the purpose of securing unity and efficiency in labor, and promoting the general interests of the cause of present truth, and of perfecting the organization of the Seventh-day Adventists," the session's enabling action declared, "we, the delegates from the several State Conferences, hereby proceed to organize a General Conference, and adopt the following constitution for the government thereof."[107] The constitution called for a president, secretary, treasurer, and executive committee. The president would have charge over all ministers and would see that they were evenly distributed. The General Conference had authority to initiate evangelism and other forms of advancement, and to issue calls for funds. The session also prepared a model constitution for local conferences.

THE FIRST GENERAL CONFERENCE PRESIDENT

The delegates unanimously elected White as president, but he refused to accept. Many opponents had claimed that White supported church organization as part of a bid for power. If he took the post, James said, it would appear to confirm their arguments. When he declined, the organizing body chose John Byington, who would serve two one-year terms. Uriah Smith became secretary, and E. S. Walker, noted for his leadership in organizing the Iowa Conference, would serve as treasurer. The executive committee would consist of Byington, White, and Loughborough. It soon added J. N. Andrews and George W. Amadon.

White was extremely pleased with the developments. That fall he happily declared: "Thank God, organization is a success; the General Conference is a success; and the Publishing Association is a perfect success."[108]

James would allow himself to be named president in 1865, and he served as General Conference president for a total of 10 years: May 17, 1865, to May 14, 1867; May 18, 1869, to December 29, 1871; and August 13, 1874, to October 11, 1880.

The new denomination—spreading across the northern United States from the Atlantic Ocean to Iowa—now had 3,500 members, who belonged to 125 congregations in 6 local conferences. There were also about 30 ministers.

---

[1] This chapter is based on George Knight, *Organizing to Beat the Devil: The Development of Adventist Church Structure* (Hagerstown, Md.: Review and Herald Pub. Assn., 2001). Besides being the most recent major work on the development of Seventh-day Adventist denominational organization, *Organizing* highlights the role James White played in that quest for organization. For an older presentation, cf. R. W. Schwarz, *Light Bearers to the Remnant: Denominational Textbook for Seventh-day Adventist College Classes* (Boise, Idaho: Pacific Press Pub. Assn., 1979), pp. 86-97.

[2] James White, *Life Sketches* (1880), pp. 351, 352.

[3] Knight, *Organizing to Beat the Devil*, pp. 17, 18.

[4] *Ibid.*, pp. 16, 17.

[5] Charles Fitch, *"Come Out of Her, My People,"* p. 9.

[6] *Ibid.*, p. 19.

[7] *Ibid.*, p. 24.

[8] George Storrs, *Midnight Cry*, Feb. 15, 1844.

[9] *Ibid.*

[10] *Ibid.*

[11] JW to J. C. Bowles, Nov. 8, 1849.

[12] Ellen G. White, *Spiritual Gifts* (Battle Creek, Mich.: James White, 1860), vol. 2, p. 93.

[13] *Ibid.*, pp. 97, 98.

[14] *Ibid.*, p. 98.

[15] JW to Gilbert and Deborah Collins, Sept. 8, 1849.

[16] *Ibid.*

[17] *Ibid.*

[18] See, for example, JW to Dear Brother, Sept. 30, 1852, and JW to Brethren Cornell and Dodge, Nov. 3, 1854.

[19] JW to Bro., Mar. 18, 1850.

[20] JW to Brethren, Nov. 11, 1851.

[21] *Review and Herald,* Aug. 19, 1851.

[22] John N. Loughborough, *The Church: Its Organization, Order and Discipline* (1906), p. 101.

[23] James White, in *Review and Herald,* Dec. 6, 1853.

[24] James White, in *Review and Herald,* Dec. 13, 1853.

[25] James White, in *Review and Herald,* Dec. 20, 1853.

[26] James White, in *Review and Herald,* Dec. 27, 1853.

[27] Ellen G. White, *Early Writings* (Washington, D.C.: Review and Herald Pub. Assn., 1882, 1945), p. 97.

[28] *Ibid.*, p. 101.

[29] James White, in *Review and Herald,* Mar. 28, 1854.

[30] Joseph Bates, in *Review and Herald,* Aug. 29, 1854.

[31] James White, in *Review and Herald,* Mar. 28, 1854.

[32] James White, in *Review and Herald,* Jan. 23, 1855.

[33] J. B. Frisbie, in *Review and Herald,* Dec. 26, 1854.

[34] *Ibid.*

[35] J. B. Frisbie, in *Review and Herald,* Jan. 9, 1855.

[36] One wonders what other offices may have been under discussion. Interestingly, Stephen N. Haskell wrote an autobiographical letter in 1914 in which he states that "sometime in the 1860s, before there was any conference or organization in the four New England States, New Hampshire, Massachusetts, Rhode Island, and Connecticut, Elder James White told me he was going to make me bishop of this country" (letter cited in Donald R. McAdams, "Reflections of a Pioneer: An Autobiographical Letter of Stephen N. Haskell" [*Adventist Heritage,* July 1974]). Was he using the term in a generic sense, or speaking tongue in cheek? Or even did some seriously consider using the title of "bishop"?

[37] Joseph Bates, in *Review and Herald,* Aug. 29, 1854.

[38] James White, in *Review and Herald,* Dec. 4, 1855; JW to Bro. Dodge, Aug. 20, 1855.

[39] John N. Loughborough, *Rise and Progress of Seventh-day Adventists* (Battle Creek, Mich.: General Conference of Seventh-day Adventists, 1892), p. 208.

[40] JW to Gilbert and Deborah Collins, Sept. 8, 1849.

[41] James White, in *Review and Herald*, June 16, 1859.

[42] James White, in *Review and Herald*, Oct. 6, 1859.

[43] James White, in *Review and Herald*, June 16, 1859.

[44] See *Review and Herald*, Sept. 18, 1856; *Review and Herald*, Oct. 23, 1856.

[45] *Review and Herald*, June 9, 1859.

[46] See, for example, JW to Gilbert Collins, Aug. 26, 1846.

[47] James White, *Life Incidents*, p. 299.

[48] James White, in *Review and Herald*, July 21, 1859.

[49] *Ibid.*

[50] *Ibid.*

[51] *Ibid.*

[52] *Ibid.*

[53] Knight, p. 46.

[54] James White, in *Review and Herald*, July 21, 1859.

[55] Knight, p. 47.

[56] *Ibid.*

[57] *Ibid.*

[58] James White, in *Review and Herald*, Feb. 23, 1860.

[59] R. F. Cottrell, in *Review and Herald*, Mar. 22, 1860.

[60] *Ibid.*

[61] James White, in *Review and Herald*, Mar. 29, 1860.

[62] *Ibid.*

[63] R. F. Cottrell, in *Review and Herald*, May 3, 1860.

[64] James White, in *Review and Herald*, Apr. 26, 1860.

[65] *Ibid.*

[66] Ellen G. White, *Testimonies for the Church* (Mountain View, Calif.: Pacific Press Pub. Assn., 1948), vol. 1, p. 211.

[67] *Ibid.*

[68] James White, in *Review and Herald*, Apr. 26, 1860.

[69] Godfrey T. Anderson, "Make Us a Name," *Adventist Heritage*, July 1974.

[70] *Review and Herald*, May 10, 1860.

[71] James White, in *Review and Herald*, Oct. 16, 1860.

[72] *Review and Herald*, Oct. 22, 1860.

[73] By 1880 the face value of each share would raise to $25. They would become a major problem when the publishing house attempted to relocate to Washington, D.C., after the 1902 fire. The publishing house had to buy back at an exorbitant price those shares held by members who did not want the Review to move.

[74] James White, in *Review and Herald*, Oct. 16, 1860.

[75] Anderson.

[76] *Ibid.*

[77] James White, cited in Anderson.

[78] Ellen G. White, *Testimonies*, vol. 1, p. 224.

[79] *Review and Herald,* Oct. 16, 1860.

[80] *Ibid.*

[81] *Ibid.*

[82] Anderson.

[83] Ellen G. White, *Testimonies,* vol. 1, p. 224.

[84] *Review and Herald,* Apr. 30, 1861.

[85] *Review and Herald,* June 11, 1860.

[86] *Ibid.*

[87] James White, in *Review and Herald,* Sept. 3, 1861.

[88] James White, in *Review and Herald,* Aug. 27, 1861.

[89] *Ibid.*

[90] Ellen G. White, *Testimonies,* vol. 1, p. 270.

[91] *Ibid.,* p. 271.

[92] *Review and Herald,* Oct. 8, 1861.

[93] *Ibid.*

[94] *Review and Herald,* Nov. 18, 1862.

[95] *Review and Herald,* Oct. 15, 1861.

[96] James White, in *Review and Herald,* Oct. 22, 1861.

[97] James White, in *Review and Herald,* Jan. 7, 1862.

[98] J. H. Waggoner, in *Review and Herald,* June 24, 1862.

[99] *Review and Herald,* July 15, 1862.

[100] *Review and Herald,* July 29, 1862.

[101] *Ibid.*

[102] James White, in *Review and Herald,* Sept. 30, 1862.

[103] *Review and Herald,* Oct. 14, 1862.

[104] James White, in *Review and Herald,* Apr. 28, 1863.

[105] *Ibid.*

[106] *Ibid.*

[107] *Review and Herald,* May 26, 1863.

[108] James White, in *Review and Herald,* Oct. 6, 1863.

CHAPTER XI

ADVENTISTS AND THE CIVIL WAR

A S THE Seventh-day Adventist movement unified, the nation itself was anything but. The Southern states seceded from the Union, and war broke out. Seventh-day Adventism had not yet spread into the American South, and few church members had any sympathy with slavery and the Confederacy.[1] Though most Adventists had abolitionist leanings, that did not mean that they were ready to pick up arms against those who supported slavery.

Many Adventists felt that the conflict was a needless distraction to their primary goal of getting ready for the Second Coming.[2] Uriah Smith saw the hostilities as leading to Armageddon.[3] James White pointed to Revelation 6:15 as evidence that slavery would continue until Christ returned.[4]

Ellen White saw the conflict as God's punishment "for the high crime of slavery"—the South for inflicting it, the North for tolerating it.[5] As the war dragged on, Adventists began to sense that slavery—at least in the United States—might cease before the Second Advent. But on a more immediate level, church members increasingly faced the pressure of military conscription.

Military service raised two fundamental issues: whether Adventists should participate in war *in any form,* and, if they did—how they could observe the Sabbath while in the army. James White touched upon both aspects in a controversial article in August of 1862. After noting that the "requirements of war" conflicted with the fourth and sixth commandments, he observed that if church members were drafted, he believed that "the government assumes the responsibility of the violation of the law of God, and it would be madness to resist." To do so would result in the church member being shot by the military, an outcome that, he also believed, "goes too far, we think, in taking the responsibility of suicide."[6]

The article stimulated extensive debate. Letters about it continued to appear in the pages of the *Review* throughout the year. Several advocated that the church take a position of total pacifism.[7] Others supported active cooperation with the government because the Union cause was just.[8] Richard Schwarz sees White's August 12 article as a trial balloon that James wrote to trigger discussion.[9]

Besides raising the sensitive issue of what should be the Adventist position toward war and the draft, White's "The Nation" article and his subsequent response to the reaction it produced helped lead the majority of members away from Uriah Smith's Civil War-Armageddon connection. James White did not believe that the draft was the imposition of the mark of the beast. "The present war, and the consequent draft, is not directed to establish idolatry, Sunday-keeping, or any system or principle in opposition to the law of God," he wrote some months later, "but to put down a rebellion resulting from the highest crimes on the part of rebeldom that man can be guilty of, and to establish a government which has, under the providence of God, secured to us the right of worshiping the God of heaven according to His word."[10]

But Adventists still had to work out some approach to the draft that would fall within the guidelines of White's position that church members should not resist the draft but at the same time not take up arms. One approach, which would work in very rare cases, involved getting a member deferred because of physical reasons. Thus James White wrote letters on the letterhead of the Office of the Seventh-day Adventist Publishing Association to get some excused from military service. On October 29, 1862, he sought to get William Hull exempted because of health reasons. White explained that Hull had been able to hold a light job at the publishing house only because of the assistance of other employees and thus was not capable of serving in the army.[11]

But health and physical disabilities would not exempt the rest of the Adventist membership. A group of Adventists in Iowa tried to get the state legislature to recognize them as pacifists. Not only did the legislators reject the petition, but Ellen White felt that their attempt had put Adventists in an even more difficult position.[12] When the United States government began offering bonuses to encourage volunteers to enlist, Adventists supported the program. James White and John P. Kellogg served on a committee in Battle Creek to solicit funds for such bonuses.[13]

The American government passed its first conscription law on March 3, 1863. It had two loopholes that Adventists could use to avoid military service. They could either find a substitute to join the army in their place, or purchase an exemption for $300. James White urged all members to share the financial burden of raising the commutation to exempt Adventist men. Then in July 1864 Congress eliminated the commutation except for conscientious objectors from recognized peace churches. On August 2 the three-member General Conference committee drew up a "Statement of principles" on Adventist noncombatancy to present to Michigan governor Austin Blair. It would be the first step of the Adventist church's negotiations to be recognized by the government as conscientious objectors.[14]

The Civil War would create difficulties for Adventists until its end. The commutation fee was a heavy financial drain. The draft removed many men from church service, and evangelism was difficult it not impossible under wartime conditions. James White feared that the war might destroy the new church. He suggested that the General Conference committee appoint the second Sabbath in February 1865 as a day of fasting and prayer both for Adventist soldiers and for a quick conclusion to the war. Shortly afterward the church leadership called for its members to set aside March 1-4 for "earnest and importunate prayer" about the situation. Within six weeks General Lee surrendered his army, and many Adventists felt that God had directly answered their prayers.[15] The Adventist Church could now devote itself more fully to its mission.

---

[1] For a summary of Adventist attitudes toward the government's tolerance of slavery, see Bill Knott, "Writing Against Wrongs," *Adventist Review*, Feb. 28, 2002.

[2] Richard Schwarz, *Light Bearers to the Remnant* (Mountain View, Calif.: Pacific Press Pub. Assn., 1979), pp. 98, 99.

[3] Uriah Smith, "The War," *Review and Herald*, May 7, 1861.

[4] James White, "The Nation," *Review and Herald*, Aug. 12, 1862.

[5] Ellen G. White, *Testimonies*, vol. 1, p. 264.

[6] James White, "The Nation."

[7] Henry Carver, "The War," *Review and Herald*, Oct. 21, 1862; Otis Nichols, "Our Duty Relative to the War," *Review and Herald*, Dec. 16, 1862.

[8] Joseph Clarke, "The Sword vs. Fanaticism," *Review and Herald,* Sept. 23, 1862; J. H. Waggoner, "Our Duty and the Nation," Sept. 23, 1862; B. F. Snook, "The War and Our Duty," *Review and Herald,* Oct. 14, 1862.

[9] Schwarz, p. 96.

[10] James White, "Letter to Bro. Carver," *Review and Herald,* Oct. 21, 1862.

[11] JW to Gentlemen, Oct. 29, 1862.

[12] Ellen G. White, *Testimonies,* vol. 1, pp. 356, 357.

[13] Schwarz, p. 97.

[14] For additional background on Adventists and the Civil War, see Peter Brock, *Pacifism in the United States: From the Colonial Era to the First World War* (Princeton University Press, 1968), pp. 852-861; R. Davis, "Conscientious Cooperation: The Seventh-day Adventists and Military Service, 1860-1945" (Ph.D. diss., George Washington University, 1970), pp. 45-48; Douglas Morgan, *Adventism and the American Republic: The Public Involvement of a Major Apocalyptic Movement* (Knoxville, Tenn.: University of Tennessee Press, 2001), pp. 31-34.

[15] *Review and Herald,* Jan. 31, 1865; *Review and Herald,* Feb. 21, 1865; *Review and Herald,* Apr. 25, 1865.

CHAPTER XII

DEFENDING JAMES WHITE

SIMULTANEOUSLY with the organization of the church, Adventist leaders had to deal with another problem: the persistent stream of allegations about White's stewardship of the publishing house (along with other matters), which again had reached flood stage, threatening to cloud the issue of organization itself. After all, James White was among organization's leading proponents. Some must have assumed, therefore, that he sought it for additional personal advantage.

Though in 1854 the publishing committee of the Review had investigated misappropriation and other financial charges against James White and found nothing amiss, some remained convinced that he was getting rich at the expense of his fellow believers or somehow misusing church money. This type of sniping and slander continued through the years.

THE 1863 INVESTIGATION

Then on March 29, 1863, the members of the Battle Creek church met under the leadership of Uriah Smith to examine the persistent attacks on White. It was an especially sensitive time for such rumors, as the church was just about to complete the first step toward a formal church structure, and Sabbatarian Adventists could not permit a cloud of doubt and suspicion to hang over the man who was spearheading that process of organization. The local church session set up a committee of three— Uriah Smith, George W. Amadon, and E. S. Walker (soon to be the first General Conference treasurer)—to examine the complaints.[1] White commented in the next issue of the *Review and Herald* that the Battle Creek congregation had "deemed it necessary, for the good of the cause, that there should be an investigation of our business career connected with the cause, and a printed report made. If flying reports be true, we should be separated from the cause. If an open and critical investigation proves them false, a printed report in the hands of the friends of the cause with which we are connected, may, in some instances at least, paralyze the tongue of slander."[2] The committee would eventually issue a 39-page booklet, *Vindication of the Business Career of Elder James White,* dealing with the investigation. It described the meeting's purpose as:

"*Whereas,* There are certain reports prejudicial to the character of Elder White, as a man of upright and honest dealing, being extensively circulated through the country, and used to cut off his influence and that of his brethren, to shut the ears of the people against the truth, and steel their hearts against its reception; therefore,

"*Resolved,* That we, the church of Seventh-day Adventists of Battle Creek, deem it our duty to take measures to ascertain the grounds of the charges, complaints, and murmurs that are in circulation."[3]

The meeting declared that "those who are engaged in the circulation of the reports . . . if they are acting honestly, think that they have grounds sufficient to sustain them. They now have not only an opportunity, but a request, to bring them forward that we may see and examine them. And let it be understood by them that if they refuse to do this, it will appear that they have been acting without even a conviction of truth upon their side, which certainly will not place them in a very enviable light; and in this case it will not only devolve upon them hereafter to ever hold their peace, but it would be well for them if the memory of their past course could be blotted from the minds of mankind."[4]

The committee members announced that they would like to hear during the next six weeks from anyone who knew of any fraud or other problems involving White's financial integrity. Also they asked those who had had good business dealings with him to present testimonials. By the time the General Conference organized about seven weeks later, the investigative committee had 74 affidavits supporting White's honesty and fairness, but not a single formal charge against him. The committee then extended the deadline for evidence another two months, until early August. The committee still received nothing against James. The little book *Vindication of the Business Career of Elder James White* printed a number of the testimonials and listed the names of many others who had also supplied them. The names are a Who's Who of the early Seventh-day

Adventist Church. The investigative committee declared that "none can claim that the notice of this matter was not sufficiently definite and extensive, and the time given, sufficiently long for all to report their complaints against Bro. White, for examination and settlement, who were disposed to do so. Yet no one has presented any complaint of being wronged by him. None have charged him with taking advantage of their circumstances to favor himself, or extorting from them means under any plea or pretense whatever."[5] Then the book goes on to ask, "And why have none come up with wrongs charged against Brother W.? Simply because no such wrongs do in truth exist."[6] As we shall see later, Uriah Smith might have his differences with James White, but they did not involve his business practices.

The 1863 committee might not find any wrongdoing on White's part, but that did not mean that the attacks would stop. On the contrary, they not only persisted but increased. Church members continued to accuse him of helping himself to the profits of the publishing house as well as donations sent to the *Review and Herald*. To meet this persistent charge, White wrote that "the *Review, Instructor,* and our publications, have not been a source of profit. Even now, with its numerous supporters and subscribers, the [Review] office is hardly self-sustaining. What I this day possess I am indebted to a few personal friends, and rise [of value] of property on three places we have owned in this city, which is equal to what we possess."[7] James had bought and lived in three houses in Battle Creek by this time. He obtained the first for $500 and sold it for $1,500. Inflation during the Civil War increased the second home from $1,300 to $4,500, and the third increased in value from $5,000 to $6,000.[8]

In addition, at the beginning of the Civil War he had bought the entire stock of a stationery store for $1,200. Even though he used some of it at the publishing house, he could still sell the remainder for $2,400.[9]

The situation was, however, a little more complicated. Friends had helped him through the years, and he had used church publications to help sell his houses and to request such favors as asking church members to can a little extra fruit for the White family. But the overwhelming majority of what he possessed he had earned himself. His financial skill had kept the publishing house afloat during its days at Rochester and during other crisis periods. The Whites paid all their own extensive traveling expenses as well as the salaries of their household and editorial staffs. In addition, James's business ability enabled him to give money to people in need. He especially enjoyed helping struggling ministers, knowing from personal experience the difficulties they faced. When the impoverished John Loughborough brought his family back from Waukon, Iowa, James lent him $300 to make a down payment on a home. James aided several other ministers in purchasing homes and helped with food and clothing for still more church members. Not only did he clothe and feed one such preacher and his family out of his own pocket; he intervened to obtain back pay for him from the General Conference. James gave from his own funds an amount nearly equal to a half year's income at the time.[10]

White's talent for making money also allowed him to finance or contribute to many church projects. For example, from 1873 to 1878 he and Ellen donated a total of $15,000 to various parts of the church program—[11] at a time when $500 was a good year's income.[12] Sometimes, to help out a church institution, he would not take money that was rightfully his. When the General Conference voted to reemburse White when he transferred the *Review* to the Publishing Association, he refused to accept anything.[13] In 1881 he mentioned to Willie that he had accepted no pay from the *Review* for nearly two years,[14] supporting himself in other ways.[15]

· But that financial skill elicited both admiration and resentment, probably from the same people. Those jealous of White's moneymaking ability would obsess on the most minuscule things. Frequently they criticized the carriage and horses the Whites used to travel to their extensive speaking appointments. When James became seriously ill, he and his wife bought a $20 easy chair so that he could rest more comfortably. A $20 chair was a major purchase during the 1860s, and some questioned the propriety of having such an expensive "luxury."

The criticism was especially severe in the hothouse climate of Battle Creek. We see this in one of the most petty complaints, an incident involving some old used bottles. The Whites were in the process of moving away from Battle Creek (partly because of the constant gossiping and criticism they endured there). As they cleaned out their cellar, they found a large collection of old glass bottles. James told Ellen to throw them away, but Willie asked for them. He planned to clean and sell them. The next time his father went to town, the boy went along, taking with him a box filled with the bottles.

On the way they offered a ride to a publishing house employee. Willie took the bottles into a store, then slipped back outside to ask James how much he might get for them. The Review employee did not say anything at the time, but five months later the Whites learned in Iowa that James was "so crazy for money" that he had begun collecting and selling old bottles.[16]

THE 1869 INVESTIGATION

By 1869 rumors and accusations about White's financial dealings again reached such a point that church leadership had once again to meet them head-on. A vocal group was absolutely convinced that James was using his leadership role for personal gain. Ellen White was also under constant attack because of her prophetic role and relationship with James. Many of these latter charges came from outside the denomination. For his fellow leaders to ignore the charges any longer would not only destroy the couple's credibility and effectiveness, but it would damage the young denomination as a whole. J. N. Andrews joined with his brother-in-law, Uriah Smith, and pioneer Adventist educator Goodloe Harper Bell to form a committee to investigate the situation. Following the same procedure used several years before, they once more invited anyone who claimed to have evidence of any financial dishonesty by White to present it. Instead of a 39-page booklet, this time the testimonials were printed in a 155-page book. Fifty-four individuals testified of their satisfaction with the way James had dealt with them. Again, no one offered written evidence against him.

Besides reprinting the material in the 1863 pamphlet, the book also included a detailed history of both James's personal and denominational business ventures, particularly dealing with certain ones that people had raised questions about. It discussed his leadership of the publishing house, how much salary he received per week during different years, how he had personally gone into debt to keep the Review going during its early years, the profit he received from the sale of his Battle Creek and Greenville homes, what he made from buying the inventory of the stationery store, the funds he personally contributed to the publishing house and other denominational institutions, and his extensive generosity to others. The *Defense* also explained some of the gifts that loyal friends had given him through the years. A number of church members apologized for misrepresenting White's transactions with them, or for questioning his character. One individual refuted the rumor that James had fired him from an important position.

In addition to financial matters, the *Defense* commented on even wider issues, refuting other charges made not only against James but Ellen as well. It dealt with doctrinal issues and the role of Ellen White's visions in the church.[17] The book also had to denounce such sad slander as that Ellen White had borne children out of wedlock[18] and that she had visions that advocated wife swapping.[19]

Uriah Smith saw the persistent attacks on White as being really aimed at the church itself. "The great enemy of all righteousness knows that one of the most effectual means by which he can hinder the progress of the work he hates, is to blast the reputation of those who are called to act a prominent part therein before the people."[20] Though the report cleared James, he expressed his personal frustration. In a response to the committee, he wrote, "To me it is very humiliating that a state of things should exist to make it necessary that this pamphlet should go out to our people. For while the statements and explanations contained in it will relieve some, many will be pained to learn that such a state of things ever existed with Seventh-day Adventists. . . .

"I am not only humbled in spirit as I turn over the pages of the foregoing, but my feelings are touched with tenderness as I read the frank expressions of regret on the part of some, and the full expressions of confidence and regard on the part of all. I have felt sad, grieved, and sometimes discouraged. May God forgive me. And as I would be forgiven of God, so must I from my heart forgive others."[21] Unfortunately, his opponents would continue their criticisms against him the rest of his life.

---

[1] References to the investigation appear in the following issues of the *Review and Herald:* Mar. 31, 1863; May 26, 1863; and Aug. 15, 1863.

[2] *Review and Herald,* Apr. 7, 1863.

[3] *Vindication of the Business Career of Elder James White* (Battle Creek, Mich.: Steam Press of the Seventh-day Adventist Publishing Association, 1863), p. 5.

[4] *Ibid.,* p. 6.

[5] *Ibid.,* p. 38.

[6] *Ibid.,* p. 39.

[7] James White, in *Review and Herald,* Mar. 26, 1867.

[8] See *Defense of Eld. James White and Wife. The Battle Creek Church to the Churches and Brethren Scattered Abroad* (Battle Creek, Mich.: Steam Press of the Seventh-day Adventist Publishing Association, 1870), pp. 12, 13.

[9] *Ibid.,* p. 13.

[10] JW to WCW, July 5, 1881.

[11] James White, in *Review and Herald,* Sept. 12, 1878.

[12] Income statistics are difficult to determine for the nineteenth century, but see such sources as *The Statistical History of the United States From Colonial Times to the Present* (New York: Basic Books, 1976), pp. 163-165.

[13] *Review and Herald,* Jan. 2, 1872; Uriah Smith, in *Review and Herald,* Jan. 16, 1872.

[14] JW to WCW and Mary White, Feb. 17, 1881.

[15] Additional examples of the generous financial assistance White offered others appears in Virgil Robinson, *James White,* pp. 207-218, and *The Spirit of Sacrifice & Commitment: Experience of Seventh-day Adventist Pioneers,* comp. James R. Nix (Silver Spring, Md.: Stewardship Department, General Conference of Seventh-day Adventists, 2000), pp 152-159.

[16] Ellen G. White, *Testimonies,* vol. 1, p. 605.

[17] See, for example, *Defense of Eld. James White and Wife,* pp. 118-137.

[15] *Ibid.,* pp. 143-145.

[19] *Ibid.,* pp. 145, 146.

[20] *Ibid.,* p. 1.

[21] *Ibid.,* p. 154.

Chapter XIII

INVALID

POOR health and sudden death were a constant litany in the lives of the Seventh-day Adventist pioneers.[1] Disease and illness were an inescapable fact of life. Before the development of modern medicine and sanitation, each season had its specific health dangers, and children were especially vulnerable. When an epidemic swept through, parents could expect only the worst.

DR. JAMES CALEB JACKSON

During the winter of 1862-1863 diphtheria raced across the nation, perhaps aggravated by large-scale movements of people and other conditions caused by the ongoing Civil War. The White family children soon had high fevers and sore throats, classic symptoms of the disease. At first all their parents knew to do was to pray. But then someone gave them a clipping from the *Yates County Chronicle,* a rural New York newspaper. In it a Dansville, New York, physician named James Caleb Jackson offered a way of curing diphtheria through the use of water. Jackson employed a hot bath/cool wet-pack treatment which, he claimed, had never failed for him. Ellen White tried it on her sons, and it worked.

Dr. Jackson belonged to one of the health reform movements that had begun to explode across the United States. He had been on the staff of the prestigious Philadelphia Medical College and had served as an adviser to Horace Mann on the latter's famous educational report of 1842. Then many Americans began to reject the sometimes barbarous and generally unsuccessful practices of contemporary medicine.[2] Jackson not only shared their concerns, he had joined the stream of the health reform movement that started with Sylvester Graham during the 1830s. Graham, a Presbyterian evangelist, advocated a meatless and stimulant-free diet along with fresh air, sunlight, exercise, and frequent bathing.[3] Many accepted his ideas, including a number of Millerites. Early Adventists were active in a wide range of reform movements, often participating in the abolitionist, temperance, and other social and religious reforms. Naturally, some would be attracted to the health and medical reform campaigns, though the Millerite belief that Christ would return in a very few months tended to lessen their expectation of any substantial change in society. Two of Graham's supporters were Charles Fitch and physician-preacher Larkin B. Coles. Coles wrote a book titled *Philosophy of Health: Natural Principles of Health and Cure.* He claimed to have sold 35,000 copies within five years of its release.

During the 1840s another reform movement merged with the Grahamites. In Europe a Silesian peasant named Vincenz Priessnitz developed a technique of treating disease with water. The method, now known as hydrotherapy, soon spread to the United States, appearing first in New York City in 1844.

By the fall of 1858 Jackson and another physician, Harriet N. Austin, had purchased a failed water cure on a 44-acre wooded tract near Dansville, about 50 miles south of Rochester. He would be medical director and business manager, and Austin would be in charge of the women's program. Renamed "Our Home on the Hillside," it became one of the most successful water therapy institutions. Its 300-foot main building consisted of a maze of corridors and small uncurtained rooms. Woodburning "box stoves" struggled to heat the place during the cold New York winters.[4]

Dr. Jackson's patients followed a regular routine at his Dansville institution. A Chinese gong each morning at 6:00 announced the beginning of the day. Some might make sure they were fully awake by plunging into cold water (icy in winter). At 6:30 everyone assembled in a large parlor for a lecture by Jackson. Then they had a vegetarian breakfast. Jackson assigned his patients by lot to the long common tables. He wanted to make sure they mixed with each other. Americans of the time wanted everything to be done democratically. Unlike most water cures, Jackson served only two meals a day—breakfast at 8:00, dinner at 2:30. The menu consisted of Graham bread, vegetables, and fresh fruit. He disapproved of meat, white-flour bread, butter, tea, and coffee.

During the rest of the day the patients had various water treatments such as half-baths, sitz baths, plunges, and being draped in dripping sheets. They also did simple exercises and amused themselves with card playing and dancing. By 8:30 everybody was supposed to be asleep on the hard mattresses filled with sea grass.

Jackson believed in using only natural remedies: "First, air; second, food; third, water; fourth, sunlight; fifth, dress; sixth, exercise; seventh, sleep; eighth, rest; ninth, social influences; tenth, mental and moral forces."[5] One of his favorite mottoes was "Nature is a mistress gentle and holy. To obey her is to live."[6] He refused to prescribe the harsh drugs of the time, once claiming that "in my entire practice I have never given a dose of medicine; not so much as I should have administered had I taken a homeopathic pellet of the seven-millionth dilution, and dissolving it in Lake Superior, given my patients of its waters."[7] Homeopathic medicine was noted for its incredibly dilute mixtures. While such dosages could not really help anyone, they did no harm. Jackson also opposed the use of to-bacco and alcohol. He believed that they not only weakened the body but hindered self-control. As a result he emphasized the moral implications of the care of the body.

A number of aging Millerite Adventists visited Jackson's institution, including Joshua V. Himes. Himes wrote of Jackson's books and water cure center in his *Voice of the Prophets* magazine and printed articles by Jackson in his later periodical, *Voice of the West.* Sabbatarian Adventists who also had an interest in health would read Himes's publications and learn about Jackson.

A GROWING ADVENTIST INTEREST IN HEALTH

Joseph Bates had long been interested in health and temperance top-ics, and he was one of the few Seventh-day Adventist pioneers with con-sistently good health. As the years had gone by articles occasionally appeared in the *Review and Herald* against tobacco and tea, though the op-position was based more on biblical and economic, as opposed to medi-cal, reasons. Other articles rejected pork and supported vegetarianism. James White endorsed good ventilation in both houses and public build-ings. His Wood Street home had been designed around the best contem-porary ideas of ventilation and light. White told his readers that "air, water, and light, are God's great remedies. If the people would *learn* to use these, doctors and their drugs would be in less demand."[8] He also said that he had cross ventilation in his bedrooms all winter, and that he took a cold-water sponge bath each morning. When one remembers the cold Michigan winters, it reveals his dedication to have the windows open in an unheated bedroom.

A week after his "Pure Air" article, James reprinted Jackson's "Diphtheria" clipping that he and Ellen had followed to help their sons.[9] He commented in an editorial note that he had "a good degree of confidence" in hydrotherapy treatments. Unfortunately, he did not follow his own advice some months later when Henry Nichols White contracted pneumonia. He had sent for Jackson's books on health, but because of a heavy travel schedule he had not yet read them. They still remained in their wrappers. Instead of trying hydrotherapy, the Whites called in a local doctor and stood by helplessly as the man used the conventional poisonous drugs. They would turn to hydrotherapy, however, when Willie White came down with pneumonia in February 1864.

ELLEN WHITE'S HEALTH VISION

Health had become a real problem among the emerging Seventh-day Adventist Church. John N. Andrews, J. N. Loughborough, Uriah Smith, and others were frequently sick. James White was on the verge of physical and mental collapse. Ellen had long suffered from fainting spells. Something had to change. And the spark for it came in a vision Mrs. White had on the eve of June 6, 1863, near Otsego, Michigan.

The Whites had come to the town 30 miles northwest of Battle Creek to attend some evangelistic tent meetings. Friday evening they visited the home of Aaron Hilliard. James White had become depressed about some problems that he and Ellen had been struggling with in Battle Creek. The Hilliards asked Mrs. White to have prayer at their family worship. James knelt near her. As she prayed she moved toward him and placed her hand on his shoulder, then went into a vision. It lasted about 45 minutes.

The vision presented health principles applying to everyone—such as the use of natural remedies and the avoidance of the dangerous chemicals used by physicians of the time—and specific counsel for both her and her husband. They should not drive themselves to exhaustion and James should not dwell on "the dark, gloomy side" of life.[10]

The next morning Ellen recorded her vision in a 16-page manuscript. In it she stated that "it was duty for everyone to have a care for his health, but especially should we [the Whites] turn our attention to our health, and take time to devote to our health that we may in a degree recover from the effects of overdoing and overtaxing the mind. . . .

"It is not safe or pleasing to God to violate the laws of health and then ask Him to take care of our health and keep us from disease when we are living . . . contrary to our prayers. I saw that it was a sacred duty to attend to our health, and arouse others to their duty."[11] She also wrote that God wanted her and James to tell others about health.

Intrigued by her manuscript, James—remembering the newspaper clipping by Dr. Jackson—contacted Dansville for a sampling of the water cure's books and pamphlets. Apparently his wife was not fully aware that he had ordered the material. With the books came an invitation from Dr. Jackson to visit his water cure at the clergy rate of $2.50 a week.

At first Ellen hesitated to discuss with others what she had seen in visions. But one day she rode in a carriage with Horatio S. Lay, a largely self-taught physician from Allegan, Michigan (though he would work for a time at Jackson's Dansville institution). Several of her comments caught Lay's attention. On June 23 the Whites visited Allegan. Lay invited them home for dinner, then began questioning her about the vision. At first she hesitated to say much, explaining that she did not know medical terminology. But when he persisted, she discussed the vision with him for four hours.

The White family began to adopt the principles she had seen in vision, though at first she had a hard time because she was a "great meat-eater."[12] By the next year, though, she could comment that the simple food she had served twice a day she now "enjoyed with a keen relish." "We have no meat, cake, or any rich food upon our table," she reported. "We use no lard, but in its place, milk, cream, and some butter. We have our food prepared with but little salt, and have dispensed with spices of all kinds. We breakfast at seven, and take our dinner at one."[13]

A few years later James White expanded on the changes in his home. He told how Willie had been a finicky eater and never wanted anything they served. But when they stopped preparing greasy and spicy foods and switched to just two meals a day, the boy would respond to his mother's question of what he wanted, "'Victuals, mother, victuals.' The simplest and most healthful food could then be received with a relish far exceeding that enjoyed in eating the greatest delicacy before his appetite was restored by proper habits."[14]

In the spring of 1864 Ellen published her first health materials—*An Appeal to Mothers* in April and a 30-page chapter on health in volume 4 of *Spiritual Gifts*. Then she began a series titled *Health: or How to Live*. The series consisted of a six-part essay, "Disease and Its Causes," that she personally wrote, and the rest of the material was excerpted from the publications of popular health authors. James White signed the preface to the first volume and must have selected much of the material.

VISITING OUR HOME ON THE HILLSIDE

During a September 1864 trip to the eastern United States the Whites decided to stop by Dansville and see Our Home on the Hillside for themselves. James reported in the *Review* that "the health question is much agitated among our people. The Dansville institution has its warm friends, and strong prejudices against it. We wish to investigate as far as we can spare the opportunity to do so, that we may be able to speak more understandingly."[15]

"I am pleased with the Philosophy of Health taught here generally," he wrote after a few days. "The American Costume [a dress style advocated by Jackson's associate, Dr. Harriet Austin] and their Theology I regard very doubtful. But in these things you are at liberty to please yourself."[16]

His wife was more critical. "You may ask what we think of this institution," she wrote to a Mr. and Mrs. Lockwood. "Some things are excellent. Some things are not good. Their views and teaching in regard to health are I think correct. But Dr. Jackson mixes up his theology too much with health questions; which theology to us is certainly objectionable."[17] The card playing and dancing bothered her, and she felt that he served too much food. Then, after describing the daily bath routine, she observed, "I do think we should have an institution in Michigan to which our Sabbathkeeping invalids can resort."[18] Many Seventh-day Adventists were already patronizing Jackson's establishment.

The Whites stayed three weeks at Our Home on the Hillside. Ellen felt that some of its health practices disagreed with her health vision. When they finally returned from their itinerary in the East, she finished the *Health: or How to Live* tracts and published them early in 1865. Within a few months the publishing house issued them bound together in a 400-page volume. "We are deeply impressed with the great fact that grains and fruits are the proper food for man," James said in his introduction. "These are best, and generally far the cheapest, which is a worthy consideration for the poor. Cheerful toil, or exercise, proper rest in sleep, air, water and light, are Heaven's great remedies. To use these properly should be the study of the people. This leaving our souls with the ministers, and our bodies with the doctors, and we pass along ignorant of our real hold of either earth or Heaven, is bad business."[19] The book also described the Whites' visit to Dansville in what would seem to many a complete endorsement of their program.

A convention of "friends of health reform" met December 22, 1864, in Battle Creek. It appointed a 12-woman committee to compile a healthful cookbook. Ellen White and a number of ministers lectured on health both to church members and to those who attended their evangelistic meetings. But many Adventists wondered what health had to do with the church's doctrines. "The health reform, I was shown, is a part of the third angel's message and is just as closely connected with it as are the arm and hand with the human body," she would tell Adventists in 1867. "I saw that we as a people must make an advance move in this great work."[20]

In a way, non-Adventists recognized the significance of the church's health reform program better than did its own members. In 1865 Dr. Jackson had written to the editor of *World's Crisis* magazine that Seventh-day Adventists "publish books and tracts on the subject, arousing the attention of their people, until really as a denomination, they are in advance of any denomination of Christians in the United States. I think the effect of this must be very conducive to a high spirituality."[21]

But Adventists accepted health reform only slowly, despite its great need, as exemplified during the summer of 1865, when so many church leaders became ill that church headquarters came to a virtual halt. The sickness of two of the three General Conference Committee members forced them to suspend its meetings. (The only one not ill was longtime health reformer Joseph Bates.) Health problems paralyzed the Michigan Conference Committee. Illness forced Uriah Smith to quit as editor of the *Review and Herald* for a time. And perhaps the most important person struck down was James White himself.

The third session of the General Conference had met in Battle Creek on May 17, 1865. The nominating committee had brought in White's name for president. Though protesting at first, he did accept. Uriah Smith took over as *Review* editor.

The Whites immediately plunged into a hectic round of travel and appointments. First they made a difficult trip to Wisconsin. A Mrs. T. M. Steward had claimed to have had visions, and the local Adventists had split among themselves on how to respond. James referred to "Sister Steward" as "a little homely dark-eyed piece of intelligence who has much influence I judge."[22] Then James and Ellen rushed to Iowa to deal with a split in the churches caused by B. F. Snook[23] and W. H. Brinkerhoff, the president and secretary, respectively, of the recently organized Iowa Conference. Opposing a strong form of church organization, the two men criticized not only church leadership as a whole but the Whites in particular. They rejected the whole concept of her visions. Confronting the dissidents and their followers would have been particularly stressful to James since he and his wife were the targets of the bitterness. At best, their efforts provided a temporary truce only. The Iowa membership replaced Snook and Brinkerhoff with George I. Butler. Eventually the two men left Seventh-day Adventism to form one of the few offshoots that still survives—the Church of God (Seventh Day).

Returning to Battle Creek from that exhausting experience, the Whites received an urgent message asking them to help the Memphis, Michigan, church. This involved getting up at midnight to walk a mile to the train station. After a long Sunday night meeting and not falling asleep until midnight, they arose at 3:00 in the morning of August 14 to ride a stage-coach to the depot. Their train missed its connection at Detroit, so they did not reach Battle Creek until midnight. Although James slept only fitfully, he was in the office the next day, and handled many urgent problems. By the time he reached home that night he was exhausted, but he still did not sleep well.

STROKE

The next morning around 5:30 he and Ellen went out for a walk. As they stopped at the home of a neighbor named Lunt for some milk, James noticed that the family's corn was ripening. Breaking off an ear, he began to strip off the husks. Suddenly he groaned and staggered. His face was flushed and his right arm paralyzed. Ellen rushed to support him as he staggered into the Lunt Home. Once inside, he could manage only one word—"Pray!"[24] He had just suffered the first of at least five strokes that would haunt him until death. James had ignored the message of Ellen's vision not to drive himself so hard. His body, reaching the point of collapse, now rebelled.

Mrs. White and the Lunts knelt beside James and prayed. Before long he could again speak and raise his arm. Word raced through the Adventist community that he had suffered a possibly fatal stroke. Ellen sent for a physician, and James received electrical stimulation treatments using a battery, but she then decided to use only simple hydrotherapy techniques. Two days later friends took him to his own home. The physicians were not encouraging. But she continued to pray for his healing, assuring him that family and friends "will present your case to God, dear James, every time we pray, and will press our petitions to the throne [of God]. . . . Be of good courage, my poor suffering husband, wait patiently a little longer and you shall see the salvation of God."[25]

On August 27 White dressed for the first time since the stroke and managed to take a few steps without assistance. Then two weeks later he walked to the *Review* office. Ellen continued to nurse her husband until she had exhausted herself. She could find no one willing to care for him.

Dr. Lay, a staff member at Our Home on the Hillside, heard of White's condition and came to see him. By now Ellen had decided to take him to Dansville. Lay would accompany James and Ellen to Dr. Jackson's water cure. But they were not the only ones going. The "Seventh-day Adventist invalid party" left Battle Creek by train the morning of September 14.

When Jackson examined White, the doctor told him and Ellen that James should expect to stay in Dansville for six to eight months. Jackson explained that White had, through overwork, driven himself to a nearly fatal stroke. Now the Adventist leader must have complete physical and mental rest. Ellen would also take treatments.

H. S. Lay reported in the *Review* that the Whites and Loughborough, another ailing leader, must have time to rest and recover. As for James, Lay described him as having experienced a "shock of paralysis, leaving his nervous system, as a matter of course, in a shattered condition, and his brain somewhat disturbed."[26] (Today such a press release would be unlikely to discuss the mental condition of an ill church leader in such blunt terms.)

As happened so often throughout his life, friends once again came to White's aid. Encouraged by Joseph Bates, the Monterey, Michigan, church sent James $60, and a woman named Gates offered $10 (about a week's income for the average person) along with a note declaring, "It is impossible for us to know that you are in infliction, and we not suffer with you."[27]

CONVALESCENCE AT DANVILLE

People offered him nearly $1,000 during his stay at Dansville. Although he would frequently accept gifts, he was somewhat ambivalent toward them. For a long time he refused to accept direct financial aid, explaining that he would let his friends know when he really needed help. He had determined, if possible, to be financially independent. White even had declared in the *Review* that "we have never been what might be termed a church pauper, and we expect, with the blessing of Heaven, never to be. By the grace of God we will eat no man's bread for naught."[28] But they were running out of resources. The time would quickly come when they would have to accept even more help, though the Whites attempted, by selling their furniture, to make it on their own as long as possible. When their only milk cow died, James wrote to a man who had previously offered help. But the church member had changed his mind. Now he accused White of being "insane on the subject of money."[29] The experience left them feeling "humbled into the very dust and distressed beyond expression."[30]

The Adventist invalids rented some small rooms near the water cure. Ellen made the beds and cleaned the rooms not only for her husband but also for the Adventist ministers who shared adjoining quarters. When she and James were not taking water treatments, the couple walked around the institution's grounds. Three times a day the Adventist patients—now including Daniel T. Bourdeau from Vermont—met to pray for James, who at night suffered from so much pain that he could not sleep. Sometimes he managed only an hour or two of rest. His wife would rub his arms and shoulders to bring temporary relief.

During the first part of October the rest of the General Conference Committee requested the church to fast and pray for James White on October 14. The afternoon of that Sabbath the Whites, Loughborough, Bourdeau, and Uriah Smith prayed together as a group. The next day James seemed on the road to recovery. But a relapse occurred in mid-November. Soon he became so weak that he could no longer walk the short distance up to the dining hall. Loughborough brought baskets of food to James's room.

Because the Whites had by now been away from their sons for some time, they arranged for them to stay at a friend's home in Rochester. Ellen went to spend a few days with them. While there she had a dream or vision that suggests a growing friction between her and the staff at Dansville, most likely over her disapproval of Jackson's prescription that her husband should confine himself to complete mental and physical rest. James had always been constantly busy, and the inactivity at Dansville was wearing on him. Her husband, she concluded, would respond best to "exercise and moderate, useful labor."[31] Dr. Jackson had told James that any return to physical activity would cause another stroke. As a result he would avoid physical exertion as far as possible for the next couple years. Instead of helping him, though, the inactivity made his condition worse.

Ellen had still another reason for wanting to leave Our Home on the Hillside. As on her previous visit, Jackson's religious teachings and the card playing, dancing, and other amusements continued to bother her. It was time for a decision. Because her husband was not improving as quickly as she thought he should, she could see no alternative except to have him in a different environment.

As December began, Ellen was herself approaching exhaustion. Then on December 4 James had an especially bad night. Mrs. White decided it was time to leave. The next morning, when she told Dr. Lay of her intentions, he protested that her husband was not strong enough to travel. She explained that they would make the trip back to Battle Creek in several stages. They would rest for a while in Rochester, then in Detroit. The morning of December 6 she bundled James up and they left in a driving sleet storm. The couple planned to remain at the Bradley Lamson home in

Rochester for several weeks.

J. N. Andrews had been preaching in Maine. James, who had great respect for and confidence in Andrews' prayers, now asked the young minister and friend to come pray for him. Andrews did, and the prayers seemed to help. On Christmas he and several other friends conducted three special prayer services. During the evening Ellen had a vision, in which she was assured that her husband would recover and that she should immediately take him back to Battle Creek. But even more significantly, the vision called for Adventists to start their own institution for the sick.

New Year's Day the Whites departed Rochester and headed by train straight back to Battle Creek without pausing anywhere. By now James had lost 50 pounds, but once back home he began to walk slowly around the West End neighborhood. The first Sabbath he managed to preach 45 minutes, then conducted Communion that evening. When the weather was good he and Ellen would take a carriage or sleigh drive in the countryside. But his progress still appeared too slow for Ellen. He seemed unable to gain weight and found it difficult to read or write. Also he struggled with bouts of depression and seemed convinced that he was not improving even though others thought he had gotten better.

The fourth session of the General Conference met in Battle Creek on May 16. Its delegates reelected White to a second term as president.

WHITE'S STRUGGLE TO REGAIN HIS HEALTH

Church leaders set May 20 as another day of fasting and prayer for White. Two days later James wrote to the *Review* that "you will be able to form some idea of our [the editorial "we" that he loved to use] sufferings, when we say that for the past nine months we have not been able to obtain sleep without artificial heat in some form, either a jug of hot water or a hot stone, or hot blankets applied to the feet; and that for the last five months we have not had more than one hour's sleep out of twenty-four, and that often disturbed by unhappy dreams. . . .

"For two nights past since the season of fasting and prayer, Sabbath, May 20th, we have slept more than for the two weeks previous, and our feet were warm without the use of artificial heat."[32]

Because James did not have the strength to go to his office, staff from the publishing house would come to him with its unending problems. The other General Conference officers would also consult with White. He could not escape the pressure of either responsibility, and the stress, besides keeping him awake many a night, was hindering his physical recovery.

Ellen had to do something drastic. She concluded that she had to rescue her husband from the constant burden of leadership. He needed to be away from Battle Creek so that she could employ the kinds of treatments that she believed would be efficacious. But when she mentioned her concerns and ideas, she ran into great opposition. Many in the Adventist community thought it would be a terrible mistake to take James elsewhere. To try what she had in mind would not help her husband, they believed, and it would destroy her own health. Her fellow Adventists "all felt that I was sacrificing my life in shouldering this burden; that for the sake of my children, for the cause of God, I should do all in my power to preserve my life. His own father and mother remonstrated with me in tears."[33] The local physicians announced that she would fail. Their experience had convinced them that it was impossible for a stroke victim—"paralysis of the brain"—to recover. But she told them all that "God will raise him up."[34]

LEAVING BATTLE CREEK

Her insistence on taking care of James someplace other than in Battle Creek drove a wedge between the Whites and many members of the local Adventist congregation. In closely knit communities such as the Adventists of Battle Creek, everybody knows everyone else's business and has an emotional investment in what happens. The Whites' fellow church members had definite ideas of what they thought Ellen should or should not do. They firmly believed that she was endangering her own life by spending so much time taking care of her husband. When she ignored their ideas and suggestions, it hurt. The bitterness created would last for years, intensifying into criticism and rumor that threatened to destroy the Whites' influence in both Battle Creek and the denomination as a whole.

At last Mrs. White made her decision to leave Battle Creek. On a bitterly cold December 19, 1866, a friend named Rogers drove her, James, and 12-year-old Willie through a snowstorm to the home of E. H. Root in Wright, Michigan, about 80 miles away. The fact that she left in such bad weather upset some. The cold, they believed, would kill James. After spending the first night of their journey at a local hotel/tavern, they stopped for breakfast at the home of the Hardys, the African-American family Ellen had admired years before. James's account of the visit indicates not only that he was well-acquainted with the family but that the Hardys had apparently accepted health reform.[35]

The Whites stayed six weeks with the Root family. James and Ellen visited the local churches and held meetings. Friends gave them money and other gifts, including a sleigh worth $75, an amount equal to about six weeks' pay for James. From Wright the Whites went to Greenville, Michigan. Again they spoke at area churches. After living six weeks with the A. W. Maynard family, they liked the area so much that they decided to move there. Maynard helped them to find farmland to build a house on.

By March 1867 James's health had improved so much that Ellen decided that they could return to Battle Creek for a while. They had been away from denominational headquarters for nearly three months. She thought that their fellow believers would be happy to see them, especially since James was so much better, physically and mentally. But she was shocked to discover how the bitterness toward them had festered. It took a year before some of the hostility and suspicion began to ebb. At times during the next few years they would find themselves tempted to return to the farm at Greenville permanently. The unhealthy relationships in Battle Creek would concern Ellen for years, to the point that she would urge Adventists to move away from the little city.

The March 19, 1867, *Review* carried a petition from the 68 Adventist church members living in Montcalm and Ionia counties asking that the Whites settle in their area. James resigned from the church's Publishing Department and put his Battle Creek home up for sale.

The fifth session of the General Conference convened May 14. The lingering estrangement between the Whites and certain members of the Battle Creek church cost James a number of votes, and the session elected John Nevins Andrews as president. James decided to sever his ties with the publishing house. J. M. Aldrich, who had chaired the session that organized the General Conference, took his place. In addition, White withdrew from leadership in the new Health Reform Institute.

The Whites returned to Greenville after the session closed, taking strawberry plants with them to set out on their new property. Soon after they arrived back, James came down with a toothache. After enduring the pain for several days, he went to a dentist and had five teeth pulled. A few days later (in what was a common custom), he had his remaining teeth removed—all six of them. Because of limited and primitive dental care, people would frequently have all their teeth extracted—sometimes in their late teens or early 20s—and wear dentures the rest of their lives. That way they would not have to bother with toothaches or other dental problems. Having one's teeth pulled almost became a rite of passage into adulthood. Some also believed that getting rid of the teeth would prevent certain health problems. J. N. Andrews and Uriah Smith each sent White $10 to help pay for the dentures, and Mrs. M. J. Cornell sent $5.

James wrote in the *Review* that he was "still making up lost time in sleeping, which is relieving my head. With my present labor, mental and physical, in the heat of midsummer, and loss of teeth and of blood when they were extracted, I think I fully hold my own." Then he concluded, "In my toothless condition which may continue some months, I choose not to go among strangers. Wherever I go brethren must not expect too much of me. I will, in the strength of the Lord, do what I can. Brethren, pray for us."[36]

To Mrs. White's continued frustration, James could not forget Dr. Jackson's warning to avoid physical activity lest it trigger another stroke. But she was convinced that physical exertion was exactly what her husband needed. During his youth he had done a lot of hard labor and had robust health. Somehow she had to get him physically active again.

One weekend the Whites visited Franklin L. Howe and his wife in Orange, Michigan, 30 miles from Greenville. Sunday morning, after worship and breakfast, James asked the Howes to place a couch by the front door so that he could rest and look outdoors. Soon he saw Mrs. Howe begin to hoe in the cornfield. After a few minutes his embarrassment at lying on a couch while Mrs. Howe worked in the field began to overcome his fear of another stroke. He asked his wife to bring him his clothes, and a few minutes later he joined the farmer's wife and hoed a row of corn. Franklin Howe later considered the incident a turning point in James White's recovery. But the return to full physical activity would be a hesitant one, and Ellen would have to nudge her husband along.

Hay was an important crop to all nineteenth-century farmers. It fed their horses and cattle. When the Whites' hayfield was ready to cut, James found someone to mow it for him. He also planned to have neighbors gather and pile it in a haystack. But before he could contact them, his wife went around to each neighbor and convinced them not to help. When James did request help, all said that they were too busy. Then Ellen suggested that she and James harvest the hay themselves. She and their son Willie would pitch the hay up to James in the wagon. He would spread the hay in the wagon, then drive it to where they had the haystack. Ellen and Willie would then unload it.[37]

Realizing that physical labor would not lead to another stroke, James became more active and, as a result, his strength increased. Soon he was able to load and move 3,000 feet of heavy lumber for his house and barn. Slowly but surely he recovered.

JAMES WHITE, NURSERY OWNER

The Whites had acquired a 45-acre tract of land east of Greenville. Greenville was on the Flat River in Montcalm County, about 30 miles northeast of Grand Rapids. The town had been founded in 1844 in a rich agricultural area. It would not be incorporated until 1870. There James built a large house and barn for $2,400 one mile east of the town's Ionia and Lansing Railroad station. He improved 20 of the 45 acres during their years there, planting an orchard of 100 apple trees, 400 grapevines, an acre of strawberries, plus raspberry and blackberry patches.[38]

Besides the ripe fruit he raised, he also began to sell plants and rootstock by mail order. His interest in growing fruit led him to publish a small book, *How to Cultivate and Can Small Fruits,* for 10 cents a copy. "It contains valuable information," he said, "gleaned from larger books, and from personal experience on this subject. It is just what the people need to teach them in the selection of proper grounds, and the best kinds of fruit, in planting, cultivating, and in pruning, the Strawberry, the Raspberry, the Blackberry, and the Grape, and how to can all kinds of fruit."

In addition to explaining how to get abundant fruit "with but little labor," the book also contained "a list of the most valuable varieties, and their prices, for the benefit of those who wish to purchase the best and purest roots and plants. . . . Send for this book immediately, as you will want it to assist you in making out an order for roots and plants, which order should be received by the first of March."[39] He promoted fruit raising not only in *The Health Reformer* but also in the *Review and Herald.*[40]

James involved his sons in the fruit business. Willie's name appears on the stationery of White's mail-order nursery: "Office of the Hygienic Institute Nursery: Willie C. White, Manager." Edson also participated. In one letter, perhaps an indication of the growing strain between father and son, James scolds Edson for not sending complete orders for the plants. White wrote that "delays, and indefiniteness relative to pease, plants, etc. showing a lack of interest on your part in our matters, discourage us as to our [my] interest in your matters."[41]

James apparently worked his own sons as hard as he did himself. In one letter to Willie, after telling him not to work too hard, he then gave him a list of chores (though he also asked what Willie would like his father to bring him from Battle Creek).[42]

The Whites' Greenville neighbors took good care of them. One of the things James and Ellen were especially appreciative of was the light carriage that friends bought them after seeing the couple traveling about in an uncomfortable old wagon. But some would resent the carriage, just as church members today may get upset over their pastor having a fancy automobile. (Perhaps it did not occur to the complainers that the Whites spent much time traveling to area churches, and that a carriage would be less exhausting to ride in than a farm wagon.)

The Whites enjoyed Greenville. As problems in Battle Creek worsened, especially those involving the publishing house and health institute, they considered remaining in the rural town.[43] It became a refuge away from the turmoil in Battle Creek and seemed more like home. The tranquillity of Greenville allowed them to rest after long trips and permitted them time to write.[44]

FIRST SEVENTH-DAY ADVENTIST CAMP MEETING

While at the Greenville farm James and others developed plans for Seventh-day Adventist camp meetings. The first one convened at Johnstown Center, Wisconsin, September 19-22, 1867.[45] Although 1,500 people attended the convocation, which was held on a cow pasture, the camp meeting in Wright, Michigan (September 1-7, 1868) has tended to overshadow it, and many have assumed that it was the first Seventh-day Adventist one.

The idea of a camp meeting, borrowed from the Methodist and other frontier churches, had been an important part of the Millerite movement[46] and frontier evangelism. For the Seventh-day Adventist Church it also provided a powerful means of evangelism. Thousands of non-Adventists attended some of the camp meetings. Railroads offered them special fares, ran extra trains, and occasionally even built special spur tracks to reach them. For Adventists themselves the sessions offered the church a means to teach scattered members, to give them a sense of belonging to a large community, and to bond them together. The Whites became popular speakers on the camp meeting circuit, and each conference tried to make sure that the couple attended its session. Each year the Whites would attend more and more, sometimes speaking at as many as 15 a year throughout the country.

---

[1] In 1974 historian of science and medicine Ronald L. Numbers published a seminal article ("Dr. Jackson's Water Cure and Its Influence on Adventist Health Reform," *Adventist Heritage,* January 1974) on the development of the health reform movement in the Seventh-day Adventist Church. He later issued the material in his highly controversial *Prophetess of Health* (New York: Harper and Row, 1976). While neither I nor the church as a whole agrees with all the conclusions of Numbers' book, his research cannot be ignored. I have found the *Adventist Heritage* article a helpful guide to these events as they touched upon James White's life.

[2] For an overview of what American medicine was like during much of the nineteenth century, see Mervyn Hardinge, *A Physician Explains Ellen White's Counsel on Drugs, Herbs, and Natural Remedies* (Hagerstown, Md.: Review and Herald Pub. Assn., 2001) and George W. Reid, *A Sound of Trumpets: Americans, Adventists, and Health Reform* (Washington, D.C.: Review and Herald Pub. Assn., 1982).

[3] Interestingly, modern medical science is struggling with the return of many infectious diseases that had almost vanished. They are rising again simply because people no longer wash their hands as often.

[4] At the time of this writing the massive successor building can still be seen from the parking lot of a McDonald's restaurant just off one of the I-390 Dansville, New York, exits.

[5] James C. Jackson, *How to Treat the Sick Without Medicine,* pp. 25, 26.

[6] Jackson, in George W. Reid, *A Sound of Trumpets: Americans, Adventists, and Health Reform* (Washington, D.C.: Review and Herald Pub. Assn., 1982), p. 8.

[7] William D. Conklin, *The Jackson Health Resort* (Dansville, N.Y.: privately distributed by the author, 1971), p. 81.

[8] James White, "Pure Air," *Review and Herald,* Feb. 10, 1863.

[9] James C. Jackson, "Diphtheria, Its Causes, Treatment, and Cure," *Review and Herald,* Feb. 17, 1863.

[10] EGW manuscript 1, 1863, in *Selected Messages,* book 3, p. 280.

[11] EGW letter 4, 1863, cited in Reid, pp. 101, 102.

[12] Ellen G. White, *Testimonies,* vol. 2, p. 371.

[13] Ellen G. White, *Spiritual Gifts* (Battle Creek, Mich.: Steam Press of the Seventh-day Adventist Publishing Assn., 1864), vol. 4a, p. 154.

[14] James White, in *The Health Reformer,* 1872.

[15] JW letter, in *Review and Herald,* Sept. 6, 1864.

[16] JW to Myrta E. Steward, Sept. 6, 1864.

[17] EGW to Brother and Sister Lockwood (letter 6, 1864), Sept., 1864.

[18] *Ibid.*

[19] James White, *Health: or How to Live* (Battle Creek, Mich.: Steam Press of the Seventh-day Adventist Pub. Assn., 1865), p. iii.

[20] Ellen G. White, *Testimonies,* vol. 1, p. 486.

[21] "The Health Reform," *Review and Herald,* June 13, 1865.

[22] JW to EGW, Nov. 4, 1860 [date uncertain].

[23] Earlier James had been quite favorably impressed with Snook. See JW to EGW, Oct. 16, 1860; JW to EGW, Oct. 22, 1860; JW to EGW, Oct. 24, 1860.

[24] The type of stroke that White apparently suffered often leaves the victim able to say only a single one-syllable word, frequently an expletive.

[25] Ellen G. White, *Daughters of God,* pp. 260, 261.

[26] *Review and Herald,* Oct. 31, 1865.

[27] *Ibid.*

[28] *Review and Herald,* Feb. 2, 1864.

[29] Ellen G. White, *Testimonies,* vol. 1, p. 582.

[30] *Ibid.,* p. 583.

[31] EGW to J. M. Aldrich (letter 8, 1867), Aug. 20, 1867.

[32] James White, *Review and Herald,* May 22, 1866.

[33] EGW manuscript 1, 1867.

[34] *Ibid.*

[35] James White, in *Review and Herald,* Jan. 15, 1867.

[36] James White, in *Review and Herald,* July 16, 1867.

[37] EGW manuscript 1, 1867.

[38] Information from his "Farm for Sale" notice in the February 1871 *Health Reformer.* He happily announced that land had doubled in value in the Greenville area during the previous two years. The house still exists as of the time of writing.

[39] *Health Reformer,* January 1871. He includes a "Reduced Price List" with the notice for his fruit-raising book, giving the varieties and prices of his mail order offerings.

[40] *Review and Herald,* July 16, 1867.

[41] JW to Edson White, Apr. 10, 1871.

[42] JW to WCW, Oct. 6, 1867.

[43] *Review and Herald,* Mar. 30, 1869.

[44] *Review and Herald,* Apr. 27, 1869.

[45] Adriel D. Chilson, "Don't Be Wrong About Wright (It Wasn't Our First Campmeeting)," *Adventist Heritage,* Winter 1987, pp. 3-8.

[46] See Everett N. Dick, *William Miller and the Advent Crisis* (Berrien Springs, Mich.: Andrews University Press, 1994), pp. 37-58.

CHAPTER XIV

BATTLING IN BATTLE CREEK

WHEN the Whites first returned to Battle Creek, the local Adventists had greeted them with indifference, even hostility. James and Ellen saw part of the problem as spiritual lethargy. Secularism was creeping into the community. The couple attempted to revive some spirituality in the denominational headquarter's congregation, but received only more hostility and resistance. Others, such as Uriah Smith and longtime Review employee George Amadon, both elders in the local church, attempted to remain neutral in the controversy. But then Amadon began to criticize the Whites. "I know what is the matter with you," he told them. "You have overlabored, and it is sin. You hold too many meetings. [While recently in the Eastern states] you went too fast from place to place. It is wrong. The Lord has cautioned you in this matter. Brother White takes too many burdens on himself in office."[1]

Maybe Amadon's words were true, but the timing couldn't have been worse. The criticism discouraged the exhausted Whites. Amadon's comments were probably leaked to the closely knit Adventist community, further undercutting James and Ellen's credibility. In mid-April 1869 the Whites moved back to Greenville. Ellen told Smith and Amadon that they "had all the evidences you will ever have to establish your confidence that God is with us."[2]

FINANCIAL CRISES

The church elected James White as General Conference president again in 1869, as well as president once more of the publishing association. Still recovering from his stroke, he nevertheless faced a number of major financial crises among the church's institutions. The health institute, the health magazine, and the publishing house were bleeding red ink. Perhaps his greatest concern was the Review and Herald. After all, he had founded and built it up. White had resigned as head of the publishing association in 1867 and J. M. Aldrich had taken over. During his absence the Review had raised the salaries of its staff quite significantly above other denominational employees, not increased the prices of its publications to meet increased overhead and expenses, and otherwise operated in a way that had caused the institution to lose thousands of dollars. The house had to borrow large sums at 10 percent interest to meet its cash flow.

Throwing himself into the struggle to restore the economic health of the publishing house, James expended time and energy he didn't have. One of the first things he did was to appeal to church members to loan money interest-free to the publishing association in order that it could pay off the 10 percent interest notes. He and Ellen had to confront Aldrich with his poor administration. James was, apparently, blunt in his opinions of Aldrich's management style. After White discussed the mismanagement of the publishing house with Aldrich, the administrator resigned. Rumors raced through the Battle Creek community that James had fired him, a fact that Aldrich some months later had to refute publicly.[3]

As White struggled to get the publishing house back in the black, nerves frayed. James had long had a tendency to be "exacting toward those who were wrong and had injured him."[4] He could be quite blunt about people, especially those who saw things differently. For example, in his autobiography he described a man who had criticized him: "To see a coarse, hard-hearted man, possessing in his very nature but little more tenderness than a crocodile, and nearly as destitute of moral religious training as a hyena, shedding hypocritical tears for effect, is enough to stir the mirthfulness of the gravest saint."[5] In the early days of the Sabbatarian Adventist movement, he referred to nonbelievers as "*swine*" and referred to those attending a funeral he conducted as "a congregation of old, hard, ugly Congregationalists and Methodists."[6] And in a letter to Willie, James alluded to some problem by observing that a certain individual was still "the same ugly simpleton."[7]

The struggles James now faced, along with the effects of the stroke he was probably not completely recovered from, only aggravated the trait. George Amadon's diary for 1870 contains a litany of James White criticizing him, and Amadon trying to take the rebuke positively.[8] Finally Amadon resigned from the Review and Herald on March 22 and received an indefinite leave of absence on April 4. He would not return to work until that November. Even then he would still continue to find himself in trouble with White. James drove others as hard as he did himself. In February and March of 1874 he would tell the Review employees that they were not doing enough, even though they labored 50-70 hours a week. Amadon recorded how he worked every day, including Saturday night after sunset, and received only $9 to $11 a week. After a March 2 reprimand, Amadon remained at his job 22 hours nonstop.[9]

To complicate the situation, factions in the Battle Creek church began to purge the church membership of those whom they felt were not living up to Adventist standards. For example, on April 6, 1870, a church meeting dropped all but a handful of the congregation's approximately 400 members. The factions employed censure and disfellowship against their opponents. Many of those who were dropped went to the West Coast. Ellen White was sick and homebound part of this period. As soon as she recovered she wrote a formal rebuke to those who had treated even erring church members with such harshness. Such constant turmoil made James White's task that much more difficult.

CONFRONTATION WITH SMITH AND ANDREWS

Frustrated, James criticized not only Aldrich but those he felt had not done enough during his absence to prevent the financial disaster. We know that he targeted Uriah Smith (who had served as Review editor, member of the publishing committee, as well as treasurer for 1868 under Aldrich) and J. N. Andrews. One wonders how much the Review administration would have listened even if Smith had protested the money-losing business practices. But James criticized Smith for remaining neutral on some issues that White felt the Review editor should have taken a strong position toward.[10] Smith responded that while he always defended whatever he understood to be right, he could not do so when he did not have enough information to decide whether something was right or wrong. Perhaps, Smith suggested, White did not clearly remember one particularly contentious case. If White had forgotten, Smith was "willing to let this pass, the sooner to get through, or avoid an unpleasant controversy.

. . . But if I am a person who will not, when I see the right, stand up for it, I pray the trustees [of the publishing house] to dismiss me from the office, and get a person of moral integrity in my place."[11]

In response to White's reply, Smith wrote, "I shall be happy to receive any explanation wherein I misjudge. But of two things I am certain. 1. That your place is in Battle Creek, and 2. That if we cannot cooperate it is my place to leave, not yours."[12] And Smith did exactly that. He took a year's absence during 1869-1870. But before he left he offered $450 to the publishing house and the rest of his property to the health institute "to relieve the cause of the burden and curse" he had brought upon it.[13]

When Smith eventually resumed his publishing house duties, White commented in an editorial note about Uriah's restored health, consecration, and courage. In addition, he reminded *Review* readers that "when helpers were few, nearly eighteen years since, God raised him [Smith] up to help us in the work that was then increasing upon our hands. Side by side we labor on, never with better courage and brighter hopes than at the present time. We each have our part to act in close connection."[14] But the good feelings would unravel. Smith's temporary departure had only postponed the explosion between them.

A gulf not only separated Smith from White, but one now also yawned between White and Smith's brother-in-law, Andrews. The relationship between the Whites and Andrewses seemed through the years to swing in a cycle between fond closeness and estrangement. An undated document titled "Statement of Wrongs in the Course of J. N. Andrews" seems to belong to this particular crisis. In it John admitted that he had "failed in very many respects" when he should have assisted the Whites. He confessed that he had not recognized the financial irresponsibility of Aldrich's administration. In the past, Andrews said, he had tended to take positions contrary to those of James White, but now "whenever I have the united judgment of Brother and Sister White, it will be my duty to accept it and set mine aside."[15] Andrews was "willing to yield to them—each— all the deference that it is proper to yield to mortal man."[16] He left for Boston to continue revising his book on the history of the Sabbath, and the situation at church headquarters continued to worsen.

Eugene Durand, Uriah Smith's biographer, feels that an undated letter gives some background to the increasing tension between White and the *Review* editor. In it James claims that Smith had been impatient with him and that Uriah needed to remember the "feebleness and overwhelming discouragements" that White struggled with. Even if White had been wrong, Uriah still had "caused me so much suffering much of the time for more than fifteen years" while he (James) had been "trying to help him [Smith] in every way possible."[17] The reference to suffering may have been an allusion to the tensions created when he confronted the Smith and Andrews families in Paris, Maine, and the feud they carried on with him afterward. James goes on to protest, however, that "I have not had, neither have I any controversy with Brother Smith. If he had not risen up against me . . . we might now be enjoying the sweetist union."[18]

Perhaps White's reaction may at least partly have been aggravated by his stroke. But Smith may have been still wondering about the objections that Edward Andrews and Uriah's father-in-law had raised about James and Ellen for so many years. Could there be some truth in them after all? Was James an unfit leader, and Ellen a false prophet? Although he does not mention the previous tension between the Whites and Smith's family, Eugene Durand suggests that the present dispute did involve the special authority of the Whites.[19] This would fit in with the pattern of conflict between the Whites and the Smith and Andrews families. But documents of the time carefully avoided giving any reason for the dispute between James and Uriah, even as they reported the confrontation itself.[20] Durand states that he examined the correspondence of James White, Ellen White, Willie White, George I. Butler, and John Harvey Kellogg for the year 1873, and that they offered no explanation for the conflict. A letter White sent to a church member named Abbey indicates that James felt that both Smith and Butler resisted White's efforts to remedy problems in the Battle Creek Adventist community.[21]

During the early part of 1873 General Conference president George I. Butler tried to overcome the tensions between the Whites and the two brothers-in-law, Smith and Andrews. After the General Conference session that year, Butler met with the Whites, Andrews, and J. H. Waggoner on March 20 to find some way to reconcile Andrews with the Whites. The Battle Creek Adventist community seemed to be well aware of the problem. Longtime Review and Herald Publishing Association employee George Amadon tersely recorded in his diary on March 21 that it was a sorrowful period in the church's young history.[22] At issue was James White's role as leader in the church. With Smith questioning his decisions, and Andrews not providing the support that James felt that he could have, it made White even more vulnerable to criticism from other quarters.

Finally, on May 15, 1873, things came to a head and Smith lost his job. Harmon Lindsay, acting as spokesperson for the Seventh-day Adventist Publishing Association, informed the Whites of the decision to fire Smith. He wrote that the trustees had invited Harriet Smith to meet with them, but she would not discuss the situation. Apparently she still had strong feelings toward the Whites, just as she had so many years before. The investigative committee then met with the members of the Battle Creek church and explained what they saw as the Whites' unique roles in the denomination and how Smith's actions had been undercutting them.

The next morning George I. Butler called the publishing house employees together to announce the trustees' decision about Smith. Harmon Lindsay added that the publishing house board had met several times with Uriah in an attempt to explain the situation from the perspective of Ellen White's testimonies. Smith, Lindsay said, had told them that "he had done all he could and could not promise to do better in the future. He seemed rather to justify his course."[23] Butler concluded that the board had no choice but to tell Smith that "as long as he viewed things in this light . . . we did not think he had better stay longer. Therefore he was discharged from the office [of *Review* editor] until things assumed a very different shape."[24]

Amadon continued his sketchy allusions to the trauma tearing the Adventist community apart:

"May 17—In afternoon, special meetings for investigating Brother Smith's case. Brother Smith said nothing. . . .

"May 20—Searching meeting at office. Prayers for behavior at Society. Batchelor and Whitney [apparently two sympathizers with Smith] suspended for the present.

"May 23—Brother Smith calculates to leave for Saginaw."[25]

The May 27, 1873, issue of the *Review* lacked the name of Uriah Smith as editor but offered no explanation for its disappearance. Smith went to Grand Rapids, Michigan, where he worked as a wood engraver at twice what he had received as *Review* editor. John Harvey Kellogg wrote to Willie White that Smith had "a corner in the [Grand Rapids] *Democrat* office and the last I heard he was doing very well, earning about $25 a week."[26] Butler, recognizing the stir Smith's dismissal had caused, told the Whites, "I am sure there are whisperings all through the State [of Michigan] over Uriah's case."[27]

Smith's brother-in-law, however, tried to support White despite what had happened. Andrews wrote in the *Review* that he had "not one doubt in my heart that this is the cause of God" and that "God has been leading in this work by his Holy Spirit. It is not the work, nor the cause, of man."[28] Some months later he also published a *Review* editorial entitled "Duty Toward Those That Have the Rule." Referring to those "called to bear the chief responsibility in the work of God," Andrews observed that "it is in the highest degree reasonable to believe that those thus chosen should have clearer and juster ideas by far of the steps that should be taken." As far as he was concerned, it was "an honor to be the helpers of such, and no disgrace to stand in a position where we are more ready to receive counsel than to give it ourselves, or to find fault with that which is given." "Shall we always be fault-finders and murmurers, and think our dignity sacrificed by our acknowledging others to have clearer views of God's work than we ourselves possess?" he asked his readers. He pled for all church members to be "true helpers" since it was the only way not to displease God as well as being "reasonable and just."[29]

George Butler began speaking at camp meetings on the need to obey church leadership[30] and writing on the topic. Ultimately he would produce a booklet on leadership that reflected Butler's own authoritarian management style more than it did what the Bible taught.[31] Interestingly, James White, who could be rather authoritative at times himself, fought the trend to have the church centered around a powerful human leader. He ran a series of editorials on leadership in the new *Signs of the Times* that "Christ is the only authorized leader of His people."[32] (His emphasis on Christ as only true leader of the church is clearly a reflection of his growing awareness of the preeminence of Christ in Scripture and salvation and not just the old Christian Connexion concept that the church should have no strong human organization because Christ was its only leader; see pp. 213-216). He saw the concept of one person over the church as marking "the progress of different forms of corrupted Christianity," especially Roman Catholicism.[33]

Eventually James would deal with the trend toward strong one-person rule in an editorial in 1878. "It is very well known to most of the readers of the *Review* that some five years since a mistaken view was taken . . . that one man was to be recognized as the visible leader of Seventh-day Adventists, as Moses was the visible leader of the Hebrews; and what made this a very painful subject to us was the fact that the position was taken that we should be recognized as that leader."[34] Again he reiterated that "we have but one leader, which is Christ, and the entire brotherhood of the ministry, while they should counsel with each other out of due respect for the judgment of each other, should, nevertheless, look to our great Leader as their unerring guide."[35] He signed the editorial as "a servant of the church and counselor with the brethren, James White." As a human being, though, formulating the ideal for James was easier than living it.

Although Uriah Smith left Battle Creek, he kept in communication with church leadership, as we see briefly outlined in Amadon's diary.

"Sept. 8—Presentation of Uriah's case. . . .

"Nov. 5—Brother Smith came yesterday. . . . Sessions being held with Brother Smith by General Conference Committee and picked men.

"Nov. 6—Brother Smith is not doing well. Brother White writes he will not come [to the General Conference session scheduled for that month]."[36]

The Whites, who had been in Colorado for some time, had planned to go to California instead of attending the meetings in Battle Creek. But although they had already gone as far as Cheyenne, Wyoming, they felt a strong conviction that they should turn around and head for Michigan. Shortly after she reached Battle Creek, Ellen White stated in her diary that she and her husband had met with Andrews, Smith, Butler, and Waggoner to pray and work out their differences.[37] Apparently Butler was attempting to reconcile the various parties. On November 17 the annual meeting of the publishing association elected James White its president and editor of the *Review and Herald*. Then on November 26 the association appointed Uriah Smith and Andrews as additional editors. George Amadon recorded in his diary on November 29: "Business meeting of the [Battle Creek] church to half past twelve." [The Battle Creek congregation, because so many denominational leaders belonged to it, often served as a forum for dealing with denominational problems.] "Brother White perfectly free and happy," Amadon went on. "U.S. [Uriah Smith] back at the office."[38]

Each of those involved in the crisis contributed an article assuring the *Review* readership that harmony had returned to church leadership. In them we can find allusions that point to the Whites' authority—especially James's—as underlying the confrontation. In his first article after his mysterious absence Smith wrote that "the time has fully come for the people of God to take their stand like a well-disciplined army, the ranks all closed up, and all alienation of attitude or feeling banished from their counsels." The restored editor went on to note that "by the evident workings of the providence of God, and much to the joy of our hearts, Brother and Sister White are present with words of counsel and good cheer." Such "words of counsel" had been a point of contention with Smith and others. "We believe that those who should especially stand by him [James White], as well as believers everywhere, will be ready to second his efforts as they have not been seconded in the past. Those who have made failures [including Smith himself?] are determined to retrieve them. The time that has been lost shall be redeemed."[39] The next week Smith spoke about a lack of "true blending of spirit and union of heart" in the denomination and urged members to "close up the ranks."[40] During the following weeks he would describe the role of both James and Ellen White as a great blessing to the church.[41] The December 9 issue of the *Review* would list him as editor with James White and John Nevins Andrews.

On December 1 the Adventists in Battle Creek prayed and fasted. The local church, under the leadership of James White as its pastor, chose Uriah Smith as a local elder. Smith and White could now work together again.

Uriah's wife, Harriet, was also more open to the Whites. "Perhaps you can endure one more letter in proof that I have not forgotten or grown indifferent to the great work wrought for us in connection with your visit last fall," she wrote that winter to Ellen White. "I can never be thankful enough to God, or express how greatly it has endeared you both to my, I should say our, hearts, for I know Uriah's is drawn toward you as never before. It is my rest when weary, and a joy that will not let me be sad. . . .

"I cannot forbear one more word about Uriah. His heart is surely in the work as never before. . . . Brother White's words of encouragement in a recent letter to him gave him a cheerful countenance."[42]

[1] George Amadon, quoted in EGW to Uriah Smith and George Amadon (letter 3, 1869), Apr. 23, 1869.

[2] *Ibid.*

[3] *Defense of Eld. James White and Wife,* p. 37.

[4] Ellen G. White, *Testimonies,* vol. 1, p. 614.

[5] James White, *Life Incidents,* p. 116.

[6] JW to Gilbert Collins, Aug. 26, 1846.

[7] JW to WCW, May 28, 1877.

[8] Cited in Milton Raymond Hook, *Flames Over Battle Creek* (Washington, D.C.: Review and Herald Pub. Assn., 1977), p. 61.

[9] Hook, p. 64.

[10] Smith and White had differing perspectives on a number of issues, including biblical interpretations. For example, see Donald Ernest Mansell, *Adventists and Armegeddon: Have We Misinterpreted Prophecy?* (Nampa, Idaho: Pacific Press Pub. Assn., 1999), pp. 32-45. White and Smith disagreed on what would be the final power predicted in Daniel 11. James made a 70-minute public rebutal of Smith's presentation at a camp meeting, then published part of it as a to-be-continued article in the *Review.* Ellen White counseled her husband not to pursue the issue. She did not want denominational leaders disputing in public and thus eroding the members' confidence in them. White accepted the warning and did not print any more articles on the topic. Interestingly, White's position is closer to that of twenty-first-century Adventism than was Smith's.

[11] Uriah Smith to JW, Apr. 23, 1869.

[12] Uriah Smith to JW, May 4, 1869.

[13] Uriah Smith to JW, Nov. 16, 1869.

[14] James White, in *Review and Herald,* Dec. 20, 1870.

[15] J. N. Andrews, "Statement of Wrongs in the Course of J. N. Andrews," undated manuscript, in Joseph G. Smoot, "John N. Andrews: Humblest Man in All Our Ranks," *Adventist Heritage,* Spring 1984, p. 29.

[16] *Ibid.*

[17] In Eugene Durand, *Yours in the Blessed Hope, Uriah Smith* (Washington, D.C.: Review and Herald Pub. Assn., 1980), p. 273.

[18] Durand, pp. 273, 274.

[19] *Ibid.,* pp. 275, 277.

[20] *Ibid.,* p. 275.

[21] JW to Brother Abbey, May 12, 1873.

[22] Cited in Durand, p. 274.

[23] Durand, p. 274.

[24] *Ibid.*

[25] *Ibid.,* pp. 274, 275.

[26] J. H. Kellogg to WCW, July 8, 1873.

[27] G. I. Butler to JW and EGW, Aug. 6, 1873.

[28] J. N. Andrews, "The Cause of Present Truth," *Review and Herald,* June 24, 1873.

[29] J. N. Andrews, "Duty Toward Those That Have the Rule," *Review and Herald,* Sept. 16, 1873.

[30] D. T. Bourdeau, "Testimony No. 23," *Review and Herald,* Oct. 14, 1873.

[31] Ellen White would later have to deal with the philosophy behind Butler's article. See Knight, pp. 68-75.

[32] James White, "Leadership," *Signs of the Times,* June 4, 1874.

[33] *Ibid.*

[34] James White, "Leadership," *Review and Herald,* May 23, 1878.

[35] *Ibid.*

[36] Cited in Durand, pp. 275, 276.

[37] Durand, p. 276.

[38] Cited in Durand, p. 277.

[39] Uriah Smith, in *Review and Herald,* Nov. 18, 1873.

[40] Smith, in *Review and Herald,* Nov. 25, 1873.

[41] See, for example, "The Visit of Bro. and Sister White," *Review and Herald,* Dec. 2, 1873.

[42] Harriet Smith to EGW, Feb. 21, 1874.

CHAPTER XV

JAMES WHITE, COLLEGE PRESIDENT

THE publishing house was not the only financial problem White had to solve. By 1870 the denominational health journal, the *Health Reformer,* was losing readership and money because of poor editorial management. At first its editor, Dr. H. S. Lay, had to depend on Adventist ministers for his articles (the denomination had few medically trained people). Then Dr. Russell Trall visited the Health Reform Institute and presented a series of health lectures. Impressed by the Adventist interest in health, he offered to turn over to the *Health Reformer* the subscription list to his own periodical, the *Gospel of Health,* as well as to write a column for the Adventist health journal.

The new names from the *Gospel of Health* helped increase circulation for a time, but Dr. Trall's column soon began to alienate the readership of the *Health Reformer.* Adventist readers were uncomfortable with Trall's rejection of salt, sugar, milk, butter, and eggs. Because many lived in areas where fruit and fresh vegetables were scarce most of the year, they hesitated to drop dairy products from an already limited diet. They protested Trall's position by canceling their subscriptions. Assuming the editorship, James slowly began to turn the publication around.

White soon sought the help of a young man whom he had known for years. John Harvey Kellogg, at his suggestion, had begun to learn printing at the age of 12. The lad set type for the *How to Live* series, then spent several months with the Whites on their Greenville farm. Although an enthusiastic follower of health reform principles, he decided to become a teacher and enrolled at the state teacher's college in Ypsilanti, Michigan.

John's older half brother, Merritt Kellogg, had taken the short medical course at Russell Trall's Hygieo-Therapeutic College. Merritt, who had gone to California in 1859 and established the first Seventh-day Adventist congregation there, had studied medicine in order to strengthen his witness. Now, wanting to repeat the course in order to increase his medical background, he suggested that White's sons, Edson and Willie, might accompany him. Then both he and James White decided to encourage John Harvey Kellogg to join them.

When medicine captured John Harvey's interest, James and Ellen financed him for a year at the University of Michigan, and then a year at New York's Bellevue Hospital Medical College, a leading medical college.

Because White had more leadership assignments than he could handle, he made John Harvey Kellogg his chief editorial assistant for the *Health Reformer* as soon as the 21-year-old finished the program at Trall's school. Soon Kellogg persuaded White to drop the column by Trall. A year later Kellogg became full editor, a position he would hold until his death.

Besides the health journal, White also had to do something about the church's new health institute. The Health Reform Institute had opened in 1866 under the leadership of Drs. Lay and Phoebe Lamson (both had also worked at Jackson's Our Home on the Hillside in Dansville, New York). The church had it incorporated as a stock-issuing organization, a move that would cause great problems in later years. The institute began with just one patient in the remodeled former residence of a local judge, but within four months had filled every room of its three buildings, and soon they had to find more space. By the end of the year its directors declared a 10 percent dividend on all stock certificates. Dr. Lay now outlined a large expansion program.

Ellen White opposed any rapid growth, however. The American landscape was littered with health institutions that had briefly flourished, then vanished. She also feared that the Health Reform Institute might adopt some of the amusements that she had disliked at Dansville. In addition, she did not approve of making a profit from treating illness. Along with her husband she persuaded most of the stockholders to sign agreements in 1868 to use any future profits for charity cases.

The directors began to accept needy Seventh-day Adventists at half rates, and they soon filled the facility to the point that it could not accept regular rate patients. After only three years the institute had fallen $13,000 in debt. But after James White became president of the board of directors, things began slowly to improve. The directors appointed Dr.

William Russell as chief physician. But White concluded that the institute would not be successful until it had stronger leadership and a better-trained medical staff.

For a time James considered Merritt Kellogg as head of the institute. After working in Battle Creek for a while, Kellogg became acutely aware of the limitations of his medical training and decided to repeat the course. It was at this point that he and White encouraged his younger brother John Harvey to accompany him to Trall's school.

When John Harvey Kellogg returned from Bellevue Hospital in New York City in 1875, he joined the medical staff of the Health Reform Institute. He continued as well to edit the *Health Reformer*. Soon White campaigned for Kellogg to become chief physician, even though John Harvey was only 23. At first Kellogg resisted the idea, but finally on October 1, 1876, he accepted the position just for one year (it would stretch out to 67 years). A few months later he changed the name of the facility to Battle Creek Sanitarium and then renamed the *Health Reformer* to *Good Health*. Kellogg would make Battle Creek Sanitarium a successful and internationally recognized institution. In the process he would make White feel unneeded. Eventually tension grew between young Kellogg and his mentor.[1]

About the same time, the tract and missionary program Stephen N. Haskell had started in the New England Conference caught James's interest. He wanted a more effective way of selling books and other printed materials than personally hauling them from place to place in his luggage. The program had begun when Haskell's wife, Mary, started a prayer group with three other women (Mary Priest, Roxie Rice, and Rhoda Wheeler) to pray for their children, neighbors, and former members of the Adventist Church. Stephen Haskell encouraged his wife and other women to form the Vigilant Missionary Society, the first lay-organized ministry of the new Seventh-day Adventist Church. Soon the VMS members began sending out at their own expense hundreds of tracts and booklets, first across New England and then in foreign countries. They worked to get Adventist books in local libraries. The women also wrote letters to individuals interested in the Seventh-day Adventist message. White helped spread the new system through the church. He, Ellen, and Haskell encouraged the women to form the New England Tract and Missionary Society in 1870.

The next year Haskell presented the concept to the General Conference session. A committee appointed Haskell to encourage tract and missionary societies in the state conferences, while the VMS focused on creating societies in local congregations. White published a book in support of the societies. He saw them as a powerful tool to fulfill the mission of the church, one that would involve more of a too-passive membership. "Our people generally are spiritual dwarfs," he declared in the volume, "when they might be giants in the Lord. They are waiting for the few ministers among us to warn the world, and, at the same time, carry the churches on their shoulders, while they feel at liberty to plunge into the world, and become buried up in its rubbish. The only remedy we have to suggest for them is to lay aside unnecessary cares of this life, and to put forth individual effort for the good of those around them. In fact, this is, in our opinion, the only remedy."[2]

By 1874 the General Conference Tract and Missionary Society organized with James White as its first president. He published a monthly periodical, _The True Missionary,_ to promote its program. The various societies were already distributing nearly 5 million pages of material a year, resulting in as many converts as produced by traditional evangelistic preaching series. During the 1880s the state Tract and Missionary Societies would develop the colporteur system of door-to-door book salespeople.[3] In later years, however, as White planned a large-scale colporteur system, he would have conflicts with some of the tract societies.

James urged the establishment of a fund to pay for distribution of denominational books, especially to those unable to afford them, another manifestation of the Puritan New England tradition that stressed education and reading. His letters also show him planning a nationwide system of colporteurs, or door-to-door book salespeople. By 1880 someone had drawn outline maps for him of each county in the United States.[4] He wanted Adventist book distribution on a massive scale,[5] at one point hoping to put 500 literature evangelists in the field.[6]

In 1868 Goodloe Harper Bell (who would serve a year later on the committee to investigate White's finances) started a school in the building that had first housed the Review and Herald.[7] It caught James's attention because of his own interest in education. The General Conference adopted the school in May 1872. The next year its enrollment exceeded 100.

Sidney Brownsberger, who held a degree from the University of Michigan, replaced Bell as its principal.

James and Ellen White persuaded the March 1873 General Conference session to vote a Seventh-day Adventist Educational Society and to begin to raise funds for a college building. The man who had had no opportunity to attend college now organized one for the Seventh-day Adventist Church. He especially saw it as a way of preparing young people to serve in leadership roles and responsibilities of the growing denomination. Ellen White had begun publishing her views on education the previous year.

Because he was now president of the Educational Society, James thus served as nominal president of the college. By the end of 1873 George I. Butler, Stephen N. Haskell, and others had raised or received pledges of $54,000.

The Whites wanted to establish the college in a more rural area than Battle Creek. First they looked at a 160-acre farm on Goguac Lake, several miles south of town. When the owner demanded $50,000 for it, the couple turned their attention to a 50-acre former fairgrounds on the western edge of the city. The Educational Society, however, felt the site was too far away from the denominational institutions in Battle Creek. The students would either work at or live with their parents near the publishing house and the Health Reform Institute, and transportation between the two sites was limited. The Educational Society purchased a 12-acre property across the street from the health institute and only five or six blocks from the fairgrounds they had previously considered. They soon sold off five of those acres as building lots as a way to help finance the school.

Battle Creek College opened on August 24, 1874, with 100 students, though its three-story building would not be finished and dedicated until January 4, 1875. The school did not yet have any dormitories, and the students had to find their own places to live. Some lived in local homes, others boarded together. The ages ranged from 7 to 45, for the college also provided elementary and high school classes. The fact that so many students were young and living in unsupervised situations created problems.

Also the school struggled to define its educational philosophy and mission. Its administrators and teachers followed the then-popular Greek and Latin classics-oriented curriculum; Ellen White, in contrast, urged a program that would not only prepare students to serve the church but give them practical skills enabling them to earn a living wherever they went. The discussion went on for many years.

A number of staff members from the publishing house taught classes at the college. Review translators offered courses in foreign languages, and for a time Uriah Smith was the only Bible instructor. Students did not consider him a scintillating teacher.

White hoped his family would take advantage of the opportunities at the new institution. James wrote to Edson and his wife, Emma, that he wanted "all my children to go to school at Battle Creek College." He offered both his sons room and $100 a year to each son to attend, paid tuition for their wives, and the use of his house.[8] (Some years before he had told his sons that they should go to school six months of each year and work the other six for him.)[9]

James would also write letters of recommendation for other young people he saw as potential students.[10] He was particularly impressed with the sons of some wealthy families. A few disappointments, though, made him more cautious about whom he endorsed.

By 1881 Battle Creek College had 490 students. Through the years up to a fifth of the student body had consisted of non-Adventists from the surrounding community. In 1880 James White recommended that Brownsberger be college president instead of principal.[11]

After a number of frustrating difficulties in Battle Creek, the college moved in 1901 to rural Berrien Springs, Michigan, and renamed itself Emmanuel Missionary College. In 1959 the church merged it with Potomac University, the denomination's graduate school, and the combined institution became Andrews University, honoring Adventism's first scholar, John Nevins Andrews. The university combined its various book collections to establish the James White Library in honor of the denominational founder.[12] Perhaps White would have been pleased that when the university dedicated the new building on October 24, 1962, the individual listed in the program to offer the dedicatory prayer was Harry M. Tippett, associate book editor at the Review and Herald Publishing Association. Tippett, who had been an English teacher at Emmanuel Missionary College, represented both White's love of education and of publishing, especially book publishing.

In addition to the college, White was involved in the construction of a new building for the local Adventist congregation. The Dime Tabernacle received its name from Willie White's suggestion that church members throughout the country contribute dimes to finance it. Besides serving the Battle Creek church, the Tabernacle was also the college chapel and the largest auditorium in the city. James White was pastor of the congregation and spoke at worship and chapel services whenever he was town. Both he and Ellen held revival series for the students, and those who attended the college long remembered the couple's sermons and talks there.[13]

---

[1] The best source on Kellogg and the Battle Creek Sanitarium continues to be Richard W. Schwarz, *John Harvey Kellogg, M.D.* (Nashville: Southern Pub. Assn., 1970).

[2] James White, *An Appeal to the Working Men and Women in the Ranks of Seventh-day Adventists* (Battle Creek, Mich.: Steam Press of the Seventh-day Adventist Pub. Assn., 1873), p. 19.

[3] Schwarz, *Light Bearers to the Remnant,* pp. 152-154; Brian E. Strayer, "Called to Witness," *Adventist Review,* Jan. 24, 2002.

[4] JW to WCW, Nov. 10, 1880.

[5] See some of his plans in JW to WCW, Oct. 15, 1880; JW to WCW, Oct. 16, 1880.

[6] JW to WCW, Nov. 3, 1880.

[7] Bell's was not the first Adventist school in Battle Creek. A Mrs. M. M. Osgood had begun one in a little house in 1856 (see Emmett K. Vande Vere, *The Wisdom Seekers* [Nashville: Southern Pub. Assn., 1972], pp. 15, 16). It did not impress James White, who wrote, "We have had a thorough trial of a school at Battle Creek, under most favorable circumstances, and have given it up, as it failed to meet the expectations of those interested" (*Review and Herald,* Sept. 24, 1861).

[8] JW to J. Edson White and Emma White, Mar. 8, 1879; JW to WCW, Mar. 10, 1879.

[9] JW to Edson White and WCW, Dec. 30, 1872.

[10] See, for example, JW to Dear Brother, Dec. 21, 1876; JW to WCW, J. H. Kellogg, and S. Brownsberger, Nov. 21, 1878, and Dec. 2, 1878. If their parents were wealthy, he would note in the letter that the student should not receive any discount in tuition.

[11] For a more detailed account of James White's involvement in Battle Creek College, see Emmett K. Vande Vere, *The Wisdom Seekers.* This volume was condensed from a longer manuscript preserved in the archives of the Heritage Room at Andrews University.

[12] The library was not the first institution named in his honor. The denomination designated its first residence for the aged as the James White Memorial Home. Funded by the General Conference, it existed on West Emmett Street in Battle Creek from 1894 to 1905. Later the Lake Union Conference operated another James White Memorial Home at Plainwell, Michigan, from 1921 to 1940.

[13] Vande Vere, pp. 37, 38.

CHAPTER XVI

AN EVER-EXPANDING VISION

A S ALWAYS, James White had continued to drive himself, and by 1872 his health had, again, deteriorated. Almost completely disabled, he had retreated to another of his homes, that in Washington, Iowa. Despite his condition, however, he planned a heavy schedule of camp meetings and other appointments. Then in June Ellen received a letter from Merritt G. Kellogg, who some time before had left Battle Creek in frustration and settled in California. He had also taken a medical course from Russell Trall's medical school in 1868 and begun practicing medicine. Ellen held the letter for a few days, then showed it to her husband.

"I am grieved to learn that Brother White is so poorly," Kellogg wrote. "He has worked himself down and must have rest. Do come immediately to California and rest. Brother W. MUST cease brain labor for a time. . . . I suppose he feels that he must WORK, WORK, WORK and that the cause will suffer if he does not work, but if he works into the grave, then we will have to get along some way without him."[1] James White's health seems to have been a topic of discussion wherever the Adventist grapevine extended, including California. Having heard about James's condition, Kellogg felt free to urge his opinions.

Even though the Whites had previously decided to go to California in the fall, they now decided to leave much sooner. The Michigan Conference eventually offered to pay travel expenses if the trip would help the Whites regain their health. But instead of heading directly to California, James, Ellen, Willie, and Ellen's assistant and close friend, Lucinda Hall, would first hold some meetings in Missouri, then stop in Ottawa, Kansas, the home of Ellen's older sister, Mrs. Caroline Clough. The two women had not seen each other for 25 years, and they now spent 13 days together. While there the Whites received an invitation from Mr.

and Mrs. William B. Walling, Caroline's daughter and son-in-law. The Wallings ran a lumbering business and had a water-powered sawmill in Gregory Gulch, at the foot of the Rocky Mountains. The sawmill provided timbers for the nearby gold mines. The couple told the Whites that they would have a cabin ready for them near the mill.

A MOUNTAIN RETREAT[2]

The ride in a poorly ventilated train across the stifling heat of the plains of Kansas exhausted the already weakened James, and by the time they reached Denver, the others had to help him off the train. Unable to sit up on the benches in the railroad station waiting room, he sprawled on the floor. He spread a shawl for a mattress and tucked a sleeping bag under his head as a pillow. His wife sent their son to find Mr. Walling, who arrived with a carriage and drove them to his home.

When James regained some of his strength a few days later, Walling loaded a chuck wagon with camping equipment and took everyone on a trip over the Snowy Range. They would spend three nights and four days on the way. Most of the party went by horseback, including Ellen, who rode sidesaddle. Social custom did not yet approve of women straddling a horse.

On the second day out the bundle of blankets tied behind her on the saddle came loose and dangled against the horse's hooves. Realizing what had happened, she pulled her foot from the sidesaddle stirrup and prepared to slide to the ground before the blankets spooked the horse. But at that moment the animal became frightened. It shied and threw her backward. She fell on her back and head. For a time she could barely breathe or talk. The others prayed for her healing, then lifted her to a makeshift bed in the wagon. The party continued on its way. Later in the day Ellen was again able to mount her horse. Though weak and suffering from pain, she still managed to ride up mountainsides that she described as being as steep as a house's roof. Despite the accident, the Whites enjoyed the mountains and stayed two months. The scenery, climate, and hospitality so impressed the Whites that they decided to make the Rocky Mountains a regular vacation spot.

During July of 1873 the Whites stayed at a house near Black Hawk, Colorado, converted from a sawmill owned by the Wallings. In a letter to his brother Edson, Willie White mentioned how well their father was as he puttered about the place, mending fences, building shelves, and doing other chores.[3] When James was physically active with something that did not involve administration, his health would improve. Many times his retreats to their houses in Greenville, Michigan; Washington, Iowa; a cabin in Colorado; or elsewhere seemed the only thing that would recharge his strength and keep him from total collapse.

Mary Clough, Mrs. Walling's sister and Ellen White's niece, had filed a claim on 160 acres and built a homesteader's cabin between Central City and Rollinsville, Colorado, in the northeastern corner of Gilpin County. Now, although by herself, she was in the process of fulfilling the five-year residency the United States required for her to secure the title for the property. Mary Clough received the patent on her homestead on October 20, 1873, and James White bought the cabin and 160 acres for $100 on September 17, 1876. Earlier he had written to Ellen about buying the land for $500, but in time he devised a plan to make $3,000 by selling wood cut from the property, more than covering his expenses.[4] Wanting more land, he added another 160 acres and intended to raise hay, oats, and potatoes as well as gather wild berries. The property was about 40 miles from Denver and about four miles south of Rollinsville at an elevation of about 11,000 feet. He planned a 28' x 32' two-story house. The Whites built a number of additions, probably using lumber from the Walling sawmill. For nearly a decade during the summers they would board the narrow gauge railroad from Black Hawk, Colorado, or the regular railroad from Cheyenne or Denver to Boulder. From there they could take a stagecoach up a newly constructed road to the cabin. After 1872 they could ride the Colorado Central narrow gauge directly from Denver to Black Hawk.[5] James continued the nursery sideline he had started at Greenville, Michigan, and grew strawberries and raspberries on the Colorado land.[6]

The times the Whites spent in their Colorado cabin were often what we would today call working vacations. During one visit James—along with his protégé D. M. Canright—held the state's first Adventist evangelistic meetings in a schoolhouse in Golden. Canright had accompanied him to Colorado as a male nurse and companion. White lodged at the home of a Mrs. Shaw, who had already been an Adventist when she had come to the Colorado territory as a young girl. Her husband and several others joined the Adventist Church.[7]

In 1878 church leaders sent Merritt E. Cornell, one of the denomination's most successful tent evangelists, to Boulder. James was at the family cabin while Ellen was making the round of camp meetings in California. Early in August, when she had finished her speaking appointments, she, along with her daughter-in-law Emma White and Edith Donaldson, took the train to Boulder. There they stayed at the home of an Amy Dartt. Mrs. Dartt, the second Adventist in Colorado, had become famous for distributing Adventist tracts to townspeople. Cornell lent the evangelistic tent for a series of community temperance meetings. Because of Mrs. White's reputation as a temperance orator, the organizers invited her to lecture them.

Still at his mountain vacation home along with Canright, White took up hiking in the cool mountain air, hoping to increase his endurance by a mile a day until he could race up the mountainside "like a deer." He also talked about swimming in the cold mountain lakes.[8] Then a Mrs. Thayer, the Adventist wife of a miner in Georgetown, Colorado, sent a letter to the men, asking that they hold meetings in her community. Cornell moved the tent to the mining town. By now all the White family except Edson had arrived at the cabin, and one weekend they all went to help the evangelist. James presented three sermons, and the others sang. The Georgetown series, though successful, did not last long. At 9,000 feet the weather soon turned too cold, and the meetings had to halt on September 22, a time that would still be mild at a lower altitude.

A MISSION TO OTHER TONGUES AND PEOPLES

As he stayed at his mountain cabin White found himself able to stand back and look more objectively at the current needs, prospects, and condition of the Seventh-day Adventist Church. On the one hand, he and Ellen were concerned about what they regarded as the Laodicean spiritual condition of the church. They saw a strong need for spiritual revival. On the other hand, James had a growing sense of its mission and what it would take to accomplish it.

He began to outline some of his ideas and proposals in a 47-page document titled *An Earnest Appeal* that he addressed to "the General Conference Committee, the 'Picked Men' at Battle Creek, the Committees

of the State Conferences, and the Officers of the Several Branches of Our
Tract and Missionary Society."

One of his primary interests, of course, concerned the denomination's
publishing program. He immediately wanted to print evangelistic material
in the various northern European languages spoken by the thousands of immigrants flocking to the United States. In 1874 he urged the General
Conference to spend $20,000 preparing, translating, and publishing peri-
odicals and tracts in German, Danish, Swedish, as well as French
(Adventists had already done some evangelism among French-speaking
Canadians). The Review and Herald would be the church's primary foreign
language publisher until the 1902 fire. With its production facilities destroyed, the Review had to turn over foreign language publishing responsibilities to a Chicago-based entity. Pacific Press would later buy the
organization and transfer all foreign language production to the West Coast.

In his special document White suggested some ways of expanding the
production capacity of denominational publishing. "We have recently been
looking over the broad field relative to our publishing interests. We think
the time has come to stereotype [a new type of printing plates] our standard books, pamphlets, and tracts, and at the same time make two sets of
plates, one for a branch office on the Pacific Coast, and one for the Atlantic.
This would reduce the cost of our publications, and the need of capital and
office room in Battle Creek. . . . The day is not far distant when our publications will be printed from duplicate plates, both on the Pacific and
Atlantic coasts. This will greatly reduce our typesetting, and our heavy
freights on publications from the interior to the east and to the west."[9]

But James's greatest concern was to extend the church's evangelistic
outreach. He mentioned a willingness by the General Conference
Committee to begin evangelism in Oregon and the Washington Territory.
And he wanted to use the foreign language publications in more than just
the United States. White urged the General Conference to "extend its missions to Europe, to the Pacific, and, in fact, in all directions, as far as the
calls can be supplied."[10]

James began negotiating with George I. Butler to call an early meeting
of the General Conference session that year in order to implement some
of White's ideas. Butler was sympathetic to the proposals. In the *Review* he
wrote of James's proposals, "We are in the fullest sympathy. We are not

ignorant of the fact that he has laid out before us an immense amount of work. Neither do we believe mere human agencies can ever accomplish it alone. . . . We believe God has a *special* work for these last days, and that work must go to 'peoples, nations, tongues, and kings.' It is worldwide."[11]

FIRST MISSIONARY TO EUROPE

On October 23 White sent a telegram from nearby Black Hawk, Colorado, to Butler, urging the General Conference session be set for November 14 to 18. One of the upcoming issues would regard a missionary to Europe. The logical candidate was John N. Andrews. But first White and church leadership would have to deal with the problems caused by the strained relations between James and Andrews' brother-in-law, Uriah Smith, as well as serious questions about Andrews himself.

The 1873 General Conference session enabled the Whites and Uriah Smith to work out their differences (see pp. 178-182), but tension continued between James and Ellen White and J. N. Andrews. Although in a separate article in the *Review* Butler had specifically mentioned Andrews learning French and German to go to Europe to head Adventist missions there,[12] the records of the meeting remain silent on the topic. Apparently James White was not ready to endorse Andrews.

His wife also had—and would continue to have—serious reservations about the evangelist-scholar. She saw the cause of many of J. N. Andrews' problems as stemming from the influence of the Smith and Andrews families upon each other. When Andrews had begun first courting Angeline Stevens back in Rochester, Mrs. White had opposed the marriage, perhaps recognizing what the interaction between the two families, with their history of fanaticism, would lead to. Finally she gave her consent, but only because the relationship had progressed so far that a breakup would have devastated Angeline.

Ellen believed that the unstable chemistry between the Smith and Andrews families had led J. N. Andrews to, in her words, "crave for sympathy, to love to be pitied, to be regarded as one suffering privation and as a martyr."[13] Andrews' character flaws were longstanding. According to a letter Ellen White wrote him a few years later, these flaws led him to dwell on self, mourn the death of his wife and daughter to the point of obsession, be driven, as a leader, to control others, and to worship intellect.[14]

During the remainder of 1873 and through early 1874 the General Conference committee stalled on any decision to send Andrews as its first overseas missionary. In a February 6, 1874, letter to Ellen White, Andrews acknowledged that the committee wanted him to prove himself before they authorized him to go—"that I should show that I was again made strong in God before being sent on this work."[15] As far as he was concerned, he "thought this all right."[16] On February 24 he wrote to James White that he would "be ready very shortly to go to Europe unless you think I should not go."[17] Then on April 21 he announced his intention to return to Rochester, sell his home there, and "start for Europe at once if there be no light to the contrary."[18] Apparently Andrews was willing to leave without official General Conference sponsorship, but not without approval from the Whites, particularly James.

As James and Ellen White procrastinated, George I. Butler decided to take action. At the August 1874 General Conference session he recommended that it make a decision, "especially in consideration that Elder J. N. Andrews is about to take his departure to engage in the cause in Switzerland."[19] The delegates voted that the executive committee send Andrews "to Switzerland as soon as possible."[20]

Whatever his own feelings or those of his wife, James White decided to support the session's decision. He gave his formal approval through an article in the *Review:* "Eld. J. N. Andrews, who had nobly defended the truth from his very youth, leaves for Europe, probably before these lines shall meet the eyes of the patrons of the *Review*. God bless him."[21] Andrews would begin James White's vision of global evangelism.

But even though White had acceded to Butler's push to get Andrews to Europe, that did not mean that James fully trusted Andrews. After Andrews had been in Switzerland a couple years and Daniel T. Bordeau had joined him, James wrote to Willie White, "You know that Andrews and Bordeau would make a fool of it if they should try."[22] White wanted to send his son to Basel, Switzerland, to manage the new publishing house. A month later White informed Willie that he would like to take Andrews and Bordeau to task for the way they were handling things in Europe.[23] The strokes James kept suffering made it increasingly difficult for him to trust others.

PACIFIC PRESS PUBLISHING ASSOCIATION

During 1873 James also conceived of and urged a weekly religious newspaper on the West Coast, as well as a publishing house. In June 1874 he founded what would become the weekly *Signs of the Times* and served as its first editor. His name would remain on the masthead as editor until his death. At first he had the magazine commercially printed in Oakland, California. As had been the case with the *Review and Herald,* White wanted a denominational publishing house to produce the periodical. An appeal at the October 1874 camp meeting in Yountville, California, raised $19,414 in gold dust and pledges to construct the church's second publishing entity. The California Adventists were much more spontaneously generous than their fellow believers in the East. Still, James White obtained an additional $10,000 in pledges in the eastern United States, and on April 1, 1875, the Pacific Seventh-day Adventist Publishing Association organized with John N. Loughborough as its first president.

O. B. Jones, who had erected the Review and Herald building in Battle Creek, now came to supervise the construction of the publishing house on Castro Street in Oakland. Duplicating what he had done in Rochester, White purchased equipment in New York and persuaded five young people to return with him to the new institution in the West. And, as with the Review and Herald, James White not only helped found Pacific Press but would provide it leadership. Though Loughborough served as president for two years, and then William C. White from 1876-1877, James White would be president 1877-1878 and 1879-1880.

White threw himself into Pacific Press as thoroughly as he had the Review and Herald. He determined to make it a success, wanting it to stand on its own, without continual support from the Review.[24] At one point he wrote to his sons—who both worked at the new institution—that "unless the manufacture of type proves a failure, and job [commercial] work fails at Oakland, I decide that the Pacific Press is the Little Giant, and does not need to be favored one mile by Review Office."[25]

Even when he was in the East he involved himself in the press. James particularly enjoyed buying and selling paper and printing supplies, and he acted as a purchasing agent for the West Coast publishing house. His letters contain many references to the jobbing of paper and of visits to paper mills.[26] The paper jobbing offered him a source of extra income, about $2 to $10 a day (at a time when a laborer earned $1 a day) dealing in paper stock.[27] Sometimes, though, his paper brokerage could be as much a problem as a help.

James had great plans for the new periodical *Signs of the Times*. "It must be and can be our best paper," he assured Willie.[28] A few months later he declared to his son that he thought *Signs* edited better than the *Review*.[29] Could there be a hint of rivalry with Uriah Smith, editor of the *Review?*[30]

But his involvement in Pacific Press created problems for his sons. He trusted them more than he did others in Oakland, but only to a point. He could not fully let go of control even to his sons, and he micromanaged Willie. White would nitpick on grammatical details of *Signs*, and though across the country, he would send Willie detailed editorial instructions.[31]

While determined to build up Pacific Press, he still didn't find it easy to get along with its management. Soon he became as frustrated with them as he was with the Adventists in Battle Creek.[32] His letters to people at Oakland could become quite critical.[33]

Also, White's financial dealings with Pacific Press created an ongoing tension. He did not feel that the publishing house paid him as promptly and fully as he thought they should. His letters to Willie during his son's years in Oakland are full of references to James's need to get cash from the publishing house or requests for Willie to prepare new notes on money owed either to James or the publishing house.[34] Besides his financial dealings with the publishing institution,[35] White wrote to his son of other financial notes and loans and rents on houses he owned. Sometimes his business dealings could become quite tangled.[36] He constantly reminded Willie to make sure his father's money was drawing a good interest[37] and would write about the price of gold and greenbacks.[38] The amounts of money involved in the various transactions were highly impressive for the time.

Because of his strokes, White was finding it harder to get along with others. But the magnitude of what he was still accomplishing would have been impressive even if done by a much healthier person.

---

[1] M. G. Kellogg to EGW, June 6, 1872.

[2] Renowned historian Everett Dick's article "For Health and Wealth" (*Adventist Heritage*, Fall 1982) explores the beginning of Seventh-day Adventists in the state of

Colorado and provides a useful source and outline to reconstruct James White's years at his beloved Rocky Mountain cabin. As was the practice with *Adventist Heritage* articles, it does not provide documentation, however, and I could not independently verify some points he made. The Dick article is interesting also in that Dick did not write much about denominational history after LeRoy Edwin Froom blocked the publication of his doctoral dissertation on the Millerites. Instead, Dick became an expert on the history of the trans-Mississippi West (see the foreword by Gary Land in Dick, *William Miller and the Advent Crisis,* pp. vii, viii). Thus he wrote this article near the end of his career.

[3] WCW to J. Edson White, July 4, 1873.

[4] JW to EGW, Aug. 30, 1878.

[5] Dick, "For Health and Wealth," pp. 18-27.

[6] JW to WCW, Apr. 27, 1879.

[7] Dick, "For Health and Wealth," p. 21.

[8] James White, in *Review and Herald,* July 25, 1878.

[9] James White, *An Earnest Appeal.*

[10] *Ibid.,* p. 29.

[11] George I. Butler, "Testimony No. 23 and Bro. White's Address," *Review and Herald,* Nov. 4, 1873.

[12] Butler, "The General Conference," *Review and Herald,* Nov. 4, 1873.

[13] Quoted in Smoot, "J. N. Andrews: Humblest Man in All Our Midst," pp. 32, 33. See the Smoot article for more background on the problems Andrews struggled with and Ellen White's evaluation of him.

[14] Smoot, "J. N. Andrews," p. 33.

[15] Smoot, "J. N. Andrews," p. 30.

[16] *Ibid.*

[17] *Ibid.*

[18] *Ibid.*

[19] Smoot, "J. N. Andrews," pp. 30, 31.

[20] Smoot, p. 31.

[21] James White, in *Review and Herald,* Sept. 15, 1874.

[22] JW to WCW, Apr. 12, 1876.

[23] JW to WCW, May 16, 1876.

[24] JW to WCW, July 5, 1874.

[25] JW to J. Edson White and WCW, July 15, 1878.

[26] See, for example, JW to WCW, Lucinda, Anna, and Mary, Aug. 1, 1875; JW to WCW, Feb. 20, 1879; JW to J. Edson White, Jan. 16, 1880.

[27] JW to WCW, Feb. 11, 1879.

[28] JW to WCW, Apr. 29, 1875.

[29] JW to WCW, July 21, 1875.

[30] Sadly, though, White became more critical of *Signs,* especially as he began to feel shut out as a writer for it. See, for example, JW to WCW, Nov. 3, 1880; JW to WCW, Nov. 13, 1880; JW to WCW, Dec. 10, 1880. *Signs* duplicated somewhat the role of the *Review,* and

this created some tensions between the editors of the two periodicals. "Had I not established that Press at great labor and expense," he told Willie, "I should feel differently. And
now as long as you, the Directors, and the General Conference Committee choose to main-
tain such rigid silence in the matter, I shall feel released from duty to the *Signs* or Pacific
Press. I shall turn my attention to the *Review,* and do all I can to increase its circulation.
The *Signs* should not supplant the *Review.* I shall do nothing directly against the *Signs,* but
I shall establish the *Review* everywhere as our church paper, this side the Rocky
Mountains" (JW to WCW, Dec. 12, 1880).

[31] JW to WCW, July 21, 1875 ("I will suggest that in one place a (;) would have been
better than a (,)"); JW to WCW, Aug. 24, 1875.

[32] See, for example, JW to WCW, Lucinda, Anna, and Mary, Aug. 1, 1875; JW to EGW,
Apr. 7, 1876; JW to WCW, June 7, 1876; JW to WCW and Mary White, July 3, 1876; JW
to WCW, Dec. 10, 1880.

[33] See, for example, JW to Lucinda Hall, Jan. 14, 1880.

[34] See, for example, JW to WCW, June 7, 1876; JW to WCW, July 3, 1876; JW to
WCW, Jan. 16, 1880; JW to WCW, Jan. 28, 1880; JW to WCW, Apr. 30, 1880; JW to
WCW, May 12, 1880; JW to WCW, June 2, 1880.

[35] See, for example, JW to WCW, Lucinda, Anna, and Mary, Aug. 1, 1875; JW to
WCW, June 7, 1876.

[36] See, for example, JW to WCW, Apr. 30, 1880.

[37] For example, see JW to WCW, June 18, 1876; JW to WCW, July 3, 1876.

[38] JW to WCW, July 21, 1875; JW to My Dear Children, Willie and Mary, July 3, 1876.

CHAPTER XVII

JAMES WHITE, TRAIL BOSS

JAMES'S health, again, through sheer exhaustion, deteriorated during the 1870s. By the late 1870s he was approaching 60 at a time when few managed to live that long. Though pleading for younger men to take over his heavy responsibilities, he found it difficult to actually let go of them.

Church leaders occasionally grumbled in denominational publications that church members took the great Advent movement too literally. Adventists were constantly moving westward with the rest of their fellow Americans to seek better opportunities. For a time the Iowa Conference was the church's second-largest conference, before the wave of westward expansion flowed on to more distant territories.

THE WHITES IN TEXAS

In June 1876 a group of Adventists left Michigan for northern Texas. The settlers included James and Roxie Cornell, William and Hannah Moore, and Hiram and Melinda McDearman, who were the parents of Emma, Edson White's wife. William Moore had consumption and hoped the Texas climate would improve his health. Unfortunately, malaria was widespread there and quickly struck the newcomers.

Word soon spread through the Adventist grapevine about their problems. An Adventist camp meeting had been planned in Texas for November 1878. The Whites decided to speak at it and to check on the condition of the McDearmans and the other Adventists from Michigan. When James and Ellen finished their appointments in Kansas, they rode the train to Callas, Texas, not far from Grand Prairie, where the McDearmans lived.

Malaria had left Edson's in-laws so weak that they could no longer work and were on the edge of starvation. Ellen White remarked that they resembled corpses. Before the Whites left for the scheduled Texas camp meeting at Plano, near Dallas, James bought them sacks of flour, nuts, a barrel of apples, sugar, codfish, potatoes, and other supplies.[1] He even purchased beds for them and handed Mr. McDearman his own coat. Ellen gave them $40. Emma White remained behind to help her parents.

A blind man in the area, named J. F. Bahler, earned a meager livelihood selling a printed life story that he had put together. White became interested in him and worked with Willie at Pacific Press to get a better edition of the pamphlet printed. Bahler also asked James to build a house for him that the Whites would share while in Texas.[2]

Shortly before Christmas what Texans call a "blue northerner" raced down the plains from Canada and plunged the temperature below freezing. At that time of year such cold fronts can drop the temperature from the 80s to the 30s or less in a few hours. But that year was even worse than usual. People who had lived in the area for a long time judged the weather the coldest they had ever seen. James White muttered that they had to chop their teeth out of solid ice each morning before they could eat breakfast. Snow began to fall. Generally the temperature quickly returns to normal and melts the rare dusting of snow. But the cold hung on long enough that the snow accumulated to the point that James had to remove the wheels from his carriage and replace them with runners. He contacted his son in Battle Creek to send him a pair of woolen socks each week until the tenth of February. But by January 23 he could report to Willie, "The winter is past."[3]

Wanting to help all the suffering Adventists, James resorted to his entrepreneurial skills. Buying buffalo and wildcat skins, he shipped them to the Northeast for a good profit and purchased Michigan butter, nuts, beans, and other items and sold them in Texas for still more profit. He used the money to help his fellow Adventists. After selling $4 worth of brooms one day, he toyed with the idea of starting a broom factory to employ the needy Adventists and even discussed with Willie about ordering equipment for it. Mrs. White did not approve of all her husband's business activities. These in Texas particularly bothered her.[4] But, as revealed in his letters, her opinions did not stop his projects. His sidelines seemed to distract him from the stress of church leadership, and his health would usually get better when he threw himself into such endeavors. And, at least as early as 1855, he had himself noticed that his health would improve when he got away from his office duties and traveled among the church membership.[5]

When he discovered that mules sold for $200 in Colorado mining country and that he could obtain them for $80 in Texas, he thought of still another way of aiding the destitute and sick Adventists. The climate of Colorado had helped his own health, so why not move them there along with a herd of mules that they could sell to pay for their expenses? He could also get $60 ponies at $25.[6]

First James had to convince the people of the advantages of Colorado. When William Moore asked if the new state (Colorado had joined the union in 1876) had chills and fever such as he had been suffering, White replied, "Nary a chill! Nary a chill!" James hired someone to buy mules and bring them to a corral in Denison, Texas, until the Adventists could start the drive north. (White predicted Denison would be one of the most prosperous and populated parts of Texas because of the four railroads that ran through it.) One day the herd broke out of the corral and fled across the rolling plains. Fortunately White had someone who knew how to round up the animals. A young minister from Iowa tracked the mules down. Perhaps it gave Arthur G. Daniells some valuable experience for his later career as General Conference president.

While in Texas, James carried on extensive correspondence with Willie on both personal and church matters. When Willie did not respond on one matter as quickly as his father thought he should have, James fired off a letter declaring, "The United States Mail still runs from Michigan to Texas."[7]

ACROSS INDIAN TERRITORY

The expedition started from Dallas on March 19 with 15 people traveling in two heavily-loaded wagons, two two-seated wagons, and the Whites' carriage. They planned to meet the others in Denison. That segment took two days, and they arrived in time to set up camp before Sabbath. The Whites had planned to speak at a May 15 camp meeting at Emporia, Kansas, but sickness and flooding along the Red River delayed the start of the mule drive. William Moore came down with food poisoning from eating partially decomposed bear meat. Even when he could travel, he had to ride on a mattress in one of the covered wagons.

Finally the expedition decided it had better be on its way regardless.

But by then James Cornell was so sick that the rest felt it would be best if they left him behind. Moore had to break the news to him. "You can dig a hole and bury me by the side of the road as easy as they can in Texas," Cornell replied in a barely audible voice. The others decided to take him with them. The 30 men, women, and children traveled in eight covered wagons and James White's two-seater spring carriage. Their equipment included three tents, two cookstoves, and a sheet-iron camp stove. The wagon train headed 45 miles up the Red River to where they could transfer the herd of mules by a crude, pole-propelled ferry to the Indian Territory (modern Oklahoma) side. Once across the river they had to drive off the ferry onto shore as quickly as possible because of quicksand. Then, under the leadership of James White and John O. Corliss, they followed the Chisholm Trail north to Kansas. Between 1866 and 1885 Texas cattlemen drove more than 6 million longhorn cattle across the Indian lands to the railroad centers in Kansas to be shipped to market in the East. Two Adventist ministers would add a herd of mules and horses to the history of the Chisholm Trail. (James had also thought to take along some cattle, but decided to sell them in Texas.)[8]

The mule drive would struggle with broken-down wagons, cloudbursts that flooded rivers, more sickness, accidents, and other delays. Before they could finish trenching around the tents on the first night on the trail a severe storm struck and flooded the tents with several inches of water. Ellen and three other women slept crosswise on her bed, and James shared a wagon with a Dr. Hardin. Along the way they encountered tarantulas. Hardin caught "two immense fellows that look frightful" and put them in bottles.[9]

At night the wagons formed a circle with the mules and horses in the center to protect them from marauders both human and animal. Two men carrying guns stood guard in two-hour shifts. The travelers feared that White men might pay Indians to stampede their herd and steal the animals. But James White thoroughly enjoyed himself as trail boss, living out the dream of so many Americans of being a cowboy. "Father rides horseback a considerable part of the time," his wife wrote. "He is enjoying the journey much."[10] Again—as so many times before when he let himself be caught up in something that did not involve church administration and kept him physically active—his health improved. In fact, he said that he had taken "this long, slow journey to save [prevent] a breakdown and improve health."[11]

The wagon train first wound its way through the Arbuckle Mountains. The 600- to 700-foot hills had unusual geological formations and scenic woodlands. Ellen White liked the scenery but little else of the trip. "It seemed very lonesome journeying in the thick forest," she recorded in her diary. "We thought what might be if robbers or horse thieves—Indians or white men—should molest us, but we had a vigilant watch guarding the animals."[12]

Leaving the Arbuckle Mountains, they crossed the Sandstone Hills region. The hills here were much lower, only 250-400 feet high and covered with blackjack and post oak forests. The eastern part of the state was the home of the so-called Five Civilized Tribes: the Cherokee, the Chickasaw, the Choctaw, the Creek, and the Seminole. They had earned their name because, before the United States government forcibly moved them from the Southeastern states, they had adopted many habits and customs of the Whites. Until the Civil War many had even owned slaves.

James and Ellen received a number of requests to speak along the way to the many non-Indians who had already settled in the territory. (Ellen wound up giving most of the devotionals in the wagon train—no one else wanted to do it.) James also spoke in the Indian council house in Okmulgee on Friday, May 9. Like a typical tourist, White wrote of the things he saw. Explaining that Okmulgee was the capital of the Creek Nation tribes, he told Willie that "we have just passed the council building, which exceeds most of the county houses of any of the new Western States" and that the Indians governed themselves through 100 councilmen who met periodically.[13]

UNHAPPY CAMPERS

Unfortunately, Ellen did not enjoy the trip, as she had to do much of the work. She and her assistant, Marian Davis, had to feed everyone. "No rest, not a bit of it, for poor Marian," Ellen later wrote to her daughter-in-law Mary White. "We have worked like slaves. We cooked repeatedly half the night, Marian the entire night. . . . Unpack and pack, hurry, cook, set table, has been the order of the day."[14] Early in the morning Ellen would pick wild strawberries and greens to stretch their limited food supply. One of the boys among them would always remember finding James sitting under a small tree eating an apple.

James explained to him that all he had had for breakfast that day was a few dry crackers.

Ellen also worried if the trip was even necessary. Should she be doing something more important? "I had rather attend twenty camp meetings with all their wear, knowing I was doing good to souls, than to be here traveling through the country. The scenery is beautiful, the changes and variety enjoyable; but I have so many fears that I am not in the line of my duty. Oh, when will this fearful perplexity end?"[15] Yet the trip did provide a break for James, and his health did improve. And he apparently did some serious thinking about his future.

He wrote to Willie that "I design to take a humble and more quiet position among my brethren, and move out as the providence of God and my brethren call me out. I felt very confident that I was doing my duty in writing the address I called back, and certain articles which have been suppressed, but the liberties taken with these has astonished me,[16] and has led me to my present position which may be stated thus:

"1: I am probably incapacitated by sickness and care, and my distance from the Lord to take a leading position in matters and things.

"2: Or my brethren, for some reasons, after putting me in high position, take strange liberties in not allowing me to speak as formerly, through the press.

"3: In either case the only consistent course for me is to retire from the fort, until it is decided fully where the fault is. At Emporia [Kansas] [camp meeting] I shall try to preach the Gospel. Then my work will be done at that campmeeting.

"4: I shall not spend these next six months in reading and answering letters pertaining to the entire cause and in writing articles to be suppressed, as I have the last six months. . . . Therefore, I shall report myself through the *Review* as refusing all correspondence on such matters, and shall refer the brethren to Elders Canright and Haskell. . . .

"6: I shall not hold myself in the least responsible for the debts upon our institutions, and shall no more commit and identify myself with the run-in-debt policy by setting example of liberality by large pledges, and encouraging the brethren to submit to the policy."[17]

It must have been extremely frustrating to the rest of the church leadership to have the president constantly questioning and challenging their decisions. Also, as we shall see, as his increasingly erratic behavior was becoming an embarrassment to them, they blocked the publication of some of his articles. Their resistance forced White to face the fact that he was no longer in complete control.

"The time was when it was my place to lead off, and where necessary to storm it through," he observed to his children. "Times changed, and organization came in. Then I had to hold the important offices from necessity. But the work became too large for any one man to stand at the head of all branches. And now the time has come for me to retire, and let younger men come to the front. I had a work to do, a place to fill. Now the work is too large for one of my age and temperament to preside over."[18]

Because of the delays James concluded that he and Ellen would not reach Emporia, Kansas, by the time the camp meeting there would start. He sent a message to Battle Creek that they would not get there by May 15. The next *Review* announced that the Kansas camp meeting would be postponed a week. When the wagon train camped near Coopersville, James sent someone to the post office five miles away. Learning that the camp meeting would start a week later, he thought he might make it there by the new date. After reaching a railroad line in Kansas, James and Ellen had less than an hour to grab their trunks and without changing from their trail clothes, catch a train to the camp meeting in Emporia. There they hired a coach known as an omnibus, pulled by four horses, and raced the two miles to the campground. By then Ellen had lost 12 pounds. She wrote to Mary White, "I am worn and feel as though I was about one hundred years old. . . . This journey has nearly killed me. My ambition is gone; my strength is gone . . . I have not had even time to keep a diary or write a letter."[19]

"I tell you, Willie," she wrote to her son, "I shall never, never consent to go any place with Father alone again. It is the last time."[20]

James White wrote to his children the same day as Ellen and reported that his health was the best it had been in four years.[21]

Two days later Corliss and the rest of the wagon train pulled into the Emporia camp meeting, where they rested. At the end of the camp meeting Corliss led them along the Arkansas River on a roundabout route toward Boulder, Colorado. Some of the wagon train stopped at Pueblo, Colorado; others at Denver. The rest arrived at Boulder on June 9.

William Moore took the mules to the Whites' cabin and sold them. James was offered $350 for a span of mules that had cost him $240 in Texas.[22] Some of the Adventists found work at the various Walling sawmills, while others cut trees for them. And true to James's promise, the Colorado climate did improve the health of those who had come from Texas, including James Cornell.

The Whites had thought to avoid the stress of a heavy camp meeting appointment calendar, but after speaking at Emporia and the Missouri camp meeting, they would now hurry from one gathering to another. First they went to Battle Creek, where James spoke at the new Dime Tabernacle Friday evening, Sabbath morning, and Sabbath afternoon. A news note in the *Review* commented on how healthy he appeared. After speaking at a number of eastern camp meetings, the Whites returned to Boulder for a few days. Then Ellen boarded the train for California, and James spent the rest of the summer at the mountain cabin.

STRUGGLING TO LET GO

As the 1870s neared their end James White continued to wrestle with whether he should retire or not. "I shall take it easy, and grow old gracefully, and make you all love me half to death,"[23] he wrote to his sons. But his personality and circumstances would not allow him to turn over leadership to others. He had personally built up so much of the church that he could not let go easily. White still felt just as intensely as he had when he wrote to Willie in 1870: "At prayers this morning a sense of the importance of our having oversight of the entire work came upon me, and for a moment I could not speak."[24] Six years later he explained to Willie that "I am doing splendidly here in getting things in real good shape at the school, Institute, and Office, and I cannot possibly leave just now, and let these institutions suffer great loss."[25]

At times he recognized his driving personality, as when he told Willie, "You and Edson will come out all right. If you did not put your whole soul into what you are doing, you would not be like your father. Neither would you amount to much."[26] He also acknowledged another problem when he wrote one time to Ellen "that Willie may be in as much danger of taking extreme views . . . as his father."[27] James admitted to Willie that "I undertake to do too much work. I shall not deny that I love to work, and am inclined to take too much on my hands."[28] And one wonders what White's fellow denominational leaders would have thought if they had seen his cryptic comment to his wife that the Spirit of God did not initiate all his feelings or the things he wrote.[29] But it is one thing to be aware of personality traits and quite another to change them. White found it impossible to step aside voluntarily and let others take charge. He would never have the chance to retire to a life of ease and family.

---

[1] JW to WCW, Nov. 12, 1878.

[2] JW to WCW, Nov. 20, 1878.

[3] JW to WCW, Jan. 23, 1879.

[4] EGW to Brother and Sister Daniels (letter 32, 1879), July 17, 1879. Later she would miss James's business talents. Three years after his death she wrote to his brother, John White, that without her husband's skill and help her financial position was deteriorating (EGW to John White, Nov. 27, 1884).

[5] James White, in Review and Herald, May 29, 1855.

[6] J. Edson White to WCW, Nov. 12, 1878.

[7] JW to WCW and Mary White, Mar. 3, 1879.

[8] JW to WCW and Mary White, Feb. 27, 1879.

[9] EGW to WCW and Mary White (letter 20a, 1879), May 3, 1879.

[10] EGW to Children (letter 36, 1879), May 4, 1879.

[11] JW to Children, May 11, 1879. Ellen White also recognized her husband's need for physical or other activity to distract him from his problems. See, for example, how she urged James to make a vacation out of his time at their Rocky Mountain cabin (EGW letter 1, 1878).

[12] EGW manuscript 4, 1879.

[13] JW to Children, May 11, 1879.

[14] EGW to Mary White (letter 20, 1879), May 20, 1879.

[15] EGW to WCW and Mary White (letter 20a, 1879), May 3, 1879.

[16] Apparently White had written articles that upset other church leaders. Most likely they involved criticism of decisions and policies made by others (probably financial matters).

[17] JW to Children, May 11, 1879.

[18] Ibid.

[19] EGW to Mary White (letter 20, 1879), May 20, 1879.

[20] EGW to WCW and Mary White (letter 20a, 1879), May 3, 1879.

[21] JW to Children, May 20, 1879.

[22] JW to WCW, July 28, 1879.

[23] JW to Children, May 20, 1879.

[24] JW to WCW, Lucinda, Mary, and Anna, June 17, 1870.

[25] JW to WCW, Oct. 31, 1876.
[26] JW to WCW, July 15, 1878.
[27] JW to EGW, Apr. 18, 1880.
[28] JW to WCW, May 4, 1880.
[29] JW to EGW, July 4, 1880.

Ch∱PTER XVIII

RECONCILIATION

B Y THE late 1870s James and Ellen White felt increasingly concerned about the lack of Christ-centered sermons in Seventh-day Adventist churches and evangelistic series.[1] James more and more expressed a desire to write and to avoid wearing himself out attending every camp meeting.[2] He dreamed of his writings being printed by the millions and translated into other languages.[3] In 1881 James and Ellen decided to stop their exhausting schedule of camp meeting and other speaking appointments and instead collaborate in preparing studies on "the glorious subject of redemption that should long ago have been more fully presented to the people."[4]

James vowed to bring the denomination to a much more Christ-oriented presentation of "present truth." "I have a burden on me to preach Christ, Christ, *Christ,* through the *Signs* this winter," he had written the previous September, "then in the spring have a volume to be translated in all the languages where there is a call for the book."[5] The book, one that colporteurs could sell, would center around a revised version of his allegorical engraving on the plan of salvation, "The Way of Life."[6] White told Willie that "God has pressed upon my soul the subject of Redemption through Christ, and I must devote myself to it. The subject is opening to me with still greater power. I design to give it in articles through the *Signs,* then revise it for a book of ten forms [signatures], 320 pages, large type headed, and thick paper to make up a bound book of the clearest cut matter. And as it will be put in French, German, Danish and Swedish, it should be carefully written and brief."[7] In his mind White named it *Christ, the Way of Life: From Paradise Lost to Paradise Restored.*[8]

Although it has been suggested that Ellen White instigated the more Christocentric "Christ, the Way of Life,"[9] James's letters indicate that he was already consulting with the engraver on changes that he wanted to make. In fact, he planned to call the new version "Behold the Lamb of God" and specifically said that he already had a sketch of it with the "Law tree" removed and a larger Christ on the cross placed in the center of the engraving.[10]

He told the church that "we feel that we have a testimony for our people at this time, relative to the exalted character of *Christ,* and his willingness and power to save." We can see certain themes running through his writings. Earlier we noted his 1850 statement that salvation was all through Christ. In his 1868 *Life Incidents* he declared, "The hope of eternal salvation hangs upon Christ. Adam hung his hope there. Abel, Enoch, Noah, Abraham, and the believing Jews, hung theirs there. We can do no more. The hope of the next life depends upon Christ. Faith in his blood can alone free us from our transgressions."[11]

James developed the themes even more fully in several tracts that he published. In one that he had written in 1877 he declared that "the Scriptures reveal but one plan by which fallen men may be saved," and that was that "Jesus Christ is the Redeemer of sinners in all the ages of probation."[12] Furthermore, he proclaimed that "the church of all ages is the church of Jesus Christ. He is the world's only Redeemer."[13] "When sin had separated man from God, the plan of redemption made Christ the connecting link between God and the offending sinner."[14] He demonstrates in the tract that Jesus was the channel through which God communicated the plan of salvation to humanity.

That same year in another tract he spoke of "our adorable Redeemer as the only means of redemption from sin."[15] "The kingdom of grace is God's plan to save men by grace. It was established as early as mercy and grace were offered to fallen man. Adam, Abel, Noah, Abraham and Moses were as truly the subjects of the kingdom of grace as the apostles and martyrs of Jesus were, or as the followers of Christ now are. If it be said that the kingdom of grace was set up by our Lord Jesus Christ at his first advent, then we inquire, Had God no kingdom of grace before that time? If not, then Enoch, Noah, Lot, Abraham, Isaac, Jacob, Moses, and the prophets, have perished without hope; for certainly no man can be saved without grace."[16]

In a tract on the law and its relationship with the gospel, while he, as

always, staunchly defended the continuing relevance of God's commandments in the life of the believer, James powerfully emphasized that the law
never had and never would save anyone—only Christ could. "But here let
it be distinctly understood that there is no salvation in the law. There is no
redeeming quality in law. Redemption is through the blood of Christ. The
sinner may cease to break the commandments of God, and strive with all
his powers to keep them; but this will not atone for his sins, and redeem
him from his present condition in consequence of past transgression.

"Notwithstanding all his efforts to keep the law of God, he must be
lost without faith in the atoning blood of Jesus. And this was as true in the
time of Adam, of Abel, Enoch, Noah, Abraham. Moses, and the Jews, as
since Jesus died upon the cross. No man can be saved without Christ."[17]
It was a refrain that permeated his writings. "Jesus Christ is the Redeemer
of sinners in all the ages of human probation. . . . Without the gospel of
the Son of God none of the men of the patriarchal and Jewish ages could
be saved."[18]

He concluded his tract on the law and the gospel with the observation
that "the hope of eternal salvation hangs upon Christ. Adam hung his hope
there. . . . We can do no more. The hope of the next life depends upon
Christ. Faith in his blood alone can free us from our transgressions. And a
life of obedience to the commandments of God and the faith of Jesus will
be a sufficient passport through the golden gates of the city of God."[19]

Ellen White would go further in emphasizing that sanctification—the
life of "obedience to the commandments of God"[20] was also God's doing.
As for the Trinity, James was in a period of transition. In his "Christ in the
Old Testament" article he stressed that the Father and the Son were not
"parts of the 'three-one God.' They are two distinct beings, yet one in the
design and accomplishment of redemption."[21] But he may have been only
still rejecting a certain Methodist view of the Trinity that declared that the
Godhead had no parts or bodies, thus merging the members of the Trinity
into an amorphous state. His wife had also combated that same teaching
when she emphasized that the Father and the Son did have bodies.[22] We
do know that he declared in a Review article that "Christ is equal with
God."[23] He was definitely on the path away from the traditional Arian
view with its core doctrine that Christ was inferior to the Father, as we see
when he declared, "The inexplicable trinity that makes the godhead three

in one and one in three is bad enough; but that ultra Unitarianism that makes Christ inferior to the Father is worse."[24] The theological direction he was traveling was definitely headed toward the Trinitarian position.

White preached his themes powerfully. D. M. Canright observed after James's death that "as all will remember, wherever he preached the past few months, he dwelt largely upon faith in Christ and the boundless love of God."[25]

Unfortunately, James White did not get to finish his mission. Perhaps if he had, we would today consider it to have been his greatest impact on the church. But his wife would continue speaking and writing on the subject of Christ and His fundamental role in our salvation. The issue exploded into the righteousness by faith controversy during the 1888 Minneapolis General Conference session. As she spoke on the subject, she would frequently mention how she had discussed it with her husband.[26]

One could even wonder if James White's increasing emphasis on Christ and His central role in salvation could have upset some traditional leaders and members, making the subject suspect in their minds.[27] Could the fact that the theme had become identified with the sometimes irrational James offer George Butler, Uriah Smith, and others still another reason to become uncomfortable when righteousness by faith became prominent at the Minneapolis General Conference session?

But if James White died before he could complete what he wanted to say to the church about Christ and salvation, he did something that on a personal level was just as important. He achieved reconciliation with his family and many others in the church. It had been an estrangement that had been growing for many years. For all his abilities and accomplishments, James White was a difficult man to live with.

Between 1865 and his death in 1881 James White had at least five strokes. Though the first, as we have seen, was the most severe, the succeeding ones added to the damage. Strokes often affect the personality, causing personality traits already present to become more extreme. Common post-stroke symptoms include impulsiveness, sadness, depression, anxiety, and loneliness, traits that frequently and markedly showed up in White in the years after his first stroke. His stroke at age 44 "and his inability to trust others, slow down, or delegate authority colored the remainder of his life. Problems that had been evident in his early years became pronounced after 1865. Thus he suffered from recurring depression, was suspicious of other people, and at times made ill-advised statements and accusations. Those problems affected both his relationships with fellow church workers and with his wife and children."[28] The man who, according to his wife, had always enjoyed a good "fuss"[29] had become increasingly combative. Ellen White observed that her husband had had "to meet disaffection and murmurings on every side. These had been greatly magnified in his mind, and he has felt too keenly over them."[30]

At times James recognized the problem himself. In 1879 he had written to Willie and his wife, "I wish now to call your attention to a subject of graver importance. Probably, dear children, I may have erred in some of the sharp things I have written relative to the mistakes of younger heads. It is my nature to retaliate when pressed above measure. I wish I was a better man." Then he immediately added, "I also wish that the members of my good family had not the difficulty, of long standing, of becoming very gifted over my faults as they imagine them to be."[31]

The very strength and determination that had enabled White to organize a fractious body of believers into a church, and to establish the institutions it needed to thrive, now increasingly made him a difficult person to get along with. The drive that had enabled him to overcome so much opposition and personal animosity now saw hostility and rivalry where it did not exist. He became suspicious and demanding. His letters echo his complaints and criticism of his fellow leaders. At times he would get so frustrated that he would threaten to resign.[32] The letters also depict abrupt mood shifts, sometimes even between one sentence and the next.

Dudley M. Canright revealed the complex mixture of awe, respect, and frustration that James could inspire in those around him. In his book attacking Ellen White, Canright attempted to discredit James—and thus his wife—by arguing that he "was not a literary man, not a student of books, not scholarly, not a theologian. He understood neither Hebrew,[33] Greek nor Latin, read only the common English version of the Bible, and seldom ever consulted other translations."

White may not have been a trained theologian, but as we have seen, he had a profound impact on the theology of the Seventh-day Adventist Church through his pamphlets and books and countless periodical articles. He made Adventist doctrines understandable and convincing to both church members and converts. And he helped lay the groundwork for the emphasis on Christ and righteousness by faith.

But although he dismissed White's theological background, Canright had to admit that James "was a business man. He had large business ability, and was a born leader of men. His study and work were largely devoted to building up large business institutions, such as publishing houses, the sanitarium, the college, general and state conferences, and to finances. Here he made a success."[34] White's talents and abilities had built up the Seventh-day Adventist Church. But when crippled by illness and other problems, those same characteristics could damage all that he had accomplished—including his personal and family life, especially his marriage.

A MARRIAGE THAT ENDURED

To have a successful marriage, couples—especially those with strong personalities—must learn to respect each other's feelings. On June 6, 1863, Ellen White wrote: "I was shown some things in regard to my husband and myself. . . . I saw that we neither understood the depth and keenness of the heart trials of the other. Each heart was peculiarly sensitive, therefore each should be especially careful not to cause the other one shade of sadness or trial. Trials without will come, but strong in each other's love, each deeply sympathizing with the other, united in the work of God, [we] can stand nobly, faithfully together, and every trial will only work for good if well borne."[35] But that is easier said than done.

The Whites' marriage faced its greatest tests in 1874 and 1876. As we examine this period in their lives we see two very human beings with strong personalities struggling to relate to each other. James increasingly exhibited the damage of the crippling strokes he had suffered. White's drive and forceful personality had birthed the Seventh-day Adventist Church and enabled him to guide its various institutions through a series of crises. He was used to being in charge. But now that leadership ability was becoming more of a desire to control. And it crept over into his personal relationships. Ellen would find herself forced to confront him on how his poor work habits were injuring him and how he let his suspicions and depression drive wedges between himself and others.[36] Here we will focus on the struggles they faced in the 1876 period.[37]

Although Ellen sought to defer to him as much as possible, she still had to preserve her own individuality, especially as it related to her own role in the church. When James became too controlling, she had no choice but to resist—and at times even confront and censure some of his actions. This can be difficult for any husband, but it was especially the case with a powerful individual such as White. The stroke damage made him especially demanding, suspicious, and perhaps even bordering on the paranoid—further complicating the marriage.

Whenever possible she tried not to upset him. "It grieves me that I have said or written anything to grieve you," she wrote to him one time. "Forgive me and I will be cautious not to start any subject to annoy and distress you."[38]

Despite the fact that for years they had labored and attended camp meetings together, now they went their separate ways. Ellen lived in Oakland, California, and James worked in the Midwest and East. But apparently during the spring of 1876 he wanted her to travel with him during the upcoming camp meeting season. She did not know whether to join him or not. As she agonized over what to do, she unburdened her concerns and frustrations to her longtime friend and personal confidant, Lucinda Hall.[39]

Mentioning that she had received a letter from her husband, Ellen wrote, "Lucinda, I have no idea now of exchanging a certainty for an uncertainty. . . . Should I come east, James's happiness might suddenly change to complaining and fretting. I am thoroughly disgusted with this state of things, and do not mean to place myself where there is the least liability of its occurring. The more I think of the matter, the more settled and determined I am, unless God gives me light, to remain where I am."[40]

Ellen had long wanted to devote more time to writing, but her busy schedule had prevented her, especially without clerical assistance. Now that she had someone to help her she did not want to lose the opportunity, especially just to please her husband. "I can but dread the liability of James's changeable moods, his strong feelings, his censures, his viewing me in the light he does, and has felt free to tell me his ideas of my being led by a wrong spirit, my restricting his liberty, et cetera. All this is not easy to jump over and place myself voluntarily in a position where he will stand in my way and I in his.

"No, Lucinda, no camp meetings shall I attend this season. God in His providence has given us each our work, and we will do it separately, independently. He is happy; I am happy; but the happiness might be all changed should we meet, I fear. Your judgment I prize, but I must be left free to do my work. I cannot endure the thought of marring the work and cause of God by such depression as I have experienced all unnecessarily. My work is at Oakland. I shall not move east one step unless the Lord says 'Go.' Then, without one murmur, I will cheerfully go, not before.

"A great share of my life's usefulness has been lost. If James had made retraction, it would be different. He has said we must not seek to control each other. I do not own to doing it, but he has, and much more. I never felt as I do now in this matter. I cannot have confidence in James's judgment in reference to my duty. He seems to want to dictate to me as though I was a child—tells me not to go here, I must come east for fear of Sister Willis' influence, or fearing that I should go to Petaluma, et cetera. I hope God has not left me to receive my duty through my husband."[41]

Two days later Ellen was still wrestling with what to do, though she wrote to Lucinda that she had decided to remain in California. "I dare not go east without an assurance that God would have me go," she told her friend. "I am perfectly willing to go if the light shines that way."[42] Her reluctance to be with a difficult husband was warring with her lifelong ingrained sense of duty to God and the Adventist movement. "But the Lord knows what is best for me, for James, and the cause of God. My husband is now happy—blessed news. If he will only remain happy, I would be willing to ever remain from him. If my presence is detrimental to his happiness, God forbid I should be connected with him. I will do my work as God leads me. He may do his work as God leads him. We will not get in each other's way. My heart is fixed, trusting in God. I shall wait for God to open my way before me."[43]

Then she focused on her deepest fear. "I do not think my husband really desires my society. He would be glad for me to be present at the camp meetings, but he has such views of me, which he freely has expressed from time to time, that I do not feel happy in his society, and I never can till he views matters entirely differently. He charges a good share of his unhappiness upon me, when he has made it himself by his own lack of self-control. These things exist, and I cannot be in harmony with him till he views things differently. He has said too much for me to feel freedom with him in prayer or to unite with him in labor, therefore as time passes and he removes nothing out of my way, my duty is plain never to place myself where he will be tempted to act out his feelings and talk them out as he has done. I cannot, and will not, be crippled as I have been."[44]

Three days later she received a letter from James that greatly disturbed her. It must have reflected one of those mood swings so prominent among some stroke victims. She poured out her feelings to Lucinda that it convinced her "that he is prepared to dictate to me and take positions more trying than ever before. I have decided to attend no camp meetings this season. I shall remain [in California] and write [primarily on the manuscript that became *The Desire of Ages*]. My husband can labor alone best. I am sure I can."[45]

She worried that James wanted "the entire control of me, soul and body, but this he cannot have." Then she confessed a horrible thought: "*I sometimes think he is not really a sane man,* but I don't know."[46]

After citing some points that James was upset with her about, she quoted from his letter to her. She said that he did "not want me to make any references to what he writes till 'you [Ellen] see things differently. And be assured of this, that none of these things sink me down a hair. I shall be happy to meet you . . . at the Kansas camp meeting provided that, with the exception of a direct revelation from God, you put me on a level with yourself. I will gladly come to that position and labor with you, but while entrusted with the supervision of the whole work I think it wrong to be second to the private opinions of anyone. The moment I come to this I can be turned by the will of others' infallibility. When I cannot take this position I can gracefully cast off responsibilities. I shall have no more controversies with my dear wife. She may call it a "mouse or a bat" and have her own way. If she doesn't like my position in reference to Edson [White] or other matters, will she please [keep] her opinion to herself and let me enjoy mine? Your remarks called me out. And now that you cannot endure my speaking as plainly as you do, I have done.'"[47]

James echoed his frustration at having Ellen attempt to correct some of his actions and positions. "'As to your coming to [the] Kansas [camp meeting], I am not the least anxious. Judging from what I can gather from that last page [of Ellen's letter], I think we can better labor apart than together until you can lay down your continual efforts to hold me in condemnation. When you have a message from the Lord for me, I hope I shall be where I shall tremble at His word. But aside from that, you must let me be an equal, or we had better work alone.

"'Don't be anxious about my dwelling on disagreeables anymore. I have them in my heart. But while on the stage of action I shall use the good old head God gave me until He reveals that I am wrong. Your head won't fit my shoulders. Keep it where it belongs, and I will try to honor God in using my own. I shall be glad to hear from you, but don't waste your precious time and strength lecturing me on matters of mere opinions.'"[48]

During this same period James wrote to Willie, "I shall be glad to see mother when she can come on her own light from a sense of duty, to hold me an equal with herself, excepting in what God reveals to her, when I hope to tremble at the word of God, and obey. I shall do all I can to make her lot easy, comfortable, and happy, and will help her all I can in her work. Don't urge her to come, and don't consent to have her come on any other terms than is expressed above."[49]

On May 17 Ellen told Lucinda that another letter had arrived from her husband "expressing a very [different] tone of feelings." But she had not changed her mind, commenting that "I dare not cross the plains. It is better for us both to be separated. I have not lost my love for my husband, but I cannot explain things. I shall not attend any of the eastern camp meetings. I shall remain in California and write."[50] She also mentioned that she had sent James a letter of confession and apology about upsetting him.

In her letter to her husband she commented, "We are living in a most solemn time and we cannot afford to have in our old age differences to separate our feelings. I may not view all things as you do, but I do not think it would be my place or duty to try to make you see as I see and feel as I feel. Wherein I have done this, I am sorry.

"I want a humble heart, a meek and quiet spirit. Wherein my feelings have been permitted to arise in any instance, it was wrong. Jesus has said, 'Learn of me; for I am meek and lowly in heart; and ye shall find rest unto your souls.' Matthew 11:29.

"I wish that self should be hid in Jesus. I wish self to be crucified. I do not claim infallibility, or even perfection of Christian character. I am not free from mistakes and errors in my life. Had I followed my Saviour more closely, I should not have to mourn so much my unlikeness to His dear image.

"Time is short, very short. Life is uncertain. We know not when our probation may close. If we walk humbly before God, He will let us end our labors with joy. No more shall a line be traced by me or expression made in my letter to distress you. Again I say, forgive me every word or act that has grieved you."[51]

A few days later she decided to accompany her husband to various 1876 camp meetings, the last continuous series of camp meetings they would attend together. They went to 13 out of the 14 scheduled that summer.

FAMILY TENSIONS

A major factor that had led to the tension between them involved James Edson, who had gone through a long and turbulent adolescent rebellion brought on, perhaps, from his difficult childhood. Because of their frequent travels, his parents often had to leave him with friends and family. Then, after the birth of his more easygoing brother Willie, Ellen often compared him to the younger child, a practice that she later regretted. James also urged him to defer to Henry and Willie[52] and told him how Edson's heart would ache if Willie died.[53] Sadly, James would also discuss Edson's problems with his brother and even Edson's wife,[54] a practice that must not have helped family relations. In one letter James told Willie, "I want you to watch his [Edson's] matters and not let him lose, or bring a disgrace upon himself and the family. If he gets into a hard spot, take measures to help him out, even to raise means for him.

"He will always be a burden to us, more or less, and we must do the best we can with the matter. We should wait, however, until he gets where he must have help. Then help him as little as will possibly do."[55]

Another time he told Willie, "There are very many parents who can do but little for their children because those children have more faith in themselves than they have in their parents."[56] Did James have Edson, or both sons, in mind? While much more compliant, even Willie—as we shall see—occasionally frustrated his father.

An explosive issue between Edson and his father was how quickly the son could run through money, a habit that disturbed frugal and business-skilled James White. Once he bought and flaunted a $26 coat, a price nearly equal to an average laborer's monthly income.[57] Business deals that went bankrupt cost him large sums of money.

The more his parents warned him about his spending habits, the more money he threw away. James tried through a number of financial offers to persuade Edson to change his spending habits, but to no avail.[58] In 1870 James offered Edson the title to the home of a Mrs. Kittle if Edson would pay him $300 over a three-year period after he turned 21 and managed to stay out of debt.[59] Although for a long time James kept bailing him out of debt, finally he lost patience and tried to avoid his son and his risky business ventures. At one point he told Edson point-blank: *"I will not pay common debts."*[60] The next year he wrote Edson, "I shall help you to help yourself, so that if you are saving you need not be much in debt. . . . This, however, will depend very much upon how you manage matters."[61] A few months later he told Edson and his wife that if his son continued to follow his independent course, "we shall in future let him do it, at his own expense, and risk. I feel that it would be a sin to help him while he pursues an independent course, and cherishes hard feelings against me. I am satisfied that as he now stands, the more I might do for him the worse he would treat me, and feel toward me."[62]

White also considered Edson immature. "Edson's danger will be in feeling adequate to enter upon some important, responsible department of professional life," he said in a letter to both Edson and Willie. "But he has almost everything to learn, besides the work of overcoming the natural defect in his makeup, of thinking himself qualified to do what he really cannot do. This is worst of all. But if he looks back faithfully upon the last five years of his life, and studies closely his mistakes, he may learn the very lesson he must learn to qualify him for future success."[63] James also believed that some of Edson's behavior had hurt the family reputation among those hostile to the father.[64]

Edson, James believed, did not have enough ambition, that he was willing to settle for being "simply a mechanic in the Office."[65] James would have liked him to learn editorial duties for the *Health Reformer,* or at least teach music in California. White also wanted his sons to help more around their parents' various homes.[66]

But White's ambitions were not just for Edson. He told Willie not to learn printing, but "press in to the editorial chair. . . . Begin to write on Sabbath Schools, temperance, good morals, or most anything. Then worm into Bible subjects. Don't let the Devil fool you out of your proper place.

You know you can beat most who work for our papers. Now is your time to strike out."[67]

James felt that things would be a success if he could be in charge with his sons working under him. We see this especially in his comments about the situation at Pacific Press. He trusted them more than he did anyone else—but even that was only to a point. They needed his continued and capable guidance.

Both Willie and Edson took a six-month medical course under Dr. Trall at his Hygieo-Therapeutic College at Florence Heights, New Jersey. James told his sons not to call themselves doctors unless they obtained more medical education, were 21, and actually went into practice.[68] Perhaps practicing medicine would settle Edson down. The son had shown interest in the profession. White particularly hoped that Edson would complete a medical program at the University of Michigan at Ann Arbor.[69]

Through all the conflict, though, James's love for Edson remained. One example is seen when he explained to Willie that he had written in a way to appear to blame others about some problem at Pacific Press in order to avoid making Edson feel bad even though he had acted recklessly and had helped create the difficulty.[70]

In later years when Ellen supported Edson financially as his father had done earlier, it alienated James further. He told Willie not to let his mother take too much responsibility for Edson's financial problems.[71] The tensions rose, until James spent more and more time away and the separation between him and Ellen became more or less permanent.[72]

As with most couples, money itself could be a cause for friction between James and Ellen. While both reflected the frugalness of their Maine upbringing, they did so in slightly different ways. He would look for discounts on railroad tickets and good returns on his business dealings.[73] Writing about plans for publishing some music books, he told Edson, "Do not pay large sums for the right to print [tunes]," adding at the end of the letter, "Keep this to yourself."[74] Otherwise, he still liked to live comfortably. In 1874 he told Willie, "Do not consent to her [Ellen's] economical ideas, leading you to pinch along. See that everything like her dresses, shawls, saques, shoes, bonnet, etc., are *good*. And be sure to dress yourself in a respectable manner."[75] James commented one time to Willie that he should have bought an $800 carriage instead of a $300 one. And he had a valid point about wanting a more expensive carriage. One of the most popular horse-drawn vehicles in nineteenth-century United States was what was popularly known as the piano box buggy. Toward the latter part of the century it could be purchased for $35.[76] But it was flimsy, and the kind of extensive travel that White did on the rough American roads would have shaken such a lightly built vehicle into kindling. Most American carriage designs came originally from England, but American roads were so bad that manufacturers in the United States had to redesign the vehicles with four wheels to keep them from flipping over because of deep ruts. James White had to have a sturdier—and thus more expensive —arriage to survive the amount of traveling he had to do. He knew that one got what one paid for.[77]

In addition, frugalness for its own sake irritated him. "I am done with that economy that tends to [cheapness] of dress and equipage. . . . I am done [with] this pinching and saving, so much."[78] White liked neither wasting money nor scrimping. Ellen could at times be too frugal for his tastes . . . *and then at the same time she would indulge Edson's spendthrift ways!* It was more than James could handle.

Shortly after her husband's first stroke, Ellen White had revealed her love for both father and son and pain over the growing estrangement between them. "Yesterday after I left the [railroad] cars I rode twelve miles in the stage [coach]. The scenery was beautiful. The trees with their varied hues, the beautiful evergreens interspersed among them, the green grass, the high and lofty mountains, the high bluffs of rocks—all are interesting to the eye. These things I could enjoy, but I am alone. The strong, manly arm I have ever leaned upon is not now my support. Tears are my meat night and day. My spirit is constantly bowed down by grief. I cannot consent that your father shall go down into the grave. Oh, that God would pity and heal him! Edson, my dear boy, give yourself to God. Wherein you have erred, frankly acknowledge it by confession and humility. Draw nigh to God and do unite with me in pleading with God for his recovery. If we chasten our souls before God and truly repent of all our wrongs, will He not be entreated, for the sake of His dear Son, to heal your father?"[79]

But the resentment between father and son did not go away. In 1871 she wrote to her son again when James sent him a letter chastising his behavior and set Edson bristling. "Dear Edson, do not on any account move rashly in regard to the letter written by your father. Keep quiet; wait and trust; be faithful; make every concession you can, even if you have done so before; and may God give you a soft and tender heart to your poor, overburdened, worn, harassed father."[80]

When Ellen poured out her heart to Lucinda Hall, she said that Edson was still a problem between her and James. Her husband felt that their son was a bad influence on her. She said that James "has in his letters to me written harshly in regard to Edson, and then told me that he did not write to call me out. He did not want me to make any references to Edson."[81] In reply she told him, "Please take the same cautions yourself. When you wish to make these statements in reference to your own son, please lay down your pen and stop just there. I think God would be better pleased, and it would do no harm to your own soul. Leave me to be guided by the Lord in reference to Edson, for I still trust in His guiding hand and have confidence He will lead me. The same guiding hand is my trust."[82]

In response to one of Ellen's letters, James White wrote to Willie, "I have read your mother's letter. . . . She can go to California, and get all her relatives[83] there she pleases. But I shall wait for radical changes before I go. If mother would not always blame me when Edson abuses me, and would take a firm stand for the right with me, I think I would consent to live in the same State where Edson may reside. But until I see a radical change in both Edson and mother, I do not expect to go to California. I have not a single apology for my course toward him last winter, only that I did stay in Oakland and suffer under his abuse. And yet your mother blamed me for weeks. I am *fully settled* in my views and I conclude she is in hers. So mother will probably go to California with her friends in the fall, and I go to Texas."[84] He commented to Willie that he regretted that Ellen came to him (apparently at their cabin in Colorado). "She is quite a burden to me sometimes, and in being tended so carefully by Cinda [Lucinda Hall] has become quite helpless."[85] In the same letter he wryly observed that "Mother appears kind and well. I have no doubt in the absence of Edson, we shall get along splendidly."[86]

Three years later White commented, "I have probably been too much wounded at the perpetual faultfinding of my course by the members of my family. I am sure that if you knew the effect of this upon my mind you would change your course towards me. Your mother has pursued this course till she has broken me down—soured me. And Edson has here found grounds for his course."[87]

During the fall of 1880 he wrote Willie that he had urged "your mother to go to California to help you ship Edson here [Battle Creek]. It was well that she went. Edson will do less harm here than there. His being in California has been the only reason that has kept me from going to that State since my last recovery of health."[88]

Willie was also at times the target of his father's frustration and anger. We have already looked at James's tendency to be controlling and to micromanage his son when he was an administrator at Pacific Press. Willie could not avoid being involved in some of the conflicts between his father and other denominational leaders. Probably some individuals came to Willie seeking to influence James White. Whatever Willie did or didn't do would get him into trouble with someone. Thus James's letters to the younger son sometimes take Willie to task for his actions and comments in such awkward situations.

"You have not meant to injure me," he declared, "but you have hurt me terribly. Your assuming responsibilities in reference to my financial business at the office, of which you had no business to meddle with, led me to call money to Texas to sustain a loss of not less than one thousand dollars; and your tender regard for your brother-in-law, instead of your father last fall, who needed a quiet home away from the very center of confusion, has resulted very bad."[89] Yet he was disappointed that Willie did not share his father's interest in business matters.[90]

"The day will come when you will be sorry for casting such an influence against me with such men as Elders Butler and Whitney," he warned his son, then added, "I am rising above all the grief I have felt on this subject, and am feeling better."[91]

That fall he told him, "Nothing has grieved me, Willie, and thrown me off my guard so much as you watching and criticizing my business relations with the Offices, as though I was wanting in conscience in my deal [sic.]. I hope to be able to prove to you that I am, at least, an honest man. Your mother's testimony to me nearly a year since speaks in unqualified terms in my defense on that point."[92]

"What kind of a spirit has entered my dear Will," he demanded on

December 10, 1880, "that he imagines he can drive his father to obeisance?"[93]

On December 28, 1880, James fussed at Willie for mentioning something that the father had said in private, calling the act "unjust trickery."[94] A few weeks later he scolded Willie for allegedly making a decision without his father's authorization. Willie had not asked James about it even though his father was in town in Battle Creek.[95] And, referring to what he considered a misuse of a quote he had made about *Signs,* he almost sobbed, *"This wrong was done your father!!!* . . . Oh, my poor misled Willie! How could you be so cruel?"[96] It was a difficult period for Willie White.

Adding to his frustration with his sons was the fact that they were now adults. As a loving father, he wanted to protect and guide them, but he wanted to do it the way it had been done in the past. He wanted to cling to the old relationships. "You as children need our counsel and we need your help. Our work is important."[97] But their relationship could no longer be that of parent/dependent child. For better or worse, both sons had their own lives, their own careers. Willie did return to help his mother, but that was after James's death and a period of service on his own.[98] And Edson would work in the American South and elsewhere.

But despite all his frustrations, James still loved Willie "as my own soul."[99] And that love included Edson as well. "May God have mercy upon me," James said. "And may He remove all the sad results of my weakness and sin from our family."[100]

CONFLICT WITH KELLOGG

By the 1870s the Seventh-day Adventist Church had grown to the point that White could not personally oversee every aspect of it—and it had developed sufficient leadership that it was no longer dependent upon him. Others now had the skill and experience to make decisions without his aid. For example, as John Harvey Kellogg turned around the finances of the Health Reform Institute and made it into the world-renowned Battle Creek Sanitarium, the institution no longer needed White's hands-on leadership. Also Kellogg's personality was just as forceful as White's and threatened to overshadow that of his mentor. The two men began a struggle for control. Even though White had put his influence in support of Kellogg, the physician began to fear his desire to control and managed to get James removed from the board of directors and replaced by the more pliable Stephen N. Haskell.[101]

James's growing jealousy of Kellogg led him to make some strange statements. He wrote to Willie White, "Do not let Dr. Kellogg figure too much in business matters. He is a perfect failure at that."[102] It bothered him when his sons worked for Kellogg instead of him.[103] White, a man who drove himself relentlessly, pushed through a General Conference Committee resolution censuring Kellogg for abusing his health, not taking vacations, not going to bed for at least eight hours out of every 24, and not delegating work and responsibility to his associates.[104] Also White began to resent Kellogg's growing reputation as a writer on health. He hinted that his sons, in their positions at Pacific Press, should see that *Signs* did not publish any articles on Bible hygiene by Kellogg as James thought of the topic as "my forte."[105]

Kellogg worked to get prices as low as possible on the books he published through the Review, hurting its financial position.[106] James warned Willie, "Be on the lookout for Dr. Kellogg's tricks. While he has been telling that SDA people were of no advantage to him, he has been oppressing the *Review* office, etc., etc., under threats that he would take his work away. He has been getting even whole state tract societies on contract to canvass for his work. This is all wrong. Our people generally are not able to purchase that book. . . . Why will the tract societies, led by Elders Haskell and Whitney, rush on so wildly?"[107]

The conflict between them became so intense that Ellen White had a dream about the situation. In it she saw both Kellogg and her husband piling up stones to hurl at and destroy each other.[108]

The fact that his beloved church could survive without him and increasingly did things differently than he would have, began to frustrate and depress him. It bothered him when he was not General Conference president, though he sensed that he had created some of the hostility that cost him the office. During one such period George I. Butler sent him a letter dealing with some issues that White had created. James began his reply by thanking Butler "for the kindness and candor with which you touch points where my course may look objectionable to you," but later in it commented, "I am sorry, my dear brother, that you are compelled to fill the place God designed that I should occupy."[109] The effects of the

strokes intensified the frustration and deepened the depression and worsened a characteristic that had long been a part of his personality.

Throughout James's life, when someone disagreed with him or criticized the approach he followed, he could respond quite negatively.
Reacting to some criticism of him in 1879, James exploded, "I am a sensitive man, and you can understand that apologies will have to be made
or you will have to look for others to fill my place."[110] Notice that he
thought that it would take more than one person to replace him. Also he
found it increasingly harder to accept the fact that he was no longer the
only prominent voice in leadership. "Things go very much as I say," he
told Willie in one letter. "I tell all hands that when they put me on a level
with others, then they can get some young man to take my place and I will
quit. I will try to fill my place, 'A Counselor to the Brethren.' When they
want my counsel, I will give it. I shall accept no offices. I shall be free."[111]

When others tried to get him to do something he disagreed with, he
could become quite upset. "Never shall I consent to go here and there,
and to do this or that by the direction of others," he protested to his wife.
He would rather quit than accept being supervised by others. "When I
come to that point, it will be time for me to retire. A retreat is the most
skillful part of military action, which you and I should be considering."[112]

It especially disturbed him to watch others make mistakes that he could
not prevent. When the various church institutions in Battle Creek began to
slide into debt, he fretted, "My brethren are all crazy, and left to themselves
would soon put me in the grave. I am the only sane man in the crowd, and
hope to remain so. I will save my money to buy help and try to save myself,
and leave our institutions to the mercy of the go-in-debt men now at the
helm."[113] The next year he complained that "there seems to be a disposition
on all hands to break me down."[114] That fall he added, "I have made mistakes in being hasty and rash under cruel pressure. But if I thought that my
mistakes were half as great as those who have plunged our institutions in
debt, and then take a course to crush out of sight the only cautious, level
brain that has labored to bring them into existence, and has looked forward
and warned of dangers in the future, I should feel worse than I now do."[115]

The mood shifts seemed especially to intensify during 1880 and
1881. In his letters, especially those to Willie, he would abruptly swing
from contrition to belligerence and suspicion.

James White had many relationships to mend. He had already tried a number of times to deal with them, but with only partial success. Some he would resolve only weeks before death. But even during July of 1880 he had written to his daughter-in-law Mary White, "This has been the happiest summer of my life. I see that I have grieved over things I could not help too much. I take time to think, rest, and sleep, and keep calm and happy."[116]

About two weeks before his death he had a premonition of its approach and decided he should as far as possible heal the damaged relationship between him and Ellen. Acknowledging the mistakes he had made, he asked forgiveness for "any word or act that has caused you sorrow. There must be nothing to hinder our prayers. Everything must be right between us, and between ourselves and God."[117]

James White's strokes had drastically altered his life. His grandson, Arthur L. White, observed that during James's final years "he was convinced of his ability and insights as being superior to that of others. At times he was discouraged; at other times he was irrational and almost irresponsible."[118] But far more important than how the strokes affected his personality and relationships is the greater reality that he accomplished so much in his later years despite the physical and mental damage they caused, which created for him as much a disability to surmount as would blindness, paralysis, or any other physical limitation. We do not condemn people who are physically blind for not being able to see—instead, we extol what they accomplish despite being blind.

While the mood swings and depression might overwhelm White for a time, he never permanently surrendered. He struggled to break free. Those who have never battled depression or similar problems cannot grasp what he constantly faced. Such conditions are not something you can snap out of at someone's urging. But Ellen White gave him her support and did everything she knew to help him.

Nineteenth-century medicine had no treatment for the neurological damage caused by strokes. James had only prayer and his faith in God. "I pray much as the train is in motion," he wrote to Ellen on one trip, "that God will help us. This is my only hope, and I mean to get out of the way so that He can work. I will, I will, I shall by the help of the Lord, be where I can prevail with the Lord. I have long been backslidden from God. I must return, and be like a child before God. There is hope for us in God. "I will cry to God for myself and you."[119]

Lesser men and women would have given up. But James clung to God, letting the Lord continue to use him in spite of his illness. God can perform great things through even a stroke victim who chooses to devote himself or herself to the Savior. His life had been a continuous process of overcoming—of overcoming a lack of a formal education, of overcoming opposition and hostility as he organized and led a new church, and finally overcoming the poor health that would have destroyed a lesser man.

James made many mistakes, but ill as he was at times, he did much lasting good even in his final years for the publishing house and for the church he loved. As we have already seen, he did some of his best writing on the glory of Christ during this tumultuous period. And his final months would bring him a new sense of peace. Dudley Canright commented to Ellen White after her husband's death that "I think I never saw Brother White so tender and patient as he was these last few months of his life. I shall always remember this with pleasure. It seems now to me that the Lord was preparing him for what has come."[120]

---

[1] Woodrow W. Whidden, "Arianism, Adventism and Methodism: The Healing of Trinitarian Teaching and Soteriology" (paper presented to the Tenth Oxford Institute of Methodist Theol. Studies Working Group: History of Wesleyan Traditions: Nineteenth and Twentieth Centuries, Aug. 12-22, 1997), pp. 2, 3.

[2] See, for example, JW to WCW, June 2, 1875; JW to EGW, Mar. 20, 1880; JW to EGW, May 21, 1880; JW to WCW, Sept. 18, 1880. The sentiment is repeated continually in his 1880 letters.

[3] JW to Children, May 20, 1879. He got a bit sensitive when Willie's wife, Mary, praised Ellen's writing and not his. See JW to WCW, Nov. 3, 1880.

[4] In Memoriam, p. 54, in Bert Haloviak, "Some Great Connexions," p. 14, and "A Heritage of Freedom," p. 11.

[5] JW to WCW, Sept. 16, 1880.

[6] JW to WCW and Mary White, Feb. 17, 1881.

[7] JW to WCW, Sept. 18, 1880.

[8] JW to WCW and Mary White, Feb. 17, 1881.

[9] LeRoy Edwin Froom, Movement of Destiny (Washington, D.C.: Review and Herald Pub. Assn., 1971), pp. 182-186. Froom reproduces the two engravings.

[10] JW to EGW, Mar. 31, 1880. See also JW to WCW, Sept. 16, 1880, and JW to EGW, Feb. 7, 1881.

[11] James White, *Life Incidents,* p. 359; cf. pp. 344, 345, 354. He emphasized a life of obedience to the commandments, but he recognized that it was not salvational.

[12] James White, *Christ in the Old Testament* (Oakland, Calif.: Pacific Press, 1877), p. 3.

[13] *Ibid.,* p. 10.

[14] *Ibid.,* p. 11.

[15] James White, *The Redeemer and Redeemed; or, The Plan of Redemption Through Christ* (Oakland, Calif.: Pacific Press, 1877), p. 12.

[16] *Ibid.,* p. 43.

[17] James White, *The Law and the Gospel. The Relation Which They Sustain to Each Other in the Great Plan of Salvation* (Oakland, Calif.: Pacific Press Pub. Assn.; reprinted in The Bible Student's Library, No. 15, Apr. 9, 1889, p. 11).

[18] James White, "The Lamb of God," *Signs of the Times,* Jan. 22, 1880, p. 33.

[19] James White, *The Law and the Gospel,* p. 16.

[20] Ellen G. White, "Sanctification," *Signs of the Times,* Apr. 13, 1888.

[21] James White, *The Law and the Gospel,* p. 2.

[22] Woodrow W. Whidden, Jerry Allen Moon, and John W. Reeve, *The Trinity,* p. 210.

[23] James White, "Christ Equal With God," *Review and Herald,* Nov. 29, 1877.

[24] *Ibid.*

[25] D. M. Canright, "My Remembrance of Eld. White," *Review and Herald,* Aug. 30, 1881.

[26] EGW manuscript 5, 1889.

[27] See the apparent reluctance of *Signs* to publish an article he titled "The First and the Last" (JW to WCW, Oct. 15, 1880; JW to WCW, Oct. 31, 1880; JW to WCW, Nov. 13, 1880.

[28] George Knight, *Walking With Ellen White: The Human Interest Story* (Hagerstown, Md.: Review and Herald Pub. Assn., 1999), pp. 73, 74.

[29] EGW to JW (letter 13, 1871), Sept. 2, 1871.

[30] EGW addition to JW to WCW and Mary White, Nov. 17, 1880.

[31] JW to WCW and Mary White, Feb. 27, 1879.

[32] For example, JW to EGW, Apr. 15, 1880; JW to EGW, Apr. 16, 1880; JW to EGW, Apr. 18, 1880; JW to WCW, Apr. 21, 1880.

[33] D. M. Canright, *Life of Mrs. E. G. White: Seventh-day Adventist Prophet: Her False Claims Refuted* (Cincinnati: Standard Pub. Co., 1919), p. 65. Interestingly, he apparently did receive some background in Hebrew from a language teacher at Battle Creek College. See JW to EGW, July 4, 1880.

[34] *Ibid.*

[35] EGW manuscript 1, 1863.

[36] See, for example, EGW letters 34, 38, 40, 40a, 1874, cited in Arthur White, *Ellen G. White: The Progressive Years,* pp. 430-438.

[37] For the 1874 tensions, see Arthur L. White, *Ellen G. White: The Progressive Years,* pp. 425-445. Afterward, James sent a letter to his wife's close friend Lucinda Hall, in which he declared, "I unite with Ellen in inviting you to come to our home and rest. It is now a pleasant, happy home, and we feel anxious you should enjoy it" (JW to Lucinda Hall, Oct. 14, 1874).

[38] EGW to JW (letter 27, 1876), May 16, 1876.

[39] See Ellen G. White, *Daughters of God,* pages 260-275, for the complete letters and the context in which they were written.

[40] EGW to Lucinda Hall (letter 64, 1876), May 10, 1876.

[41] *Ibid.*

[42] EGW to Lucinda Hall (letter 65, 1876), May 12, 1876.

[43] *Ibid.*

[44] *Ibid.*

[45] EGW to Lucinda Hall (letter 66, 1876), May 16, 1876.

[46] *Ibid.* (Italics supplied.) The problem did not go away; cf. Ellen's statement to Willie and Mary several years later when she wrote: "Father has been in such a state of mind I feared he would lose his reason. But he is concluding to lay off the burdens of office matters and go to writing. I hope he will do so." She commented that "I am at times in such perplexity and distress of mind I covet retirement or death, but then I gather courage again" (EGW to WCW and Mary White (letter 1a, 1881), Jan. 6, 1881.

[47] *Ibid.*

[48] *Ibid.*

[49] JW to WCW, May 11, 1876.

[50] EGW to Lucinda Hall (letter 67, 1876), May 17, 1876.

[51] EGW to JW (letter 27, 1876), May 16, 1876.

[52] JW to J. Edson White, Jan. 12, c. 1860.

[53] JW to J. Edson White, Mar. 20, 1860.

[54] For examples of letters to Edson and his wife, see JW to J. Edson White and Emma White, Dec. 11, 1871; JW to J. Edson and Emma White, June 23, 1872; JW to J. Edson and Emma White, Dec. 30, 1872.

[55] JW to WCW, June 2, 1875; cf. JW to WCW, May 1, 1876.

[56] JW to WCW, Apr. 29, 1875.

[57] EGW to J. Edson White (letter 14, 1868), June 17, 1868.

[58] See Robinson, pp. 141-143.

[59] JW to J. Edson White, May 12, 1870.

[60] *Ibid.*

[61] JW to J. Edson White, Sept. 30, 1872.

[62] JW to J. Edson White and Emma White, Dec. 11, 1871.

[63] JW to J. Edson White and WCW, Dec. 30, 1872.

[64] JW to WCW, May 7, 1876; JW to WCW, June 7, 1876.

[65] JW to J. Edson White and Emma White, June 23, 1872

[66] *Ibid.*

[67] JW to WCW, June 3, 1875; cf. JW to WCW, July 5, 1874.

[68] JW to J. Edson White and WCW, Dec. 30, 1872.

[69] JW to WCW, July 5, 1874.

[70] JW to WCW, Jan. 17, 1879. James wrote more than one letter that day—see one addressed to "W. C. White, Dear Son."

[71] JW to WCW, Mar. 12, 1880.

[72] Some denominational historians have suggested that James may have given Ellen an ultimatum: stop giving Edson money or he would leave. But James could have stayed away for a number of reasons.

[73] James White often urged Willie to make sure James's money was drawing good interest. For example, see JW to WCW, June 18, 1876.

[74] JW to J. Edson White, Aug. 5, 1872.

[75] JW to WCW, July 5, 1874.

[76] Patricia Boland and Suzanne Jaquin, *The Carriage Collection of the Granger Homestead* (Canandaigua, N.Y.: The Granger Homestead Society, Inc., 1992), p. 15.

[77] James White sounded like a twenty-first-century American male when he wrote to his wife, "Every time we ride in the new carriage [that he had bought], we mourn that you are not here to enjoy it. I now have the best team and carriage as a whole, that I ever owned and mean to enjoy them" (JW to EGW, Apr. 7, 1880). A few days before he had told her that the cushions for the seats were "the softest I ever saw" (JW to EGW, Apr. 4, 1880).

[78] JW to WCW, July 5, 1874.

[79] EGW to J. Edson White (letter 16, 1866), Oct. 14, 1866.

[80] EGW to J. Edson White (letter 2, 1871), Jan. 30, 1871.

[81] EGW to Lucinda Hall (letter 66, 1876), May 16, 1876.

[82] *Ibid.*

[83] White's letters hint at friction with Ellen's relatives. See, for example, JW to WCW, Sept. 9, 1878.

[84] JW to WCW, June 7, 1876.

[85] *Ibid.*

[86] *Ibid.* See also JW to WCW, July 3, 1876. James told Willie that he believed Edson influenced their mother but that she was over her bitter feelings toward James (JW to WCW and Mary White, July 3, 1876). For more on her relationship with Edson, especially after James White's death, see George Knight, *Walking With Ellen White*, pp. 84-88.

[87] JW to WCW, Mar. 10, 1879.

[88] JW to WCW, Nov. 13, 1880.

[89] JW to WCW, May 4, 1880.

[90] JW to WCW, June 2, 1880.

[91] *Ibid.;* cf. JW to WCW, Nov. 13, 1880.

[92] JW to WCW, Oct. 31, 1880; cf. JW to WCW and Mary White, Nov. 17, 1880; JW to WCW, Dec. 12, 1880.

[93] JW to WCW, Dec. 10, 1880.

[94] JW to WCW, Dec. 28, 1880; cf. JW to WCW, Apr. 10, 1879.

[95] JW to WCW, Jan. 17, 1881; cf. the incomplete letter, JW to WCW and Mary White, Feb. 27, 1879.

[96] JW to WCW, Jan. 7, 1881.

[97] JW to WCW, Nov. 15, 1880.

[98] Jerry Allen Moon, *W. C. White and Ellen G. White: The Relationship Between the Prophet*

and Her Son (Berrien Springs, Mich.: Andrews University Press, 1993).

[99] JW to WCW, Nov. 17, 1880.

[100] *Ibid.*

[101] Richard W. Schwartz, *John Harvey Kellogg, M.D.*, p. 62.

[102] JW to WCW, June 18, 1876.

[103] JW to WCW, July 5, 1874.

[104] Document titled "Dr. Kellogg," dated July 1878.

[105] JW to J. Edson White and WCW, Jan. 2, 1873. White also wanted Edson to put Kellogg and Willie White through a penmanship course. Apparently James did not like their handwriting.

[106] JW to WCW, Oct. 15, 1880.

[107] JW to WCW and Mary White, Dec. 12, 1880.

[108] EGW manuscript 2, 1880. Ellen felt that she had no choice but to deal with the situation between her husband and Kellogg. On July 16, 1881, she asked James and Kellogg to meet with her privately, during which she read to them a large number of pages of counsel. Then the following Tuesday she read the same material to a special meeting of denominational leaders. Interestingly, she both chastised and defended her husband; see Herbert E. Douglass, *Messenger of the Lord: The Prophetic Ministry of Ellen G. White* (Nampa, Idaho: Pacific Press Pub. Assn., 1998), pp. 88, 89.

[109] JW to George I. Butler, July 13, 1874. The letter is an interesting mixture of deference and strong opinion. At one point he comments, "Had I been in a good state of mind and health last winter I should have written respecting the size and cost of the [Battle Creek College] schoolhouse. But as I did not, it is no time for me to arouse the jealousies of our people to your honest decisions. Hence, I only throw out hints to only the Gen. Conf. Committee." James was reelected at the General Conference session later in 1874.

[110] JW to WCW, July 28, 1879.

[111] JW to WCW, July 21, 1875.

[112] JW to EGW, Apr. 18, 1880.

[113] JW to Children, May 3, 1879; cf. JW to WCW, Apr. 10, 1879.

[114] JW to WCW, June 2, 1880.

[115] JW to WCW, Nov. 13, 1880.

[116] JW to Mary White, July 21, 1880.

[117] *In Memorium*, p. 47.

[118] Arthur L. White, "The James White Letter to D. M. Canright" (Washington, D.C.: 1978), p. 1.

[119] JW to EGW, Feb. 11, 1881.

[120] D. M. Canright to EGW, Aug. 22, 1881.

CHAPTER XIX

THE FINAL YEAR

A T the beginning of 1881 James resigned his positions on the boards of Battle Creek College and the sanitarium. He kept only the presidency of the publishing association and the editorship of the *Review*. Both he and Ellen now wrote constantly. As spring approached and the weather improved they spoke at local churches, then in May held revival meetings for the Battle Creek College students. James also spent much time working on his home and farm, putting in raspberries, an acre each of strawberries and potatoes, and several acres of corn. Also he planted peach and pear trees and 50 maple trees. Again, as always, when he worked on something physical, his health improved.

Although they had vowed not to exhaust themselves at camp meetings that summer, Ellen felt impressed to go to the Iowa one. James agreed, and they also went to the Wisconsin one. The couple felt a warm welcome at both.

Ellen continued to try to convince her husband to lighten his load before he totally destroyed his health. A few weeks before his death she urged him to take up something that would be less stressful. When he had done nonadministrative tasks such as leading the wagon train up the Chisholm Trail, his health had improved. Trying to carry the heavy responsibilities of church leadership was killing him. But he still could not let go, could not turn over church leadership to others, could not accept the fact that he was not indispensable. He told his wife of a number of problems that he felt he alone could solve, projects that he believed he had to finish before he could possibly think of leaving Battle Creek. "Where are the men to do this work?" he asked, his voice full of concern and emotion. "Where are those who will have an unselfish interest in our institutions, and who will stand for the right, unaffected by any influence with which they may come in contact?"

Tears began to spill down his face. "My life has been given to the up-building of these institutions," she would remember him saying. "It seems like death to leave them. They are as my children, and I cannot separate my interest from them. These institutions are the Lord's instrumentalities to do a specific work. Satan seeks to hinder and defeat every means by which the Lord is working for the salvation of men. If the great adversary can mold these institutions according to the world's standard, his object is gained. It is my greatest anxiety to have the right man in the right place. If those who stand in responsible positions are weak in moral power and vacillating in principle, inclined to lead toward the world, there are enough who will be led. Evil influences must not prevail. I would rather die than live to see these institutions mismanaged, or turned aside from the purpose for which they were brought into existence.

"In my relations to this cause I have been longest and most closely connected with the publishing work," he continued. "Three times I have fallen, stricken with paralysis, through my devotion to this branch of the cause. Now that God has given me renewed physical and mental strength, I feel that I can serve His cause as I have never been able to serve it be-fore. I must see the publishing work prosper. It is interwoven with my very existence. If I forget the interests of this work, let my right hand for-get her cunning."[1] He simply could not understand that if he kept on as he had been doing and drove himself into the grave, the end result would still be the same as if he had retired—someone else would have to take over his role and responsibilities.

THE LAST ILLNESS

The couple accepted an invitation to some weekend meetings in Charlotte, Michigan, July 23 and 24. They drove in their carriage, their last trip together. The morning began hot and humid, but then a cold front pushed through, dropping the temperature and chilling James. Still he preached at the meetings Sunday afternoon. On the way back to Battle Creek Monday he told Ellen that he did not feel well. During the week he mentioned pains bothering him in his arms and legs. But he attended church services at the Dime Tabernacle and offered the opening prayer.

On Monday he felt a severe chill. By Tuesday Ellen was also extremely sick. Later that afternoon Dr. Kellogg visited their home. His concern for his old mentor had bridged the gulf between them. James had a pulse of 112 and a temperature of more than 103°F. His head was congested, and he complained of severe pain of the back, arms, and legs. On Wednesday Kellogg ordered them both to the sanitarium and diagnosed them as having malaria, a disease then so common in Michigan because of the swamps and bogs that people referred to it as the Michigan shakes. Friends placed the couple on a mattress in a carriage. It would be the last time that they would be together. At the sanitarium James received hydrotherapy treatments that seemed to help. Edson White, realizing their parents' serious condition, wrote to Willie that he should come immediately.

The fact that James slept so deeply so much of the time especially concerned Dr. Kellogg. The physician wondered if White had had another stroke. When Ellen came to her husband's hospital room and saw him, she instantly recognized that he was dying. Taking his hand and kneeling beside his bed, she prayed that God would spare his life if it were His will. Then she asked her husband if Jesus was precious to him. "Yes, oh, yes!" he answered. When she questioned if he had any desire to live, he replied, "No." Perhaps he saw death as release from the emotional turmoil his strokes had put him through.

Thursday evening friends visited, but he did not say much, drifting in and out of sleep. The next morning he spoke in brief sentences, but the symptoms of paralysis that had appeared the night before now continued. Kellogg concluded that even if James survived he would have brain damage, and both the doctor and Ellen did not expect him to recover. Friday evening Uriah Smith and some other Battle Creek ministers prayed beside his bed for James's healing, then continued praying in another room.

Kellogg and his assistants worked over White during the night. The physician thought he detected signs of another stroke. At 1:30 p.m. White slipped into a coma, and at 5:00 Sabbath afternoon he quietly stopped breathing. Dr. Kellogg sent a telegram to Oakland, California, notifying Willie of his father's death. The funeral was postponed until Sabbath, August 13, so that Willie and his wife could reach Battle Creek.

Although unable to prevent the death of James, Kellogg was determined to save Ellen, also gravely ill. Her heart rate was becoming irregular. In a time long before electronic monitoring equipment, the only way he could keep track of its behavior was to have someone constantly checking her pulse. He had two women attendants take turns being on duty with her, and he himself slept with his clothes on in an adjoining room in case of emergency.

About midnight Mrs. White's pulse stopped. Kellogg immediately came to the room and, using an electric current from a battery that he had stepped up in voltage, employed it as a primitive defibrillator to jolt her heart back into a more normal rhythm. Then the two women alternately pressed ice and a hot sponge against her spine until her pulse steadied.[2]

The August 9, 1881, *Review and Herald* announced White's death under the heading "Fallen at His Post." The four columns of type bordered in black sketched the events of his final illness, gave a brief biographical note, then—perhaps with the various investigative committees convened to examine White's financial affairs in mind—extolled James's generous contributions to the church. The author, most likely Uriah Smith, said that although White possessed "rare financial capabilities, he has not devoted these to any selfish purposes, but used them in a manner to advantage the cause he loved. In all enterprises involving the necessity of raising large sums of money, he has been first to lead out with a liberal subscription, and the stock books of all our institutions (all the stock being a donation) show larger investments by him than any other person."[3]

Next the article met head-on the strong reactions that White had produced in many people. "Being thus set for the defense of a work which is in its very nature aggressive, and possessing traits of character essential to the successful maintenance of such a position, it was inevitable that he should offend prejudices, restrain unworthy ambitions, and arouse hostility on the part of some and turn them into more or less active enemies. But whatever positions he has taken in these respects, those who knew him best are persuaded that he acted from what he believed to be duty to the cause; and where the interest of the cause was involved, that was to him above friend or foe, and he would stand firmly for that, whether it brought enmity or friendship, blame or blessing."[4] It would not be considered a politically correct obituary today, but it was hard for White's contemporaries to be neutral to so larger than life a person as James White.

The editorial writer must have winced from personal experience when he wrote: "And it was also inevitable that a man in [White's] position should sometimes make mistakes. He never claimed to be infallible in judgment or perfect in character. But whenever convinced of an error, no one was more ready than he to make sincere and ample acknowledgment for the same. Even in his last sickness, when incapable of using the pen himself, with a softened and humble spirit he dictated a message expressive of regrets for any imperfection of character manifested or errors committed, desiring forgiveness of whom it may concern."[5]

WHITE'S FUNERAL

The funeral, the largest ever in Battle Creek, took place in the Dime Tabernacle on Sabbath afternoon. Though it was Saturday, a business day to the rest of the community, many stores closed out of respect. Besides his wife, his two surviving sons and their wives, his sister Mary Chase and his brother John Whitney White, and John's son-in-law all attended the funeral. John White was a minister at Worthington, Ohio, in the state's Methodist Conference and had been at one time the state's presiding elder. More than 100 employees from the Review and Herald Publishing Association sat among the mourners. Each wore a black armband. In addition to church leaders and members, the 2,500 people attending included business friends and townspeople. James had earned great respect in Battle Creek, especially among community leaders. Admirers had sent countless flowers. John Harvey Kellogg had given a floral cross and crown woven of white double pinks and tuber roses. A portrait of James White, draped in black, hung suspended from the arch above the pulpit. Black cloth also covered the arch itself and the pulpit. Ellen, who had remained in bed until the funeral, was still weak and had to be carried to the Tabernacle.

Uriah Smith preached the funeral sermon. His words hint at the conflicting emotions that must have swirled through his mind during the past few days and must have startled some in the audience, though many would have agreed with them. After sketching the vital contributions White had made to the church he had founded and led for so many years, Smith acknowledged that it was almost inevitable that the fallen church leader had enemies. "Some would misconstrue his motives and misjudge his actions. . . . The cry has been raised at various times and in various quarters . . . that Elder White was manipulating the enterprise to enrich himself. What has already been said is a sufficient refutation of the charge.

If he had insisted in keeping matters in his own hands instead of calling for organizations with their boards of trustees and directors into whose hands the entire management of the work, financially and otherwise, should be committed, there might be some better ground for the claim. That he has acquired some means, is true, but every farthing has been made in an honorable manner from a legitimate source. No individual has been wronged, and not a dollar has been taken unjustly from the treasury of any branch of this work; while he has himself, within the last eight years, put into the different branches of the cause, the sum of twenty thousand dollars of his own means."

Then, perhaps remembering some of his own traumatic encounters with James through the years, Smith added, "some have thought that he was deficient in social qualities, and sometimes rigid, harsh, and unjust, even toward his best friends." It was, perhaps, a strange statement to make at a funeral but was still a thought obviously uppermost in his mind after all the years of conflict between them. "But these feelings, we are persuaded, come from a failure to comprehend one of the strongest traits in his character, which was his pre-eminent love of the cause in which he was engaged. To that he subordinated all else; for that he was willing to renounce home and friends. No man would have been more glad than he to enjoy continuously the pleasures of domestic and social life, and the intercourse of friends, had he not thought that integrity to the cause called him to take a different course. But when this was the case, the voice of duty was first and all else was secondary. Some in whose natures this principle is lacking, cannot comprehend the actions of a man who is governed by such motives. But how would any man be fitted, without such an element as this in his character, to be the conservator of the interests of any cause whatever? In saying this I am not saying what he so often disclaimed, and what he would not wish any one to say, that he assumed never to err in judgment, or make any mistakes. The infirmities common to our nature he possessed in like manner as his fellow-men; and these he often saw and deplored. But who, in his circumstances, would have had less occasion for this than he? Utterly abhorrent to all the better sentiments of our nature would be that spirit which would suffer any feelings from this source to survive an occasion like this—that spirit which would not bury them all, and bury them forever, in the grave which will close over him today. We turn, rather, to the thousands who have loved him as a brother, honored him as a father, and revered him as a counselor and guide, and who will cherish his memory sacredly, and never cease to regret the loss they have sustained in his death.

"As left by him, his work bears the marks of a wise builder. The elements of stability and permanence are wrought into all the structure. . . . God buries the workman, but still carries on the work. His influence will still be felt, the impress of his shaping hand will still be seen, and all the future workings of this cause will revive and keep alive his memory. His love for the work, especially the publishing department, continued to the last. But a few days before his final illness, holding up his right hand, he exclaimed, 'Let my right hand forget its cunning if I forget the interests of this work.' His spirit has seemed of late to be fitting up for the great transition."[6]

Smith dealt head-on with many of the controversial issues in James's life. He told of White's love for the publishing program, his push for organization, his willingness to invest his own money in denominational institutions and projects, and his constant generosity in helping widows and struggling ministers, frequently loaning funds to enable people to buy homes. And Smith acknowledged the charges and questions about White's financial affairs. Yet above all, James's fellow minister and successor as editor of the *Review* extolled White as a human being—his strong friendships, ability to plan for the future, and avoidance of any form of fanaticism. And Smith could not forget the themes that filled James's sermons and articles—"the wonders of redemption; the position and work of Christ as one with the Father in the creation, and in all the dispensations pertaining to the plan of salvation; and finally, the glories of the coming restitution, the realities which he soon will enjoy."[7]

After Smith finished, Ellen unexpectedly stood. "I want to say a few words to those present on this occasion. My dear Saviour has been my strength and support in this time of need. When taken from my sick-bed to be with my husband in his dying moments, at first the suddenness of the stroke seemed too heavy to bear, and I cried to God to spare him to me—not to take him away, and leave me to labor alone. Two weeks ago we stood side by side in this desk; but when I shall stand before you again, he will be missing. He will not be present to help me then. . . . When my husband was breathing out his life so quietly, without a groan, without a struggle, I felt that it would be selfishness in me to wish to throw my arms of affection around him and detain him here. He was like a tired warrior lying down to rest. . . .

"I yield my precious treasure; I bid him farewell; I do not go to his grave to weep. . . . The morning of the resurrection is too bright. And then I look to that morning when the broken family links shall be reunited, and we shall see the King in His beauty, and behold His matchless charms, and cast our glittering crowns at His feet, and touch the golden harp and fill all Heaven with the strains of our music and songs to the Lamb. We will sing together there. We will triumph together around the great white throne."[8]

The congregation sang a hymn, then filed outside for the trek to Oak Hill Cemetery. Ninety-five carriages formed a procession, and hundreds more people walked. Eighty-five Review employees walked beside the carriages. James would be buried in the family plot beside his parents and his sons Henry and John Herbert. An arbor of evergreens covered the short walk from the carriage pathway to the open grave and more evergreen branches covered the grave and surrounding area. A floral anchor stood at the head of the grave, and a cross of flowers at the other end. The scent of blossoms was strong in the August heat.

MEASURED IN THE EYES OF OTHERS

The combined boards of the publishing association, sanitarium, and college had met to pass resolutions in honor of the man who had served on all of them. The resolution recognized "the special providence of God in having raised up Eld. White for the performance of a specific work, to which he was both by natural and acquired gifts peculiarly adapted; and while we mourn and deeply deplore his removal from the work with which his life had been so closely intertwined, we also recognize the far-seeing wisdom which has placed our institutions and the several branches of our cause upon a foundation so stable as to insure not only a continuance but an increase of their present prosperity and usefulness."[9]

Editorials in newspapers in Battle Creek and elsewhere in the country praised his life. Former Congressman George Willard edited and published the Battle Creek *Journal*, which in an editorial declared that James White "was a man of the patriarchal pattern, and his character was cast in the heroic mold. If the logical clearness to formulate a creed; if the power to infect others with one's own zeal, and impress them with one's own convictions; if the executive ability to establish a sect and give it form and stability; if the genius to shape and direct the destiny of great communities, be a mark of true greatness, Elder White is certainly entitled to the appellation, for he possessed not one of these qualities only, but all of them in a marked degree.

"The essential feature of his life's work was constructive. He had the rare power of social organization, and laid the foundation, and marked the design, for the erection of a social and religious structure for others to develop and further complete. Hence it is that his influence was not only commanding during his life, but will be realized long after his death. The work begun by him will not in the least flag by his departure, as the institutions so largely shaped by his practical wisdom and untiring diligence will continue to prosper and further develop in the future as in the past.

"Therefore, as with all true founders of communities, his life is not a broken shaft, but an enduring column, whereon others are to build. He lived to see the Adventist denomination, with all its various institutions with which he has been identified as founder and chief executive, firmly established upon a stable basis."[10]

Nine days after the funeral Ellen White boarded a train for California. She abandoned the brick mansion that James had so loved the last seven months of his life. "It is grandly beautiful," she wrote to friends, "but how can I ever regard it as I could if he had lived?"[11] In fact, she had no desire to remain in Battle Creek. Except for a few months when Willie was temporary president of the General Conference after the 1888 General Conference session, she would reside elsewhere. Now she would head for her home in Healdsburg, California.

The Adventist Church struggled with the question of why James White had died so unexpectedly. Some who knew him concluded that perhaps God had done a great kindness to their leader. "As I viewed him lying in the coffin so calm and peaceful," George I. Butler told Willie White, "I almost envied him. The tears flowed freely. His Heavenly Father has in mercy to him, laid him away to sleep, secure from the strife and trials of this poor life. His works remain to abundantly testify of his great efforts in the cause. His influence remains among our people and they look up to him as to the father of the cause, and always will. Had he lived he would, as he grew older and felt more the shocks [strokes] of the past and possibly of the future, inevitably [have] weakened that influence. Now his reputation is secure."[12]

James's older brother, Bishop John White, shared a similar view. "He was a man of wonderful energy," John wrote to Ellen a few months later, "but not of philosophy enough to have grown aged and feeble, and been supplanted by the younger, gracefully and happily.

"So the Good Father saw, and when he began to fail from his long, protracted effort and care, He said, 'I will call him home. He has done and suffered enough. The rear ranks won't suit his zeal and I will take him home from the front ranks.' There are some men that can't retire and God takes them."[13]

Despite all their problems, Ellen would miss him the rest of her life. Five weeks after his death she journeyed to the little Colorado cabin where she and James had spent happy times and which he especially loved. "From our cottage I could look out upon a forest of young pines, so fresh and fragrant that the air was perfumed with their spicy odor. . . . Among these mountains we often bowed together in worship and supplication. . . . Again I have been among the mountains, but alone. None to share my thoughts and feelings as I looked once more upon those grand and awful scenes! Alone, alone!"[14]

In a letter to Willie, she expressed her grief. Despite all the problems she and James had gone through, she could declare, "I miss Father more and more. Especially do I feel his loss while here in the mountains. I find it a very different thing being in the mountains with my husband and [now being] in the mountains without him."[15] That sense of loss would continue. As with the case of the Battle Creek house James had enjoyed so, she would never return to their mountain home, and eventually sold it.

In 1899, writing to a grieving mother who had lost her child to death, she declared, "Then my husband, the faithful servant of Jesus Christ, who had stood by my side for thirty-six years, was taken from me, and I was left to labor alone. He sleeps in Jesus. I have no tears to shed over his grave. But how I miss him! How I long for his words of counsel and wisdom! How I long to hear his prayers blending with my prayers for light and guidance, for wisdom to know how to plan and lay out the work!"[16]

One could summarize his life in two words: *overcomer* and *initiator*.

He had overcome many limitations and gone on to initiate and accomplish what would have been the work of several ordinary men.

James White, who had originated so much of the Seventh-day Adventist Church's structure and organization, was gone. He had driven himself until his body could take no more. Now he would rest. But his life companion would continue the work they had begun together, especially their final vow to put Christ in the center of every church teaching. She would fill that church body with a spiritual soul. When they arise from the dust of Oak Hill Cemetery, they will both marvel at what God has grown from the seeds they planted together.

---

[1] *Life Sketches* (1915), pp. 248, 249.

[2] Mrs. White recorded her experience in letter 9, 1881. For a history of other early uses of a defibrillator, see Jack Kelly, "A Shock to System," *Invention & Technology,* Fall 1999, pp. 20-27.

[3] "Fallen at His Post," *Review and Herald,* Aug. 9, 1881.

[4] *Ibid.*

[5] *Ibid.*

[6] Uriah Smith, in *In Memoriam,* pp. 34-36.

[7] *Ibid.,* p. 36.

[8] Ellen G. White, in *In Memoriam,* pp. 40-43.

[9] *Review and Herald,* Aug. 16, 1881.

[10] Quoted in *In Memoriam,* pp. 10, 11.

[11] EGW to Brother-Sister (letter 9, 1881), Oct. 20, 1881.

[12] G. I. Butler to WCW, Aug. 17, 1881.

[13] John White to EGW, May 13, 1882.

[14] Ellen G. White, "Cheerfulness in Affliction," *Review and Herald,* Nov. 1, 1881.

[15] EGW to WCW (letter 17, 1881), Sept. 12, 1881.

[16] Ellen G. White, *Selected Messages,* book 2, p. 259.

INDEX